The Bounds of Agency

The Bounds of Agency

AN ESSAY IN

REVISIONARY METAPHYSICS

CAROL ROVANE

PRINCETON UNIVERSITY PRESS

PRINCETON, NEW JERSEY

Library of Congress Cataloging-in-Publication Data

Rovane, Carol A. (Carol Anne), 1955–
The bounds of agency : an essay in revisionary metaphysics / Carol Rovane.
p.   cm.
Includes bibliographical references and index.
ISBN 0-691-01716-6 (alk. paper)
1. Agent (Philosophy)   2. Self (Philosophy)   3. Subject (Philosophy)   I. Title
BD450.R6538   1998
126—dc21   97-17514

This book has been composed in Janson

Frontispiece drawing by Marina Moevs

Princeton University Press books are printed on acid-free paper and meet the guidelines for
permanence and durability of the Committee on Production Guidelines for Book
Longevity of the Council on Library Resources

http://pup.princeton.edu

Printed in the United States of America

1   3   5   7   9   10   8   6   4   2

TO MY MOTHER AND FAMILY

$\bullet$ C O N T E N T S $\bullet$

• A C K N O W L E D G M E N T S •

I WOULD LIKE to thank several people for extensive commentary on earlier drafts of the book: Akeel Bilgrami, Michael Della Rocca, Isaac Levi, Derek Parfit, and Stephen White. I would also like to thank the following people for conversations and correspondence on a variety of philosophical subjects: Robert Adams, Patricia Blanchette, David Bromwich, Sarah and Frederick Broadie, Marcia Cavell, Jennifer Church, Donald Davidson, Daniel Dennett, Alan Donagan, Owen Flanagan, Ivan Fox, Daniel Garber, Jesse Kalin, David Lewis, Michael McCarthy, John McDowell, Mitchell Miller, Marina Moevs, Alan Montefiore, David Pears, Derk Pereboom, David Schmidtz, Sydney Shoemaker, Sir Peter Strawson, David Wiggins, Catherine Wilson, Richard Wollheim, and Allen Wood.

• PART I •

Lessons from Locke

Introduction to Part I

LIKE much recent philosophical work on personal identity, this effort takes its main cue from Locke.

Locke famously argued that the condition of personal identity is distinct from the condition of animal identity. Yet that is not where his real originality lay. Cartesians, and many others in the Platonic and Christian philosophical traditions, had embraced and defended this distinction well before he did. Locke's innovations lay rather in his particular account of the distinction, and the defense he gave of it. He produced an entirely novel analysis of the condition of personal identity, and he defended that analysis with what may have been the first philosophical thought experiment about personal identity.

According to Locke's analysis, personal identity consists in sameness of consciousness. Although it is somewhat obscure what sameness of consciousness is, this much is clear: Locke regarded it as a psychological relation that comprehends different thoughts and actions, and he held that this relation can obtain over time without being grounded either in a persisting soul or in the ongoing life of an animal. Thus his first innovation was to analyze personal identity in purely psychological terms, making no appeal to any independent, which is to say nonpsychological, ground for personal identity. What is especially striking about Locke's thinking in this matter is that his arguments against such independent grounds of personal identity took the same form no matter what sort of ground was offered—that is, regardless of whether it was the sort of ground that dualists offer, namely, the spiritual substance of a soul, or the sort of ground that materialists offer, such as the biological organization of an animal. In both cases Locke's objection was the same: he could imagine sameness of consciousness without sameness of soul or animal, and he could imagine sameness of soul or animal without sameness of consciousness. From this he inferred that the condition of personal identity must be distinct from the respective conditions of identity for souls and animals.

Locke's second innovation was to offer a thought experiment in defense of his purely psychological analysis of personal identity in terms of sameness of consciousness. He asked us to imagine that the respective consciousnesses of a prince and a cobbler were switched, each into the other's body, and to work out who would be who once the switch had taken place. He thought it was obvious that in this circumstance the prince would be the person with the princely consciousness and the cobbling body, and the cobbler would be the person with the cobbling consciousness and the princely body.

It is a testament to the power of Locke's two innovations that philosophical investigations into the person continue to grapple with them. Not only is it the case that subsequent investigations have continued to focus on the issue that he made central to his own investigation, namely, what is the condition of personal identity? But also, the central dispute in such investigations continues to be whether it is possible to secure his distinction between personal and animal identity by providing a purely psychological analysis of personal identity. And thought experiments continue to play a pivotal role in attempts to resolve this central dispute.

The present investigation into the person also bears the mark of Locke's influence. It too is concerned with the question of whether personal identity can be analyzed in purely psychological terms, thereby preserving his distinction between personal and animal identity. However, not very much of this book will be devoted to a direct examination of the issue of personal identity. And even when it does take up that issue, it will not avail itself of Locke's thought experimental method. Instead, it will take its main cue from the instruction that he offered at the start of his discussion of personal identity:

> 'Tis not therefore Unity of Substance that comprehends all sorts of Identity, or will determine it in every Case: But to conceive and judge of it aright, we must consider what Idea the Word it is applied to stands for: It being one thing to be the same Substance, another the same Man, and a third the same Person, if Person, Man, and Substance, are three names standing for three different Ideas; for such as is the Idea belonging to that Name, such must be the Identity: Which if it had been a little more carefully attended to, would possibly have prevented a great deal of that Confusion, which often occurs about this Matter, with no small seeming Difficulties; especially concerning Personal identity, which therefore we shall in the next place a little consider. (2.27.7)[1]

If we disregard Locke's nominalism, his instruction comes to just this: before we try to analyze the condition of a thing's identity, we must first take careful account of what *kind* of thing it is. Accordingly, the major occupation of this book will be to arrive at an adequate account of what kind of thing a person is. Then from this prior account of what kind of thing a person is, appropriate conclusions will eventually be drawn concerning the condition of personal identity.

It is notorious that Locke himself did not manage to clear up all of the confusions and difficulties to which he alluded in the passage quoted above. Indeed, to this day, the philosophical dispute about personal identity that he inaugurated remains disturbingly far from resolution. It will emerge that Locke's failure to resolve that dispute was really a failure to carry out his own instruction—a failure, that is, to consider the issue of kind in sufficient depth and detail before turning to the issue of identity. This same failure is also shared by contemporary proponents of his distinction between personal and animal identity. In fact, most neo-Lockeans do not even represent themselves as trying to carry out Locke's instruction. They rarely justify their attempts to

---

[1] John Locke, *Essay Concerning Human Understanding*, ed. P. Nidditch (Oxford: Oxford University Press, 1975). All future references to this work will simply indicate book, chapter, and section numbers in parentheses in the text.

analyze personal identity in psychological terms by appealing to a prior account of what kind of thing a person is. More often they attempt to justify their analyses directly, by appealing to our intuitions about the condition of personal identity itself. And their favorite tools for eliciting such intuitions are thought experiments modeled on Locke's imaginary case of the prince and the cobbler whose psychological properties are switched into each other's bodies. However, neo-Lockeans have not succeeded where Locke failed, in establishing firm conclusions about personal identity directly on the basis of our intuitive responses to such thought experiments.

This book aims to rectify these failures of the Lockean tradition by attending more scrupulously to Locke's sensible advice. It will thus proceed indirectly, first establishing an account of what kind of thing a person is, and then assessing what that account entails with respect to the issue of personal identity. The results will be threefold: (1) a new *defense* of Locke's distinction between personal and animal identity, (2) a new *interpretation* of that distinction, and (3) a new *analysis* of personal identity.

The new defense of Locke's distinction will ultimately rest on ethical considerations. In fact, the whole account of personhood and personal identity that will be developed in this book will proceed from an initial assumption about the nature of persons that is ethical in character. This procedure reverses the usual order of inquiry in the subject of personal identity. Usually, philosophers begin by making metaphysical assumptions about the nature of persons, and then they go on to draw appropriate ethical conclusions. We shall see in chapter 1 that this is true of Locke. Although he did discuss at length certain ethical dimensions of personhood that have to do with personal accountability, he nevertheless began with a strictly metaphysical characterization of personal nature, from which he directly derived his analysis of personal identity. In contrast, this book will begin with an ethical assumption about the nature of persons, which it will then take as a criterial and defining starting point for further metaphysical investigation into the kind 'person'. Thus the assumption really amounts to an *ethical criterion of personhood*. It stipulates that something qualifies as a member of the kind 'person' just in case it has the ability to engage in *agency-regarding relations*. These are relations in which one agent attempts to influence another and yet aims not to hinder the other's agency—in a very specific sense of hindering agency that will be clarified in chapter 3.

What is the distinctive ethical status of persons that this criterion claims to capture? It follows from the criterion that all persons both occasion and face the same choice concerning whether and when to engage in agency-regarding relations with one another. Furthermore, persons must always view this choice as ethically significant—whichever way they choose and on whatever ground. (So for example, even if persons should choose always to show disregard for the agency of others on egoistic grounds, they would still have made an ethically significant choice.) And finally, persons mutually recognize one another as the only agents who both occasion and face this ethical choice.

Thus persons, as defined by the criterion, must see themselves as comprising a *distinct ethical kind*, because they stand in an ethical relation in which only they can stand, by virtue of their distinctive capacity to engage in agency-regarding relations. The point of the criterion is to pick out this ethical kind.

Of course, the general idea that persons ought to display due regard for one another's agency lay at the center of much Enlightenment thinking about politics and morals, the most vivid and influential examples of which are Kant's account of respect and the idea of universal human rights. However—and this is absolutely crucial to the argument of this book—one need not embrace any particular Enlightenment agenda in order to embrace the ethical criterion of personhood. For that matter, one need not embrace any substantive moral doctrine whatsoever in order to do so. The criterion explicitly raises only one issue of ethical significance, namely, agency-regard, and it does not incorporate any specific moral injunction with respect to that issue. It does not directly *state* that persons are morally obliged to engage in agency-regarding relations. And it does not *imply* such an obligation either. Nor does it imply that agency-regard is morally right, or even morally better than agency-disregard.

Despite its deliberate reticence with respect to the ultimate moral status of agency-regard, the ethical criterion of personhood does claim one very important moral advantage, which is that it helps to define and identify a particular form of prejudice against persons. All prejudice involves some sort of differential treatment of persons that is not warranted. But the particular form of prejudice that is exposed by the ethical criterion involves a further feature, which is that it is *hypocritical*. The hypocrisy arises in the following way. Sometimes, persons want to escape the ethical pressure of the choice they face concerning agency-regard. Yet they cannot escape the ethical pressure except by escaping the choice itself, and they cannot escape the choice so long as they recognize other persons as such. This may lead—and historically has led—some persons to deny the personhood of other persons (as, for example, in the refusal to grant the status of 'person' to slaves in the American south). In this state of denial, persons can show disregard for the agency of other persons without acknowledging that anything of ethical significance has happened at all. But the ethical criterion of personhood helps us to see that such denials are almost always hypocritical, because it is in the nature of persons, qua agents who can engage in agency-regarding relations, to recognize other instances of their ethical kind. This is not, of course, to say that what is objectionable about the hypocrital variety of prejudice against persons is the hypocrisy itself. What is objectionable is the attempt to escape from an ethical relation that is, for persons, inescapable.

It might be wondered whether this last claim, that hypocritical prejudice against persons is objectionable, is consistent with the claim above, that the ethical criterion of personhood does not incorporate any specific moral injunctions with respect to agency-regard. But there is no inconsistency here.

What is being claimed as objectionable is not any particular way of treating other persons, such as showing disregard for their agency; what is objectionable is failing to acknowledge that however one chooses to treat other persons, whether it be with regard for their agency or without, one will have made a choice of ethical significance. (Thus the slave ideology mentioned above was objectionable not only because it chose to license certain sorts of treatment of slaves, but also because it conjoined that choice with a hypocritical denial of the slaves' personhood—and thereby tried to avoid acknowledging the ethical significance of the choice.) The point of the ethical criterion of personhood is not, then, to dictate or constrain what ethical choices persons make with respect to one another; it is rather to point out that there are ethical choices to be made, and that these ethical choices are uniquely occasioned and faced by persons. As a result, the ethical significance of persons and of agency-regard that the criterion claims to capture is not tied to any particular ethical position or theory, but is visible from the perspective of every such position and theory.

Having identified the kind 'person' by the ethical criterion, the book will go on to identify the metaphysical properties that distinguish its members. The resulting metaphysical account of the kind 'person' will provide us with reason to affirm Locke's distinction between personal and animal identity. Yet at the same time, the account will also require a new interpretation of his distinction because it entails two possibilities that he did not explicitly recognize, namely, the possibility of *group persons* who are composed of many human beings and the possibility of *multiple persons* who coexist within a single human being. These possibilities closely resemble the actual phenomena of joint agency and multiple personality disorder. However, the book will not argue that there are any actual instances of group or multiple persons. It will argue merely that their possibility follows from the ethical criterion of personhood, because certain groups and parts of human beings could in principle function as individual agents in their own rights, and could engage in agency-regarding relations. If such group and multiple agents were to exist, then by the lights of the ethical criterion, it would be an act of hypocritical prejudice to deny that they were persons. Obviously, these group and multiple persons would not be identical with human animals. So to accept their possibility is to embrace a version of Locke's distinction between personal and animal identity. But it is also to reinterpret his distinction, since the possibility of such group and multiple persons is not what he had in mind when he introduced his thought experiment about the prince and the cobbler.

This reinterpretation of Locke's distinction is not without some partial antecedents. The possibility of group personhood has been raised before, both in philosophy and in the law.[2] It has also been suggested (though very

---

[2] See, for example, Christine Korsgaard, "Personal Identity and the Unity of Agency: A Kantian Response to Parfit," *Philosophy and Public Affairs* 101–32; (1989): and Roger Scruton, "Corporate Persons," *Proceedings of the Aristotelian Society* 63 (1989): 239–66.

rarely) that the alter personalities of human beings with multiple personality disorder might appropriately be viewed as persons in their own rights.[3] What is novel about this book's thesis is that it affirms *both* possibilities *together*, and moreover, it appeals to exactly the *same* ethical and metaphysical considerations in each case—a single argument and basis for two quite different conclusions. The result is a much more radical rejection of the metaphysical role of the human organism in grounding personal identity than has ever been entertained in any previous discussion of the cases of group or multiple personhood.

This last point will be easier to understand in connection with the new analysis of personal identity that will be offered in this book. It is a *normative analysis* that equates the condition of personal identity with the condition that gives rise to a certain normative commitment, namely, the *commitment to achieving overall rational unity*. Thus the analysis says that wherever this normative commitment is in place, there is a single agent who can engage in agency-regarding relations; there is, in other words, an individual agent who satisfies the ethical criterion of personhood and whose personhood it would be hypocritical to deny.

So to return to the point about the book's radical rejection of the metaphysical role of the human organism in grounding personal identity: The point goes together with another closely related point, which is that the normative analysis of personal identity is *thoroughgoingly* normative. Not only is it the case that the analysis ties personal identity to a certain normative commitment (the commitment to achieving overall rational unity); but also, the analysis places no restrictions at all on how this normative commitment can fall with respect to human organisms. That is why, or rather how, the analysis manages to support the new interpretation of Locke's distinction that affirms the twin possibilities of group and multiple persons; these are possible because groups and parts of human beings can have the normative commitment that, according to the analysis, constitutes personal identity.[4] Suppose, in contrast, that only one of these possibilities were to be affirmed without the other. In that case one's approach would no longer be thoroughgoingly normative in the way that the normative analysis is; instead, one would be allow-

---

[3] See, for example, Stephen E. Braude, *First Person Plural: Multiple Personality Disorder and the Philosophy of Mind* (Lanham, Md.: Rowman and Littlefield Publishers, 1995).

[4] Subsequent chapters will describe in greater detail the precise nature of the parts and groups of human beings who would thus satisfy the normative analysis of personal identity and qualify as individual persons in their own rights. For now, the following qualifications may help to forestall unnecessary misunderstanding.

The *parts* of human beings who would constitute multiple persons cannot be characterized except in terms of a highly abstract rational structure, which will figure in the analysans of the normative analysis of personal identity. But even without yet specifying this rational structure, it is easy to say what these parts are *not*. They are not bodily parts in any straightforward sense, since at any given time one multiple person will control all of the outward bodily actions of a whole human body. They are not exactly temporal parts either, since several multiple persons can coexist within a single human being at the same time. Such contemporaneous existence is possible

ing that the human organism imposes some sort of further, *non*normative metaphysical constraint on the normative commitment to overall rational unity. More specifically, to affirm the possibility of group without multiple personhood would be to affirm something like the following: nothing prevents a group of human beings from being committed to achieving overall rational unity together, but something does prevent different parts of a single human being from having independent commitments to achieving separate pockets of rational unity within their human host; for the brute fact of the individual human being's organic unity (the fact that it has a single body and a single consciousness) imposes a normative commitment to achieving overall rational unity within its whole self. On the other hand, to affirm the possibility of multiple without group personhood would be to affirm a parallel, though different, sort of metaphysical constraint: nothing prevents different parts of a single human being from having independent commitments to achieving separate pockets of rational unity within their human host, but something does prevent groups of human beings from undertaking that commitment together; for the brute fact of the organic separateness of the group's human members (the fact that they have separate consciousnesses and bodies) makes the normative commitment to achieving overall rational unity within the group completely unfeasible. The normative analysis of personal identity does not recognize either of these metaphysical constraints. That is the sense in which it is thoroughgoingly normative. And that is why it is able to support the new interpretation of Locke's distinction that affirms both possibilities at once, of group and multiple persons.

Before proceeding further, a brief cautionary word about the term "normative." It may seem to the reader that when the word "ethical" is used to describe the criterion of personhood from which an account of the kind 'person' is to be developed, and when the word "normative" is used to describe an analysis of personal identity, these two words are synonymous and indifferently interchangeable. That is not so. On the matter of what is the kind 'person', the word "ethical" is used to describe a criterion of personhood whose content and rationale are both specifically ethical: the things that satisfy the criterion all face an ethically significant choice, and by adopting the criterion, we can help to expose a particular form of prejudice against persons. Whereas on the matter of the analysis of personal identity, the word "normative" is used, again deliberately and distinctly, in order to describe something of greater generality and perhaps greater abstraction. It would be natural to run these different things together. Because ethical considerations are in a clear

---

because their mental lives can continue even when they are not in control of outward bodily actions.

As for group persons: they must be characterized in terms of the same abstract rational structure that multiple persons instantiate. Only in their case, this structure is spread out across many human beings, rather than multiply instantiated within a single human being. The text refers in a loose way to groups of human beings, as if a group person had to be composed of *whole* human beings. But this is not so. It may be composed instead of parts of many different human beings.

sense also normative considerations, the sort of ethical defense of Locke's distinction between personal identity and animal identity that this book will offer might be characterized as a normative approach to the issue of personal identity. Yet this ethical defense will lead up to a normative analysis of personal identity that is not itself defined upon ethical considerations, but rather on considerations having to do more generally with rationality. To avoid confusion, the term "normative" will be used to refer only to the latter, non-ethical sort of normativity that resides in rationality, and will never denote anything ethical. Whenever a specifically ethical sort of normativity is in question, as in the prior issue of how to distinguish the kind 'person' from all animal kinds, that will be marked specifically by the term "ethical."

The reader is now urged to pause, in order to assimilate fully the somewhat complex and differentiated approach being taken. On the one hand, the approach is ethical and not merely normative because the ethical criterion introduces issues of ethical significance: the choice with respect to agency-regard is an ethically significant choice, and furthermore, insofar as persons are agents who face this choice, they comprise a distinct ethical kind whose members are bound to recognize one another as persons or be guilty of a certain hypocritical variety of prejudice. On the other hand, no substantive ethical position on human rights or along Kantian lines is embraced simply because of this ethical significance. Rather, this significance is supposed to be visible from the perspective of every position within ethical theory. It might therefore seem appropriate to mark out this significance by calling it "meta-ethical." This would indeed be appropriate if the term referred to whatever belongs to the entire domain of the ethical—that is, to the common subject matter of all of the different and opposed positions within ethical theory; for we shall see that the ethical significance that is being claimed here can and should be recognized in all ethical reflection, whatever its theoretical outcome might turn out to be. But in point of fact, it would be highly inappropriate to call it "meta-ethical" because in current usage the term refers to a subject with which the ethical criterion is not at all concerned, which is the logical and semantical (and perhaps metaphysical) status of ethical propositions in general. That is why the expression "ethical significance" will have to do. So to avoid the pitfalls of misinterpretation, the reader is asked always to bear in mind that the ethical significance that is being claimed here for persons is neither merely normative nor substantively moral in its connotation.

This book will be as much occupied with the question what is a person? as with the question, what is the condition of personal identity? Yet the normative analysis of personal identity is really its final end. And it will be helpful to have this end in sight as the argument of the book progresses. Unfortunately, a proper and complete statement of the normative analysis cannot really be given in advance, since such a statement would have to incorporate details that will be provided only in the course of the argument itself. We must settle at the start for a partial view of the normative analysis, a view that can be glimpsed beforehand from the perspective of Locke's original discussion of personal identity. It is the aim of chapter 1 to provide this preview of the normative analysis of personal identity.

Chapters 2 and 3 will go on to lay the groundwork and establish the point of departure for the positive arguments of Part II—in favor of the new interpretation of Locke's distinction that countenances the possibility of group and multiple persons, and the new normative analysis of the condition of personal identity, as the condition that gives rise to the normative commitment to overall rational unity.

The specific task of chapter 2 is to assess the current state of philosophical debate about personal identity, and to raise a *methodological difficulty* that has been completely overlooked in that debate. As was mentioned above, Locke and neo-Lockeans have tried to settle the issue of personal identity directly on the basis of intuition, through the use of thought experiments. But the thought experimental strategy has failed utterly. Chapter 2 will show that this failure is irremediable. Not only is it the case that our intuitions about the condition of personal identity have proved to be variable across different thought experimental settings; but what is worse, they have proved to be downright inconsistent. They reflect an underlying conflict in our commonsense outlook, concerning whether Locke's distinction between personal and animal identity obtains or not. This means that we cannot resolve the philosophical dispute about personal identity without *revising* some aspect of our commonsense outlook. Yet few philosophers have been willing to label their conclusions about personal identity "revisionist" (Derek Parfit is of course a notable exception). But more importantly, *no one* has noticed that *every* such conclusion is *bound* to be revisionist, due to the conflict in our commonsense outlook. In consequence, no one has faced up to the methodological difficulty that the underlying conflict poses for the project of resolving the philosophical dispute. Due to the conflict, *both* sides of the dispute can claim significant support from common sense. And moreover, as chapter 2 will show, neither side can be eliminated on grounds of internal incoherence or inadequacy. The methodological difficulty that ensues is acute: how are we to provide a compelling justification for taking sides in the philosophical dispute about personal identity, given that each side can claim significant support from common sense and given that each is also internally coherent and otherwise adequate? It should be clearer that there can be no strict *proof* in this circumstance. But it is far from clear what else, besides strict proof, could serve as a compelling justification. What must be justified, after all, is a revisionist conclusion that asks us to give up a significant portion of our commonsense beliefs about what we, our very selves, are.

The last section of chapter 2 and all of chapter 3 will be occupied with meeting this methodological difficulty. The effort to meet it will lead us back to Locke's original instruction, for we shall find that we must seek our reasons for taking sides in the dispute about personal identity in a substantive account of what kind of thing a person is. We shall also find that we need to impose several *methodological constraints* on ourselves as we develop this account of the kind 'person'. These constraints are designed with the express aim of meeting our methodological difficulty. Thus, when chapter 3 argues that we should adopt the ethical criterion of personhood, the argument will be, in essence, that the criterion falls within the constraints, and thereby meets the methodological difficulty. With the adoption of the criterion, the promised new ethical defense of Locke's distinction will begin, which defense will lead to the new interpretation of his distinction that countenances the possibility of group and multiple persons, and to the new normative analysis of personal identity.

Preview of the Normative Analysis of Personal Identity

A FULL STATEMENT of the normative analysis of personal identity must wait for details that will be supplied much later, in the course of the book's overall argument. But some sense of the analysis can be conveyed in advance by situating it in relation to Locke's original discussion of personal identity—more specifically, by displaying what it takes from Locke and how it departs from him.

In showing how the normative analysis departs from Locke, the aim is not to draw attention to any internal difficulty or incoherence in his position. Such difficulties have been exhaustively discussed in the secondary literature about Locke and in the wider literature on personal identity. The aim here is different. It is to give a more or less sympathetic account of his analysis of personal identity, and to give a preliminary sense of the normative analysis by bringing out various points of convergence and divergence between these two analyses.

1. LOCKE'S ANALYSIS

In the following much quoted passage Locke set out what he took the term "person" to stand for:

> . . . which, I think, is a thinking intelligent Being, that has reason and reflection, and can consider it self as it self, the same thinking thing, in different times and places; which it does only by that consciousness, which is inseparable from thinking, and as it seems to me essential to it: It being impossible for any one to perceive, without perceiving, that he does perceive. (2.27.9)

Locke regarded this brief statement of what kind of thing a person is as a sufficient basis for his analysis of personal identity, which he immediately proceeded to provide. The passage continues:

> When we see, hear, smell, taste, feel, meditate, or will any thing, we know that we do so. Thus it always is as to our present Sensations and Perceptions: And by this every one is to himself, that which he calls self: it not being considered in this case, whether the same self be continued in the same, or divers Substances. For since consciousness always accompanies thinking, and 'tis that, that makes every one to be, what he calls self; and thereby distinguishes himself from all other thinking things, in this alone consists personal Identity, i.e., the sameness of

rational Being: And as far as this consciousness can be extended backwards to any past Action or Thought, so far reaches the Identity of that Person; it is the same self now it was then; and 'tis by the same self with this present one that now reflects on it, that that Action was done.

The last few clauses lead many to interpret Locke as analyzing the condition of personal identity in terms of the memory relation. But the constant emphasis, both in his statement of what a person is and in his analysis of personal identity, is the more general epistemic relation that each person, qua self-conscious thing, bears only to itself. This relation is more general than the memory relation because it holds in the present as well as bridges the past. And what distinguishes this relation at all times and in all tenses is its reflexive character, which character Locke aimed to capture with the language of "self" that he repeatedly employed in the passage. We more commonly express this reflexive epistemic relation of self-consciousness with the first-person-singular pronoun.

This point, if correct, suggests a somewhat nonstandard interpretive proposal, and that is that the language of the first person provides a good way to state the main tenets of Locke's view of personhood and personal identity. These tenets are three in number, and when formulated in the idiom of the first person they are: (1) a person is something with a first person point of view; (2) the identity of a person consists in the unity and continuity of such a first person point of view; and (3) the first person point of view of an individual person need not coincide with an individual soul or an individual animal. Given that Locke himself avoided the language of "first person" and "point of view," it might seem odd to formulate his theses in this way. But he did avail himself of the notion of reflexive, or self-conscious, knowledge. And the only way we have of expressing the content of such knowledge is through the use of the first person singular pronoun "I" (or an equivalent locution that shares the reflexive character of "I," such as "the thinker of this thought"). Furthermore, there is just no getting around the fact that the subject of such self-conscious knowledge must have a point of view from which it can reflexively apprehend its thoughts and actions as its own—that is, a point of view from which it can apprehend them in the first person mode, as *mine*. So there is no harm in appealing to the idea of a point of view in trying to understand Locke's account of personal identity. And there can be no doubt that such a point of view must, given its reflexive character, be a first person point of view.

Once Locke's three main theses are formulated in these terms, a basic unclarity emerges. Even if thesis (1)—namely, that a person is something with a first person point of view—is allowed to stand without supporting argument, much more needs to be said about what such a point of view is. And until the notion of a first person point of view is properly developed, it is impossible to assess theses (2) and (3). For that matter, until this is done it is not really clear what any of the three theses really means. This is not to say that we cannot make out what Locke had in mind by them. It is rather to say that they may have a meaning that he did not have in mind. Indeed that is precisely what this book will argue, and precisely why it will offer a new interpretation of his distinction, via a new analysis of personal identity. But, to repeat, the aim here is not to raise any internal difficulties for Locke's own analysis, but rather to use it as a point of comparison for the normative analysis that will be put forward in this book.

At any rate, here is an account of what Locke seems to have had in mind by the three theses just attributed to him.

Thesis (1) he more or less stipulated: a person just is something with a first person point of view, which is to say, a point of view from which it can reflexively regard its thoughts and actions in the first person mode as its own. His repeated references to consciousness show that he construed this first personal relation that a person bears to its own thoughts and actions primarily in phenomenological terms—that is, in terms of a distinctive kind of phenomenological access that a person has to its own thoughts and actions, by directly apprehending them in consciousness.[1] He thought that such phenomenological access to one's present thoughts and actions is ensured just by virtue of the fact that thoughts and actions are conscious activities. And he thought that phenomenological access to one's past thoughts and actions is provided for in similar fashion by memory. In his account, to remember a past episode of one's life is literally to recall that past episode to present consciousness. As for thesis (2), Locke seemed to think that the connection between personal identity and point of view is obvious and unarguable: each person necessarily has a distinct point of view from which it has direct phenomenological access to all of its own thoughts and actions through consciousness, and to no one else's. It follows from this that whatever condition gives rise to such an individual phenomenological point of view is also the condition of personal identity. And this is the major premise from which Locke argued for thesis (3), which rejects both the Cartesian view that ties personal identity to the identity of a soul and the Aristotelian view that ties personal identity to the identity of an animal. He held that these conditions are neither necessary nor sufficient to ground a person's phenomenological point of view, and hence a person's identity.

[1] The term "consciousness" is notoriously obscure, and certainly not univocal. The use here follows Thomas Nagel (see *The View from Nowhere* [New York: Oxford University Press, 1986], chap. 2): it is a mark of *conscious* mental episodes that there is *something that it is like* for their subject to have them, and also, that by virtue of this felt quality their subject has a special sort of direct epistemic access to them—what was just referred to in the text as "phenomenological access." Thus the relevant contrast is not between the conscious and the unconscious in Freud's sense, that is, it is not between the avowed or avowable and the repressed. The relevant contrast is between that which has a felt quality and that which does not. Locke and the other modern empiricists thought that having such a felt quality, and hence actually being apprehended in consciousness, is a necessary condition for being a mental phenomenon. Nagel takes a somewhat weaker view. According to him, being the sort of thing that *could* impress itself upon consciousness in this way, by virtue of its felt quality, is a defining feature of the mental. This book takes an even weaker view: this felt quality is neither a necessary condition on nor a defining feature of the mental; but it is a sufficient condition.

The simplest way to understand why Locke held this is to consider the matter from the first person point of view. According to him, a thought or action is mine just in case I have direct phenomenological access to it, either through present consciousness or through memory. Thus my point of view—and so for Locke, my very self—consists in a certain sort of phenomenological unity that is circumscribed by the lines of my phenomenological access. Insofar as I regard this phenomenological condition as the condition of my identity, what reason do I have to embrace the Cartesian thesis that my identity consists in the identity of a particular soul? It would seem that I have none at all, since I can imagine that the lines of my phenomenological access could extend to thoughts that belong to different souls, and I can also imagine that they could fail to extend to all of the thoughts that belong to the same soul. Locke explicitly focused on identity over time, claiming that the same phenomenological point of view could be sustained through a succession of souls, and that there could be a succession of points of view within a single soul. But the claim should hold for identity at a time as well. In that case, many souls could simultaneously participate in a single, phenomenologically unified point of view, and one soul could simultaneously house many such points of view.

Locke employed the same argumentative strategy—though less convincingly—against the Aristotelian view that links personal identity with animal identity. In this case, he argued that the phenomenological unity of my point of view does not depend in any way on the identity of a particular animal. According to him, there is nothing to prevent us from imagining that the lines of a person's phenomenological access could extend to different animals and, also, that they could fail to comprehend all of the thoughts that belong to a single animal. In order to show that this is true over time, he offered two thought experiments. The first was his case of the prince and the cobbler whose consciousnesses are switched, each into the other's body. In most discussions of this thought experiment what is emphasized is that a single point of view can be sustained in a succession of animals. But of course the experiment also shows that a single animal can be the site of a succession of different points of view. In any event, Locke offered a second thought experiment in order to drive the latter point home, which asks us to imagine that a day person and a night person alternately occupy the same body.

These thought experiments do not constitute the whole of Locke's anti-Aristotelian argument. And they cannot, for they do not manage completely to divorce the phenomenological point of view of a person from the bodily perspective of a particular animal. On the contrary, they both exploit a certain intuitive connection between these two kinds of perspective. At each moment in time, the phenomenological points of view of the prince, the cobbler, the day person, and the night person are all tied, respectively, to the bodily perspectives of particular animals. And some would argue that that is precisely why we find these thought experiments intelligible. However, this was not Locke's view of the matter. He explicitly denied that there is any connection at all between the phenomenological perspective of a particular person and the bodily perspective of a particular animal—not only over time, but also at a time as well. In order to make this clear, he declared that if my little finger should be cut off and if my consciousness should leave my body and stay with my little finger, then I would literally have left my body and would reside in my little finger. In declaring this he was not suggesting that my little finger would become an independent little organism on its own, so that my phenomenological point of view could thereby be rooted in the bodily perspective of that organism. He was suggesting rather that my point of view as a conscious subject can be construed in purely phenomenological terms, and need not be seen as tied to any particular bodily perspective at all—and certainly not to the bodily perspective of a particular animal.

Locke did not deny that this suggestion is counterintuitive. Indeed, he seems to have made the suggestion expressly in order to make clear that he would not shrink from accepting the counterintuitive consequences of his analysis of personal identity. But there is another counterintuitive consequence that he ought also to have acknowledged in the same breath. And that is that a person's phenomenological point of view could in principle comprehend a multitude of animals at once, just as it could in principle be confined to a little finger. Bringing out this consequence completes Locke's anti-Aristotelian argument in much same the way that the discussion above completed his anti-Cartesian argument. In both cases, a point that Locke made about the independence of personal identity over time from certain metaphysical conditions is extended, so as to apply in analogous fashion at a time as well. There is some limited reason to think that he might have been prepared to accept the extension in both cases. And this is so even though it involves saddling him with the counterintuitive claim that there could in principle be a single, phenomenologically unified point of view that is simultaneously shared by many animals at once. In fact, it is precisely by contemplating this very possibility that we can apprehend the full meaning and radical force of his claim that personal identity consists in *consciousness alone*. And it should be borne in mind that Locke's analysis of personal identity qualifies as a *purely* psychological analysis (i.e., as an analysis that makes no appeal to any independent, nonpsychological ground of personal identity) only insofar as it carries this radical force.

Of course, once Locke's analysis is construed as being this radical—that is, so radical that it breaks all ties between the phenomenological unity of consciousness and any other independently characterizable metaphysical conditions—it loses some of its initial appeal.

For one thing, while the anti-Cartesian argument goes against no particular intuitions, the anti-Aristotelian argument does go against some of our intuitions, namely, those that link the phenomenological point of view of a person to the bodily perspective of an animal. The fact that we have such intuitions, and the fact that Locke's analysis of personal identity violates them, will be pondered at some length in the next section.

But leaving the matter of our intuitions aside, there is also a theoretical issue at stake. Locke made a deep and convincing theoretical point against Descartes the significance of which goes beyond the issue of personal identity. The point is just this: positing an immaterial spiritual substance (what Descartes referred to as the soul) goes no distance at all toward explaining the phenomenological unity of consciousness. That is, nothing in the idea of an individual immaterial substance helps us to see why it should ever give rise to a single, phenomenologically unified point of view—in Locke's terms a single consciousness—that comprehends everything within that substance but nothing without it. The anti-Aristotelian argument would seem to imply a parallel theoretical point with respect to all biological, and indeed all material, conditions, namely, that no such condition could possibly afford an explanation of the phenomenological unity of consciousness. But it is hard to be sanguine that Locke was right to dismiss the possibility of a biological, or more broadly material, explanation of the phenomenological unity of consciousness. Now, it might be protested that Locke did not actually dismiss this possibility. If he did not, then he would have had to allow that his thought experiment about the prince and the cobbler might not describe a real empirical possibility that is consistent with the laws of nature. The experiment could be taken to establish only a mere conceptual possibility. And in that case, the claim that a person's consciousness might be transferable from one body to another would be no more interesting than the claim that a human being might resist gravity and fly like Peter Pan. Perhaps it cannot be ruled out that Locke's account of personal identity has the fanciful spirit of a Peter Pan claim. But that does not square well with two features of his account: first, that it was so long and labored; and second, that it took up what must have been for Locke a very serious theological issue, which is to make sense of how an individual person whose body has perished might nevertheless face God on Judgment Day. For these reasons, this book will assume that Locke aimed to establish more than a *mere* conceptual possibility. And in any case, it is fair to say that the *interest* of his account of personal identity would be severely diminished if that were not so.

Assuming that Locke's claim is to a real possibility, there is some evidence against it—evidence that phenomenological unity is actually grounded in animal identity. For it is familiar fact that lines of phenomenological access do not, in the ordinary course of things, hold between organisms but only within individual organisms. This evidence is certainly not conclusive. And of course, it does not point to any substantive explanation of the phenomenological unity of consciousness in organic terms—that is, in terms drawn from biology, chemistry, physiology, or some other science concerned with organic nature. But all the same, the known facts, such as they are, do leave open the possibility of such an explanation. And so the most sensible position with respect to this general possibility, namely, the possibility that phenomenological unity might be explicable by appeal to facts of organic nature, is agnosticism. That, in any event, is the position that this book will adopt. Unlike

Locke, it simply will not rule out the possibility that some aspect of organic nature—perhaps even some aspect of the condition of animal identity itself—might explain the phenomenological unity of consciousness.[2]

Locke himself could not embrace an agnostic position here and also claim definitively to have established that his analysis of personal identity, in terms of the phenomenological unity of consciousness, qualifies as a purely psychological analysis. His analysis cannot be regarded as complete unless it includes, in addition to the condition of phenomenological unity itself, whatever further conditions are necessary for such unity. And to allow that such unity might be explained by appeal to facts of organic nature is precisely to allow that certain organic facts might be necessary conditions on phenomenological unity. Insofar as certain organic facts were necessary conditions on phenomenological unity, Locke's analysis of personal identity would have to incorporate them. It is obvious that the resulting completed Lockean analysis would no longer qualify as a purely psychological analysis. But furthermore, the resulting analysis might well fail to support Locke's distinction between personal and animal identity. That would be so if the added organic conditions on personal identity included the condition of animal identity itself.

2. Rational Points of View

The agnostic position of this book with respect to a possible organic basis of the phenomenological unity of consciousness compromises the pivotal step in Locke's argument for his distinction between personal and animal identity. Nevertheless, the book will defend his distinction. And in doing so it will provide an analysis of personal identity—the normative analysis—that preserves all three of the main theses attributed to him above. Those theses were: (1) a person is something with a first person point of view; (2) the identity of a person consists in the unity and continuity of such a first person point of view; and (3) the first person point of view of an individual person need not coincide with an individual soul or with an individual animal. However, despite these three points of convergence between the normative analysis and Locke's, there is also an important point of divergence. The analysis will reject Locke's specific account of what a first person point of view is. He construed it as the phenomenological point of view of a unified consciousness. In contrast, the normative analysis takes it to be the rational point of view of an agent.

The contrast between the notion of a phenomenological point of view and the notion of a rational point of view may not immediately be obvious. It certainly was not evident to Locke. He never denied that a person is a rational agent or that the point of view of a person is a rational point of view. In fact he often characterized persons as agents, and he always included rationality among the defining features of personhood. Not only did he specifically

---

[2] See section 3 of chapter 5 for further discussion of this point.

mention rationality in his famous definition of the person as a "thinking, intelligent being with *reason* and *reflection*" (emphasis added); throughout his discussion of personal identity, he used the phrase "rational being" interchangeably with the term "person". However, he also assumed—and moreover, he did so without argument—that the point of view of a rational being must be a phenomenologically unified point of view. This is a very common assumption. Indeed, it seems to be a nearly universal assumption. But all the same, this book will argue against it. Just as Locke thought that a phenomenological point of view need not be tied to a particular soul or a particular animal, likewise, this book will argue that a rational point of view need not be tied to a particular soul, or a particular animal, or a particular phenomenological point of view.[3]

What, then, is a rational point of view? And why should it be distinguished from both the bodily perspective of an animal and the phenomenological perspective of a unified consciousness? The answer to the latter question belongs to the larger argument for the normative analysis of personal identity. Since that larger argument is really the argument of this entire book, it cannot be given in these introductory remarks. On the other hand, a relatively detailed answer to the first question, concerning what a rational point of view is, can be given at this stage. This answer will accomplish three things: first, it will elucidate some of the main terms of the normative analysis; second, it will bring out part of the rationale for that analysis; third, it will clarify (though not justify) the claim that a rational point of view is distinct from a phenomenological point of view. Once these things have been accomplished, this preview of the normative analysis can be concluded, by taking stock of all

---

[3] This claim presupposes a very specific conception of what a phenomenological point of view is, as a point of view from which mental episodes are phenomenologically accessible in the sense explained above, in section 1: they can be directly apprehended in consciousness by virtue of their felt quality. This conception accords very well with the empiricist tradition to which Locke belonged, in which it is a necessary and sufficient condition for being a mental episode that it be phenomenologically accessible in this sense. But it has been emphasized that a phenomenological point of view is also a first person point of view. And of course Kant and others have provided very sophisticated arguments to show that first person ownership of mental episodes is not provided for *just* by virtue of their felt quality; they must also stand in various sorts of logical and conceptual relations, and perhaps also evaluative, and narrative relations. There is good reason to take these arguments very seriously. And those who do take them seriously are likely to conceive the phenomenological domain in a broad way, so as to include these various logical, conceptual, evaluative, and narrative relations, as well as the felt quality of mental episodes. It is unclear whether this broadening of the phenomenological domain would collapse the distinction between phenomenological and rational points of view. That depends on whether the extra phenomenological relations in question do, or do not, rest on phenomenological access in the sense that has been defined here. However, this issue need not be resolved for the purposes of this book's larger argument. No matter how it gets resolved in the end, the following will remain true (or so this book will argue): at least some mental episodes have a felt quality; such mental episodes are phenomenologically accessible in consciousness by virtue of their felt quality; there must be points of view from which such mental episodes are phenomenologically accessible in this sense; one way of individuating phenomenological points of view is by lines of phenomenological access; when phenomenological points of view are individuated in this way, they need not coincide with particular rational points of view.

unity is an ideal of rationality that *defines* what it is for an *individual* person to be fully rational.

This conceptual tie between the normative ideal of overall rational unity and personal identity has both a positive and a negative aspect. The positive aspect was just explained: the ideal defines what it is for an individual person to be fully rational. And the positive aspect automatically implies a corresponding negative aspect: the ideal does not apply to groups of persons as it does to individuals. This can best be seen by returning to the idea of an all-things-considered judgment, since these judgments are the means by which overall rational unity is achieved. The scope of the "all" in all-things-considered judgments is determined by the scope of a person's own rational point of view. That is to say, such judgments should take into account all that belongs to a person's own point of view, and they may disregard what anyone else might think or want. It follows that when I deliberate, I ought to resolve all of the contradictions and conflicts within my own point of view, but I need not resolve all of my disagreements with you. Likewise, I ought to rank all of my preferences, but this ranking need not reflect your preferences. And more generally, when I arrive at all-things-considered judgments about what it would be best for me to think and do, these judgments should take into account all of my beliefs, desires, and so forth, but not yours. This shows that the normative ideal of overall rational unity does not apply to us together; it applies rather to each of us separately. All that the ideal requires of us is that we each achieve overall rational unity just within our own respective rational points of view.

The restriction of the normative ideal of overall rational unity to a person's own rational point of view might seem implausible. After all, I often learn from others, and I also often care about what others want and think. How could I learn from or care about others' points of view unless my all-things-considered judgments took them into account as well as my own? The answer is familiar from internalist conceptions of reasoning and justification. If I am already committed to the idea that I might learn from you, or that I ought to try to satisfy your desires, then I have grounds within my own rational point of view to take your beliefs and desires into account in my all-things-considered judgments. But I need not have such grounds. I might think you a fool from whom I can learn nothing, and I might believe that there is no reason why I should try to satisfy your desires. In such cases, I am not required, by my normative commitment to realizing the ideal of rationality (the ideal of rational unity), to take your beliefs and desires into account in my all-things-considered judgments. These are of course claims about the requirements of rationality and not morality. It might be a moral failing on my part not to take your desires into account in my judgments about what it would be best for me to do. But unless I already had, within my own rational point of view, some ground for taking your desires into account, it would not be a failure of rationality on my part to disregard them in my deliberations. That is precisely why the normative ideal of overall rational unity defines what it is for an individual person to be fully rational: a person fails to be fully rational if it fails to achieve

of the various points of convergence and divergence between it and Locke's analysis.

A rational point of view is the point of view from which a person deliberates. The proper goal of deliberation is to arrive at, and also to act upon, all-things-considered judgments about what it would be best to think and do in the light of everything in the deliberator's rational point of view. This goal is achieved through the following sorts of rational activities: resolving contradictions and other conflicts among one's beliefs and other psychological attitudes, accepting the implications (both logical and evidential) of one's attitudes, ranking one's preferences, assessing opportunities for action, assessing the probable consequences of performing the actions that are open to one, determining what means are available for achieving one's ends, evaluating one's ends (and reassessing their relative preferability) in the light of both the available means to achieving them and the probable consequences of acting upon them. When rational activities such as these are fully and optimal carried out, they yield conclusions about what it would be best to think and do in the light of one's whole rational point of view. And such conclusions are the all-things-considered judgments that are the proper goal of deliberation.

This characterization of a rational point of view, as the point of view from which a person deliberates, is essentially normative. It says that a rational point of view is something in which contradictions and conflicts *ought* to be resolved, implications *ought* to be accepted, preferences *ought* to be ranked, means and consequences *ought* to be taken into account—and more generally, it is something from which all-things-considered judgments *ought* to be reached and implemented.

However, although it is possible to give a normative characterization of a rational point of view, in terms of what persons ought to accomplish in their deliberations, it must be emphasized that rational points of view are real things with causal-explanatory significance. A person's rational point of view constitutes its psychological economy. It should be clear, to begin with, that any person who deliberates and acts intentionally must have a rational point of view from which it does these things. This point of view provides the premises for its deliberations and the reasons for its choices. And in providing all this, a person's rational point of view provides the causal springs of its actions. Conversely, any phenomena that would figure in psychological explanations of a person's actions belong to its rational point of view. This includes the explananda—that is, the actions themselves—as well as the explanantia—that is, the beliefs, desires, and other psychological states and events that issue in those actions. *From here on, the phrase "intentional episodes" will denote all of these various kinds of phenomena that figure in psychological explanation.*

Before proceeding further, a brief note about the choice of the term "episode." When philosophers of mind cast about for a blanket term to cover all of the diverse phenomena that belong to a person's intentional life, they face an obvious problem, which is that these phenomena do not belong to any one ready-made metaphysical category, such as 'event' or 'state'. These phenomena include standing beliefs and other psychological attitudes that are not events in the ordinary sense of the term "event" (e.g., my knowledge of English grammar), and they include actions that are not states in any sense (e.g., my making a telephone call). Most philosophers nevertheless fasten on one of these terms (or another such term), and then find it necessary to declare that they are employing the term in a broad sense that includes phenomena to which it would not ordinarily apply. In this respect, the term "episode" probably fares no better than "event" or "state." It must also be admitted that the term has at least one unfortunate connotation, which is that it is often understood as connoting something of brief (episodic) duration. However, this connotation does not belong to the strict meaning of the term. In its primary meaning, the term "episode" refers to something that belongs to a larger temporal series or progression, and secondarily, it refers to a portion of a narrative. Here, by extension, it will be used to refer to a portion of a person's intentional life. Such an intentional episode in the life of a person may be a private thought or a public action, it may be lasting or transient, it may be important or trivial—it may be anything, so long as it may appropriately be included (either as explanans or as explanandum) in an intentional explanation of something that the person does, in the broadest sense of "do" that includes a person's thoughts as well as actions.

It is a familiar point, but still it is worth emphasizing, that the causal-explanatory significance of a rational point of view, or rather of the intentional episodes that belong to it, does not make it unfit to be characterized in normative terms; for the sorts of psychological explanations that it makes possible are reason-giving explanations in which there is a normative, or rationalizing, relation between the explanans and the explanandum as well as a causal relation. In fact, if deliberation is to be a real process with real outcomes, there must be both sorts of relations—rational and causal—between its premises and its conclusions. On the one hand, nothing counts as deliberation unless it is a rational process that is responsive to the normative (i.e., rational and/or justificatory) relations among intentional episodes. Yet on the other hand, no such rational process can be counted as real unless it belongs to the causal order. Thus not only is it the case that the normative characterization of a rational point of view, as a point of view from which deliberation proceeds, is compatible with the idea that such a point of view has causal-explanatory significance; it actually presupposes that idea.[4] Though of course the normative goals of deliberation are only partially lived up to in the actual psychological economy of any agent who is not a god or an angel.

It was promised that an account of what a rational point of view is would accomplish three things: it would elucidate some of the main terms of the normative analysis; it would bring out part of its rationale; and it would clarify the claim that a rational point of view is distinct from a phenomenological point of view.

[4] Donald Davidson, as is well known, has argued for this dual nature of the relation between reasons and actions in his seminal essay, "Actions, Reasons and Causes," in *Essays on Actions and Events* (New York: Oxford University Press, 1980), pp. 3–19.

In the first task, something has already been accomplished. the normative analysis, the condition of personal identity is the c gives rise to a certain normative commitment, namely, the co achieve overall rational unity. And both of these substantive co the analysis—the notion of overall rational unity and the notion tive commitment—can be elucidated by appeal to the above acc a rational point of view is. The account says that a rational poin point of view from which deliberation proceeds, where the pr deliberation is to arrive at and act upon all-things-considered j carrying out the rational activities described above in a ratior manner, that is, in such a way as to reflect everything within point of view. And overall rational unity is nothing else than the s achieves by realizing this goal of deliberation. The account als rational point of view can be characterized in normative terms, in which this goal ought to be achieved. And all that is meant here tive commitment" is that the agents who have the goal of achie rational unity think of the goal in this way, as having this prescrip "ought"; in other words, they think that overall rational unity i that they ought to achieve, and in that sense, they have a norma ment to achieving such unity.

This elucidation of some of the main terms of the normative ar to bring out that the normative analysis entails a perfect coincid sonal identity with rational point of view. First of all, whenev rational point of view, the condition of personal identity as it is the normative analysis is satisfied, namely, the condition that gi normative commitment to achieving overall rational unity. A rati view is a point of view from which deliberation proceeds, and th deliberation is necessarily directed toward the goal of achievin tional unity, which is to say, it is directed at living up to the nor mitment to achieve such unity. The converse holds as well: whe thing satisfies this condition of personal identity, that is, the co gives rise to the normative commitment to overall rational unity, a rational point of view, for that normative commitment is really ment to carrying out the rational activities that comprise delibe deliberation necessarily proceeds from a particular rational point

If it is taken for granted that a person is, as Locke said, a rat then the fact that the normative analysis entails a perfect coincid sonal identity with rational point of view provides a plausible r the analysis. It is, after all, plausible that something qualifies a being if, and only if, it has a rational point of view from which the rational activities that characterize and constitute deliberatio is an even deeper, and also more direct, rationale for the normat The analysis takes advantage of a direct conceptual tie betwee component of its analysans, the normative commitment to ove unity, and its analysandum, personal identity: the state of over

overall rational unity among the beliefs, desires, and other intentional episodes that comprise its own rational point of view, whereas a person does not fail to be fully rational if it fails to achieve such unity among its own intentional episodes and those belonging to other persons. And to reiterate, part of the rationale for the normative analysis lies in the fact that it thus respects, and indeed exploits, this conceptual tie between the normative ideal of overall rational unity and personal identity.

So much for elucidating some of the main terms of the normative analysis of personal identity, and bringing out the part of its rationale that can stand independently of the arguments to come later in the book. The remaining task of this section is to clarify—though again, not to justify—the claim that a rational point of view is distinct from a phenomenological point of view.

Each sort of point of view, phenomenological and rational, can claim to qualify as a first person point of view. But each implies a different account of the first person relation that a person bears to its own thoughts and actions. The first construal of a first person point of view, as a phenomenological point of view, is roughly Cartesian. It privileges the idea of consciousness, the precise idea being that I bear a first person relation to my own thoughts and actions by virtue of the fact that I have direct phenomenological access to them through consciousness. In contrast, the second construal of a first person point of view, as a rational point of view, privileges the idea of deliberation. It takes advantage of the fact that deliberation necessarily has a first personal character, a fact that can readily be seen from the nature and form of the all-things-considered judgments that are its proper goal. Such judgments are judgments in the first person mode about what it would be best for *me* to think and do in the light of *my* beliefs, desires, and so forth, that is, in the light of all of the intentional episodes that constitute *my* rational point of view. Once the notion of a first person point of view is construed in this second way, as a rational point of view, then it follows that the first person relation that each person bears to its own thoughts and actions is essentially normative. On this construal, a thought counts as mine just in case it belongs to my rational point of view, and thoughts belong to my rational point of view just in case I ought to take them into account in my deliberations, so that they are duly reflected in my all-things-considered judgments. The first person relation that each person bears to its own actions is likewise essentially normative. An action counts as mine just in case it arises as a result of my own deliberations, with the consequence that the action can be evaluated as something that I ought either to have done or not done in the light of my deliberations, that is, in the light of what I have judged it would be best for me to do, all things considered.

It is natural to assume that these two ways of construing the first person relation that a person bears to its own thoughts and actions—phenomenological and normative—should go together. After all, the normative first person relation has to do with how a person's thoughts and actions ought to figure in its deliberations, either as premises or as conclusions. And we normally think of deliberation as a conscious process that is carried out within a point of view that is, at least for the most part, phenomenologically unified. To think of deliberation in this way is precisely to think that I bear a normative first person relation to thoughts and actions just in case I also bear the phenomenological first person relation to them, of direct phenomenological access in consciousness. Nevertheless, this book will argue that having such phenomenological access to an item is neither necessary nor sufficient for bearing the normative first person relation to it.

That such phenomenological access is not necessary for the normative first person relation is not even controversial. Consider, for example, the following mundane occurrence: I often write down my thoughts in anticipation of the fact that I will later forget them, though I will not have changed my mind about their veracity. Once I no longer have direct phenomenological access to such veracious thoughts in consciousness, I am not thereby released from my normative commitment to taking them into account in my deliberations—unless of course I have changed my mind about them. But in that case I would not merely lack phenomenological access to them; I would have decided that I ought not to hold them any longer.

It is hard to produce a similarly mundane example to illustrate that phenomenological access to a thought is not sufficient, any more than it is necessary, to put me in a normative first person relation to it. But consider the following fact: not everything that enters my consciousness is worth taking into account in my deliberations; it is only those thoughts to which I assent, or about which I have feelings of great certitude, that I ought to take into account. And it is simply not guaranteed by the fact that I have phenomenological access to a thought that it be accompanied by such an act of assent or feeling of certitude. Phenomenological access, as it has been defined here, is just a particular form of epistemic access, which does not in itself imply any particular normative relation to its object.[5]

Despite these countervailing observations, intuition is likely to remain on Locke's side: a rational point of view must also be a phenomenologically unified point of view. But however much intuition may be on Locke's side in this matter, this book will argue against him. And the argument for this departure from Locke will involve an even more fundamental departure from him. This more fundamental departure concerns the place of explanation in the project of analyzing personal identity.

3. The Explanatory Goal of the Normative Analysis

What Locke took to be the condition of personal identity, namely, the phenomenological unity of consciousness, he took to be a brute fact that has no underlying explanation. This is not to say that he offered no positive reason for taking this brute fact to be the condition of personal identity. He of course

---

[5] See footnote 3 for further discussion of this point.

did. But his point in arguing against both the Cartesians and the Aristotelians was that nothing—not the immaterial substance of a soul nor the organic unity of human being—explains the phenomenological unity of consciousness. So in taking such unity to be the condition of personal identity, he took that condition to be a brute fact. That is why he insisted that personal identity consists in consciousness alone: nothing else supports its unity, or as he would say, its sameness.

This book has already declared its agnostic stance with respect to the possibility of an organic explanation of the phenomenological unity of consciousness (though it does agree with Locke's anti-Cartesian point: the soul affords no explanatory insight into the phenomenological unity of consciousness, or any other form of psychic unity, and can safely be set aside in philosophical discussions of personal identity). But not only does this book refuse to assume that Locke's phenomenological analysans is a brute fact; it also refuses to assume that its own normative analysans—the condition that gives rise to the normative commitment to overall rational unity—is a brute fact. Indeed, that is why the analysans is formulated in the way it is: the point of equating the condition of personal identity with the condition that *gives rise* to the normative commitment to overall rational unity is to invite the question, *why* does the condition of personal identity give rise to this normative commitment? And it is an explanatory goal of the normative analysis that the condition it specifies should answer this question. That is, the normative analysis aims to disclose what it is about a person's identity that ensures that an individual person will recognize, and be committed to satisfying, the normative ideal that defines individual rationality.

If Locke had adopted a parallel explanatory goal, he would not have equated the condition of personal identity with the phenomenological unity of consciousness. He would have equated it with the condition that gives rise to such unity. And he would have allowed that a full analysis of that condition should disclose what it is about a person's identity that grounds the unity of its consciousness. But of course, Locke did not try to meet, nor did he even articulate, this explanatory goal that is naturally invited by his analysis of personal identity. That is why it is fair to say that he regarded the phenomenological unity of consciousness as a brute fact. It is conceivable (though not probable) that he was right. But we are not entitled to his conclusion by setting aside, as he did, the explanatory goal that is invited by his analysis of personal identity. We would be entitled to his conclusion only insofar as we tried to meet the goal, and then found that it was unmeetable. The same goes for the normative commitment to overall rational unity. It is conceivable that this commitment is a brute fact. But we would be entitled to that conclusion only insofar as we tried, and failed, to find an explanation for the fact.

But there is one crucial difference between the explanatory issue that is raised by Locke's analysis of personal identity and the explicit explanatory goal of the normative analysis. The issue raised by Locke's analysis would best be resolved through the empirical methods of science, whereas the explanatory goal of the normative analysis can be met without waiting for the deliverances of any scientific investigation of the nature of persons. Here is why. The normative ideal of overall rational unity can apply only if it is recognized, and indeed embraced, by the person to whom it applies. As a result, the question—what condition gives rise to the normative commitment to satisfying this ideal?—is not, strictly speaking, a causal question. It is rather a *justificatory* question, about what would qualify as good and sufficient reason for persons to undertake this normative commitment, and hence to embrace this ideal of rationality. Thus when we set the explanatory goal for the normative analysis of personal identity, and ask what is it about the condition of personal identity that gives rise to the normative commitment to overall rational unity, we must ask our question in an appropriately normative spirit. We must ask, what is it about the condition of personal identity such that a person might regard the obtaining of that very condition—that is, the condition that constitutes its own existence as an individual person—as sufficient reason to embrace, and indeed to strive to meet, the normative ideal of overall rational unity?

Two related reservations are likely to arise about the explanatory goal of the normative analysis of personal identity. Both concern the direct conceptual tie that the analysis exploits, between the normative ideal of overall rational unity and personal identity. The first reservation is this: given that the ideal defines what it is for an individual person to be fully rational, to ask what reason a person has to embrace the ideal might seem tantamount to asking why be rational at all—and this question threatens to be unanswerable, at least if what is wanted is a non-question-begging answer. However, it will soon emerge that the normative question that is raised by the explanatory goal of normative analysis is somewhat different, and also subtler than the very broad question, why be rational at all? Just why this is so can best be brought out by addressing the second reservation that is likely to arise about the explanatory goal of the normative analysis.

Like the first reservation, the second arises because the normative ideal of overall rational unity defines what it is for an individual person to be fully rational. If this definitional tie is taken as given, and if it is also taken as given that persons are rational beings, it would appear that the normative analysis of personal identity must itself be a conceptual truth. That is, it would appear to be a conceptual truth that the condition of identity for persons—at least insofar as they are rational beings—is the condition that gives rise to the normative commitment to achieve overall rational unity. It is of course no cause for reservation that an analysis should state a conceptual truth. On the contrary, it would seem to be the one indisputable sign of analytical success. What is perhaps problematic, however, is the idea that a conceptual truth should stand in need of explanation. And yet in this case the demand for an explanation is perfectly natural, for that is the only way in which we shall be able to make full sense of our very selves. It is, after all, a conceptual truth about *us* that we do have reason to embrace the normative ideal of overall rational unity within ourselves. And we naturally want to know, what *is* it about us, and about the condition of our identity, by virtue of which this is true?

This latter question remains even after the first reservation, concerning the question, why be rational at all? has been set aside. For the sake of argument let us set the first one aside, and assume that rationality is in general a good worth having and pursuing. To assume this is to assume that the sorts of rational activities that were cataloged above as comprising deliberation are worthy of pursuit. Such activities include: resolving conflicts and contradictions, ranking preferences, accepting implications, and the like. In principle, there is no reason why these activities must in every case be confined to the single point of view of an individual person. There is no reason, for example, why conflicts among intentional episodes belonging to distinct persons cannot in principle be resolved, no reason why desires belonging to distinct persons cannot in principle be ranked together so as to yield a single preference ordering, no reason why one person cannot in principle accept the implications of another person's beliefs, and so on. Precisely because rational activities *can* thus encompass intentional episodes belonging to distinct persons, we need an explanation of why an individual person is not obliged, by the normative ideal of rationality, to consider intentional episodes belonging to other persons, but is obliged to consider only those episodes that belong to its own point of view. That is to say, we need an answer to the normative question that has been raised: why—where this means *for what reason*—ought a person to achieve overall rational unity among all and only the intentional episodes that belong to its own rational point of view?

To discover that this justificatory question is unanswerable would be to discover that it is after all a brute fact about persons that they recognize and embrace the normative ideal of overall rational unity. Such a discovery is clearly among the logically possible outcomes of investigation. However, to set this justificatory question aside from the start would be to prejudge the issue in favor of that outcome.

4. Meeting the Explanatory Goal

The explanatory goal of the normative analysis will figure centrally in the argument to come against Locke's analysis of personal identity—and in parallel arguments against the Cartesian, Aristotelian, and standard neo-Lockean analyses. Without yet trying to make these arguments convincing, or even plausible, here is a brief outline of their common strategy.

In all cases, the Cartesian, Aristotelian, and Lockean, the question is raised whether the condition of personal identity that each one offers serves to explain why an individual person ought to achieve overall rational unity. And the claim in each case is that it fails to do so.

The claim is relatively uncontroversial when it is applied to the Cartesian view, and the view will not be considered again in this book. When Locke

argued that the immaterial simplicity of the substantial soul does not explain the phenomenological unity of consciousness, what he really established was that it does not serve to explain any psychological phenomena
whatsoever. And that includes the phenomenon to be explained here,
namely, that individual persons embrace the normative ideal of overall rational unity.

In application to the Lockean and Aristotelian views, the claim is much
more controversial. Against Locke, the claim is that phenomenological unity
within a set of intentional episodes does not explain why a person ought to
achieve overall rational unity among them. For the fact that intentional episodes belong to the same unified consciousness might fail to provide a reason
to achieve overall rational unity among them, and the fact that intentional
episodes belong to different consciousnesses does not preclude there being a
reason to achieve overall rational unity among them. Ditto for the Aristotelian view: the coexistence of intentional episodes within the life of a single
animal does not explain why a person ought to achieve overall rational unity
among them. For again, the fact that intentional episodes belong to the same
animal might fail to provide a person with reason to achieve overall rational
unity among them, and the fact that they belong to different animals does not
preclude there being such a reason.

Thus it will be argued with respect to both phenomenological unity and
animal identity that each condition is neither necessary nor sufficient to provide a reason to achieve overall rational unity within the set of intentional
episodes that the condition circumscribes. It will also be argued these conditions are not jointly sufficient either. And of course, since neither condition
is by itself necessary, they are not jointly necessary. On the other hand, it will
emerge that something like the condition of personal identity as specified in
standard neo-Lockean analyses is necessary—but not by itself sufficient—to
provide a reason to achieve overall rational unity within a set of intentional
episodes.

Neo-Lockean analyses depart from Locke in a number of ways.[6] For one
thing, they place less explicit emphasis on Locke's idea that an individual
person must have a single, unified consciousness. But even when they take this
idea for granted, neo-Lockeans also affirm that there are other psychological
relations, besides Locke's 'sameness of consciousness', that are important ingredients in personal identity—especially over time. In addition to the back-
ward-looking relation of memory, neo-Lockeans standardly include in their
analyses certain forward-looking relations such as anticipation, and the relation that obtains between an intention and its subsequent execution. Neo-

---

[6] The most influential neo-Lockean analyses of personal identity in psychological terms are to
be found in Part 3 of Derek Parfit's *Reasons and Persons* (New York: Oxford University Press,
1984); and in the following works by Sydney Shoemaker: "Persons and Their Pasts," *American
Philosophical Quarterly* 7 (1970): 269–85; "Personal Identity and Memory," in *Personal Identity*, ed.
J. Perry (Berkeley: University of California Press, 1975); (with R. Swinburne) *Personal Identity*
(Oxford: Basil Blackwell, 1984).

Lockean analyses also standardly include relations of psychological similarity and/or stability over time.

When these psychological relations that are standardly included in neo-Lockean analyses of personal identity obtain within a set of intentional episodes, this does not guarantee that there is a reason to achieve overall rational unity within the set. In addition, the set must include certain substantive practical commitments that serve as *unifying projects*. Such unifying projects have two defining features: first, they can be neither conceived nor executed except in a context where psychological relations of the sorts just mentioned obtain among a set of intentional episodes, and second, their execution depends upon achieving (or at least approximating to a high degree) overall rational unity within the set. Given their defining features, the presence of such unifying projects within a set of psychologically related intentional episodes would clearly provide a reason to achieve overall rational unity within the set. And the normative analysis meets its explanatory goal by including commitments to such unifying projects within the condition of personal identity, as well as the specific psychological relations on which those projects depend, both for their conception and for their execution.[7]

So to sum up: The guiding idea of the normative analysis is that the condition of personal identity should be equated with the condition that gives rise to the normative commitment to achieving overall rational unity. This equation ensures a perfect coincidence of a person's identity with a single rational point of view, for whatever condition gives rise to the normative commitment to overall rational unity also gives rise to a single rational point of view, and vice versa. In making the equation of the condition of personal identity with the condition that gives rise to the normative commitment to overall rational unity, the normative analysis sets a certain explanatory goal, namely, to explain why an individual person embraces the normative ideal that defines individual rationality. However, this explanatory goal poses a justificatory, rather than a strictly causal, question. What is wanted is an explanation of why it is that an individual person recognizes a *reason* to embrace the normative ideal of overall rational unity and to strive to meet it. When there is a set of intentional episodes that stand in suitable psychological relations so as to accommodate a unifying project, and when the set includes a commitment to such a unifying project, that provides a reason to achieve overall rational unity within the set. And according to the normative analysis, such a set of intentional episodes constitutes an individual person with its own distinct rational point of view.

---

[7] The full statement of the normative analysis that appears in chapter 4 does not actually use the term "psychological relation." It refers rather to *rational* relations, which are species of psychological relation that are psychological only in a very broad sense. Rational relations are explicitly defined in a way that abstracts from the differences between certain strictly intrapersonal psychological relations and certain sorts of interpersonal relations that closely resemble them. (The reasons for this terminological innovation will emerge in the course of chapter 4's argument for the possibility of group persons.)

5. A FINAL COMPARISON WITH LOCKE

The foregoing summary of the goal and content of the normative analysis was necessarily brief and abstract. It was so brief and so abstract that it may have failed altogether to enlighten. But this cannot be helped. Further details can be supplied only as the book's larger argument unfolds. All that can be done now is to conclude this preview of the normative analysis by reviewing the various points of convergence and divergence between it and Locke's analysis.

There are three main points of convergence, insofar as the normative analysis preserves Locke's three main theses about personal identity. They were: (1) a person is something with a first person point of view; (2) the identity of a person consists in the unity and continuity of such a first person point of view; and (3) the first person point of view of an individual person need not coincide with an individual soul or an individual animal.

However, in preserving these theses the normative analysis will also transform them, thereby making its very points of convergence with Locke points of divergence as well. Thus with respect to the first thesis, whereas Locke said a person is something with a phenomenological point of view, the normative analysis says that it is something with a rational point of view. With respect to the second thesis, whereas Locke located personal identity in phenomenological unity and continuity, the normative analysis locates personal identity in the normative commitment to achieve overall rational unity. And with respect to the third thesis, whereas Locke took the phenomenological unity of consciousness to be an inexplicable brute fact that holds independently of the identities of souls and animals, the normative analysis takes the normative commitment to overall rational unity as something that admits of explanation. It is in seeking this explanation that the normative analysis arrives at the conclusion that the normative commitment to overall rational unity need not be grounded in the simplicity of the soul, or the organic unity of an animal, or the phenomenological unity of consciousness. It is grounded rather in unifying projects, and in the psychological relations among intentional episodes on which such projects depend.

Some effort was made in section 3 to explain why a rational point of view— that is, a point of view that is governed by a normative commitment to achieve overall rational unity within it—qualifies as a first person point of view, and why it need not coincide with a particular phenomenological point of view. It was claimed first that there is a specifically normative first person relation that a person bears to those thoughts that it ought, given its commitment to overall rational unity, to take into account in its deliberations, and to those actions that are assessable as warranted or not in the light of its deliberations. It was claimed further that direct phenomenological access to thoughts and actions is neither necessary nor sufficient to secure this normative first person relation. These claims can be elaborated just a bit more in the light of the details of the normative analysis of personal identity that began to emerge in the last section. What really grounds the normative first person relation, at least according to the normative analysis, is a unifying project. In providing a reason to achieve overall rational unity within a set of intentional episodes, such a unifying project provides both a perspective and a focus for deliberations that proceed from the set—thereby providing for the normative first person relation that arises within a rational point of view. So in claiming that a rational point of view need not coincide with a phenomenological point of view, it is really being claimed that phenomenological unity is neither necessary nor sufficient for the planning and execution of the unifying projects that ground rational points of view. If there were doubts about the claim before, these added details may have done little to assuage them. But at least they may have brought the object of doubt into sharper relief.

Even if it should be granted that a rational point of view can be prised apart from a phenomenological point of view, doubts will also naturally arise about whether a rational point of view can similarly be prised apart from the bodily perspective of an animal. After all, a rational point of view is the deliberative point of view of an agent, and prima facie, agents are embodied things. So how is it that the rational perspective of an agent can be divorced from its bodily perspective? In a sense it cannot. But it will be argued here that the particular kind of agency that persons possess is different from the kind of agency that animals possess. Animals do not have commitments to unifying projects; only persons do. And it will emerge in Part II that some unifying projects do not require the practical resources of an entire human life, while other unifying projects require the practical resources of more than one human life. So although a person must in some sense have a body in order to be an agent, its body need not be identical with any particular animal's body. This, of course, is just the new interpretation of Locke's distinction that was promised in the introduction to this first part of the book: there can be multiple persons within a single animal, and there can be group persons who are composed of many animals. That is what it means to say that the rational point of view of a person need not be tied to the bodily perspective of a particular animal.

The attempt to decouple the rational point of view of an individual person from the bodily perspective of a particular animal may seem even more counterintuitive than the attempt to decouple such a rational point of view from a particular phenomenological perspective. The truth is that both attempts deliberately run counter to intuition. They are *revisionist* suggestions.

Locke did not think that it was in any way a mark against his analysis of personal identity that it should have counterintuitive consequences. But on the other hand, he did not think of himself as making a revisionist proposal. He simply thought that we are a little confused, in a superficial sort of way, because we do not always keep clearly in view what we mean by the term "person." If we were to fix the idea clearly in our minds—the idea of a thinking, intelligent being, and so forth—then we would no longer be confused. It would be plain to us that a person's identity consists in consciousness alone, and that it depends on no other independent metaphysical ground, such as the simplicity of the soul, or the organic unity of an animal.

There is a temptation to agree with Locke on the more general point, that if we fix the idea of a person clearly enough, then it will also be clear what the condition of personal identity is. And indeed the argument of this book can be portrayed as an attempt to do just that. Moreover, it can be portrayed as an attempt to do it in a way that is faithful to Locke's own account of our idea of a person. Although his famous statement of what a person is, is long and complex, he often summarized it by saying that a person is a rational being. And he could not possibly deny that the point of view of such a being must be a rational point of view. Therefore, the argument of this book can be seen as levying the charge that Locke simply failed to get right what a rational point of view is. He wrongly assumed that it must be, or at least must coincide with, the phenomenological point of view of a unified consciousness.

However, this way of portraying the book's argument leaves out another crucial disagreement with Locke, which is that any consistent and systematic account of personhood and personal identity must necessarily be revisionist. While Locke was certainly right that we must fix the idea of a person clearly before attempting to pronounce on the issue of personal identity, he was wrong to think that it is always clear which of our ideas—once suitably fixed and clarified—ought to be accepted as the idea of a person. The task of the next chapter is to show just how far this is from being clear.

On the Need for Revision

LOCKE did not present his thought experiment about the prince and the cobbler as the sole ground for his analysis of personal identity in terms of consciousness alone. Nor did his early opponents fasten their critical gaze on that step. They did not question whether his thought experiment was legitimate, nor did they report intuitive responses to the experiment that were contrary to his own response. Their main concern was to show that whatever our intuitions may be, Locke's analysis of personal identity is ultimately incoherent.

Thought experiments have played a much more dominant role in recent attempts to carry out the neo-Lockean project of providing a purely psychological analysis of personal identity. Indeed, the thought experimental method has entrenched itself as a staple component of virtually all neo-Lockean efforts. Furthermore, it seems to be a significant matter of intellectual-biographical fact that many convinced neo-Lockeans first arrived at their conviction through their own intuitive responses to thought experiments modeled on Locke's prince and cobbler. Yet if it is a fact, it is a curious fact, for fairly early on in the contemporary debate, Bernard Williams demonstrated that our intuitive responses to such experiments are inconstant.[1]

Accordingly, the guiding question of this chapter is, what does this inconstancy of intuition in response to the Lockean thought experiments signify for the philosophical study of personal identity? The answer is twofold. First, it signifies a basic conflict in our commonsense beliefs about personal identity. Second, it signifies a need for revision. If there really is a conflict in our commonsense outlook, then clearly, any tenable view of personal identity must revise some aspect of common sense.

The conflict arises because common sense both denies and affirms Locke's distinction between personal and animal identity. On the one hand, it is deeply rooted in our commonsense thinking that persons are human beings whose life spans are constituted by the biologically defined sequence of birth, maturation, and death. Yet on the other hand, it is just as deeply rooted in our commonsense thought that a person's life can in principle diverge from any particular human life—as when we imagine life after death, reincarnation, other kinds of metamorphosis, and even possession. It would be a mistake to suppose that this latter conception of ourselves, as distinct from the human being, is exclusively the product of religion and myth or that it arises only in connection with spiritual matters. Some hard-line materialists and other

---

[1] He demonstrated this in "The Self and the Future," *Philosophical Review* 79 (1970): 161–80, reprinted in Perry, *Personal Identity*, and in Bernard Williams, *Problems of the Self* (Cambridge: Cambridge University Press, 1973).

naturalists (as opposed to supernaturalists) have their own ways of conceiving the ongoing life of a person as independent of any particular animal life— usually by imagining technological advances such as artificial brains (often in the form of computers), brain reprogramming, and teletransportation, to name just a few. It must be admitted that these quasi-scientific possibilities depend for their intelligibility on recently devised hypotheses about the nature of mind and its relation to matter (most often on the functionalist theory of mind and its corollary that the mental supervenes on the material). So perhaps it is not fair to attribute our recognition of the possibilities directly to our common sense. But all the same, these possibilities have been raised in an effort to make theoretical sense of a *prior* commonsense inclination, the inclination to suppose that the life of the person need not coincide with the life of a particular animal. And even if theoretical reflection should lead us to conclude that this inclination to distinguish personal identity from human (animal) identity is mistaken, that would not show that the inclination had never truly been a part of our commonsense outlook. It has been and is. The trouble is that this inclination to affirm Locke's distinction is directly opposed to an equally strong tendency to deny it, by equating the condition of identity for persons and human beings.

This basic conflict in our commonsense outlook is all too evident in the philosophical literature devoted to the topic of personal identity. The central dispute in that literature has been whether Locke was right to draw a distinction between personal and animal identity, by analyzing personal identity in purely psychological terms. This central dispute has not generally been portrayed as deriving from a basic conflict within common sense. But the very fact that the dispute has dominated so much of the philosophical discussion for so long is a sure sign that each party to the dispute can lay claim to some support from common sense. And since the parties are opposed, the different aspects of common sense from which they draw support must also be opposed. In consequence, no well-considered philosophical conclusion about personal identity can resolve this opposition without proposing some revision of our commonsense outlook.

It would of course be misguided to suppose that the central philosophical dispute about personal identity, concerning whether Locke's distinction obtains, actually exhausts the possible philosophical positions. There are, after all, only two parties to this central dispute. The first is the Lockean party, which includes only those who follow Locke in analyzing personal identity in purely psychological terms. The second is the animalist party, which includes only those who equate personal identity with animal identity. Thus the dispute leaves out of account all *non*psychological analyses of personal identity that fail to equate personal identity with animal identity. That is, it leaves out of account all analyses that support *a* distinction between personal identity and animal identity, but without supporting *Locke's* distinction. Not only does this mean that the dispute excludes the Cartesian analysis in terms of immaterial substance; the dispute also excludes all physical analyses of personal identity that fail to equate personal and animal identity. The most influential such analysis equates personal identity with the identity of the human brain.[2] However, there is no reason why a physical analysis of personal identity must necessarily restrict itself to biological terms. Nor is there anything to bar a hybrid analysis that incorporates both psychological and physical terms.

In face of all of this variety of possible philosophical response to the problem of personal identity, this book will nevertheless begin by restricting its attention to the central dispute, between the proponents and opponents of Locke's distinction. In doing so, it will initially lump all purely psychological analyses of personal identity together as parts of a single neo-Lockean project that is aimed at securing some version or other of Locke's distinction. And it will simply ignore all nonpsychological analyses besides the animalist analysis.

There are several reasons why it makes sense thus to confine the philosophical dispute about personal identity.

By far the most important reason is that it allows us to see the philosophical dispute as a direct reflection of the basic conflict in our commonsense outlook. When common sense denies Locke's distinction, it displays no commitment to any physical analysis of personal identity besides the animalist analysis—that is, persons are identified as human beings and not as brains or as any other physically defined entities. And insofar as common sense accepts Locke's distinction, it does not discriminate between the different possible versions of it that rest on different psychological analyses of personal identity. Common sense is vague about precisely what psychological conditions would be necessary and sufficient for the continuation of a person's psychological life in independence from a particular animal's life. In fact, common sense is so vague about this matter that it does not really distinguish between the purely psychological analyses of the sort that Locke and neo-Lockeans have put forward and the Cartesian analysis in terms of an immaterial substance. However, to repeat once again, this book has already set the Cartesian analysis aside on Lockean grounds. And it is perfectly justifiable to set it aside, even from the point of view of common sense. The only interest that common sense takes in the Cartesian analysis is as a way of making sense of the idea that a person's psychological life might be independent of a particular animal's biological life span. And that, of course, is the very idea on which Locke and neo-Lockeans want to insist.

Second, despite the diversity of analyses of personal identity that have been put forward in recent years, the wider philosophical dispute to which they belong was originally framed by Locke's question, concerning whether the identity of a *person*, qua rational being, comes to the same thing as the identity of an *animal*. There is therefore a certain propriety in taking his question as a starting point for investigation.

A final reason for confining the philosophical dispute about personal identity in the way suggested has to do with the specific analysis of personal

---

[2] This analysis was put forward by Thomas Nagel in chapter 3 of *The View From Nowhere*.

identity that will be defended in this book, namely, the normative analysis. What the book will eventually have to say about why the normative analysis is preferable to the animalist analysis is generalizable, and would apply to *any* position that analyzes personal identity in nonpsychological terms. So in the end, no harm will have been done by concentrating on just one nonpsychological analysis. And in the beginning, it will simplify matters enormously to do so. As for the Lockean side of the dispute, the normative analysis does differ in crucial respects from all other psychological analyses. Some of these differences, and the reasons for them, were briefly anticipated in chapter 1. They will be more fully displayed and discussed in due course. But they do not matter for the purposes of this chapter.

The chapter actually has two purposes. The first has already been announced, which is to show that the inconstancy of our intuitive responses to Lockean-style thought experiments reveals a basic conflict in our commonsense beliefs about personal identity—and hence a need for revision. Showing this will be the task of section 1. Subsequent sections will go on to consider the main strategies of revisionist response to the conflict.

Since the conflict in our commonsense outlook is directly reflected in the central philosophical dispute about personal identity, many of the strategies of response are familiar from the recent philosophical literature. But even before delving into that literature, it is easy to see that there are only four possible strategies, and that there is a definite order in which they should be pursued.

One strategy would involve trying to show that the conflict is merely apparent. This is naturally the first strategy to try, because if it succeeded, then we would be spared the embarrassment of being caught out in believing a contradiction. Yet the strategy has little chance of succeeding. We are clearly disposed both to affirm and to deny Locke's distinction, and this disposition of ours constitutes the strongest possible evidence that we actually do believe a contradiction. Locke argued that it is not really a contradiction, but only a semantical confusion. If he had been right, then there would be no need to revise our commonsense beliefs after all, but only a need to clarify them. Section 2 will argue that he was wrong on this score. It will also argue against another attempt to remove the appearance of contradiction, which proposes to relativize all claims about personal identity to social contexts. The main merit of the relativistic view lies in the fact that it can accommodate all of our apparently conflicted intuitions about the condition of personal identity. However, although the view can preserve all of our specific intuitions about the various conditions in which we are prepared to suppose that a single person exists, it is nevertheless a revisionist view. We do not believe, as a matter of common sense, that the condition of a person's identity is relative to a social context. Section 2 will raise some important ethical reasons for resisting this particular revision. (The same ethical considerations will be brought to bear in the arguments of the next chapter.)

Once the conflict in our commonsense outlook about personal identity is acknowledged as genuine, the second natural strategy would be to defend one side of it by showing that the other side is incoherent. This has been the strategy of choice among philosophers, because it holds out the prospect of conclusive *proof* in the philosophical study of personal identity. This would be a proof by elimination, in which all but one analysis of personal identity are eliminated as incoherent. Although the proclaimed results of this second strategy are rarely labeled revisionist, revision is nevertheless its aim. It asks us to give up—and in that sense revise—some of our commonsense beliefs. In actual practice, the strategy has most often been wielded against the neo-Lockean project of analyzing personal identity in purely psychological terms. But section 3 will argue that neither side of the philosophical dispute between the neo-Lockeans and the animalists can be eliminated on grounds of incoherence. The same goes for the underlying conflict in our commonsense beliefs from which this central philosophical dispute derives.

Once we have granted that there is a genuine conflict in our commonsense beliefs about personal identity, each side of which is perfectly coherent, we face a *methodological difficulty*. Since by the laws of classical logic everything follows from a contradiction, it would seem that every view of personal identity can be proven on the basis of premises drawn from common sense. Yet it would also seem that every view can be refuted on the same basis. This will be so insofar as we take the fact that a view contradicts *some* aspect of common sense as a sufficient reason to reject it. Minimally, this means that we cannot expect to establish firm conclusions about the condition of personal identity through any simple appeal to our commonsense beliefs. But in addition, it means that we shall have to settle for something less than strict proof in the philosophical study of personal identity. The third strategy therefore proposes to resolve the central philosophical dispute about personal identity, and the underlying conflict in our commonsense beliefs, on grounds that fall short of strict proof. It proposes to do this by seeking positive reasons to embrace one side in the dispute, but without seeking to eliminate the other side as untenable. Rather, it will leave the other side standing as a logically coherent alternative that can claim some support from common sense.

If this third strategy were to fail, then we would have no option but to pursue a fourth strategy, which is extremely unattractive. Instead of resolving the central philosophical dispute about personal identity, this final strategy would opt for a *non*solution that turns its back on both sides in the dispute, the Lockeans and the animalists alike. This last strategy of response is the most radical of all. It would require us to abandon all of the beliefs that generate the dispute to begin with—and that would include, quite probably, all of our commonsense beliefs about personal identity. Prima facie, this seems inappropriate, given that the concept of a person occupies a central role in the day-to-day affairs where common sense naturally prevails. But in any case, it is not clear that the fourth strategy can coherently be pursued at all. It asks us to reject both sides in the central philosophical dispute about personal identity. And if we describe that dispute in general enough terms, as a dispute about whether Locke's distinction obtains or not, then the two sides of the dispute would seem to exhaust the logically possible positions—unless we want to eliminate the concept of a person altogether.

Clearly, it would be preferable to avoid the fourth strategy of response if we can. But of course, we cannot simply wallow in the conflict of our common-sense outlook either. And since both sides of the conflict are coherent, we cannot expect to prove one by eliminating the other. So we are left with little choice but to pursue the third strategy, and seek positive reasons to embrace one side or the other anyway—which is exactly what this book will do. In seeking such reasons, we shall be led back to Locke's original instruction. We shall find that we have to develop an adequate account of what *kind* of thing a person is in order to arrive at a firm conclusion about the condition of personal identity.

NOTA BENE: Some readers may already be convinced that there is a basic conflict in our commonsense outlook, in the form of beliefs that both affirm and deny Locke's distinction between personal and animal identity. Anyone who is convinced of this, and who is also convinced that each side of the conflict is perfectly coherent, already agrees with the main conclusions of sections 1, 2, and 3. Such readers may safely skip ahead to section 4, where the third strategy of revisionist response that will be pursued in this book will be discussed in greater detail.

1. WHAT THE LOCKEAN THOUGHT EXPERIMENTS REALLY SHOW

When Locke asked us to imagine who would be who if the respective con-sciousnesses of a prince and a cobbler were switched, he thought it would be intuitively obvious to all who considered the matter that the prince would be the person with the cobbler's former body and vice versa. The only support-ing rationale that he offered was drawn from ethical considerations. He asked who, after all, could possibly be held responsible for the prince's past actions except the person who could remember them and claim them as his own—that is, the person who retained the prince's consciousness and later came to have the cobbler's body? This ethical leg of Locke's argument is significant for the arguments to come in section 4 and in the next chapter. But the pres-ent issue is whether our *direct* intuitive responses to Locke's thought experi-ment, regardless of the ethical considerations that might be brought to bear in support of them, universally affirm his distinction between personal and animal identity.

It seems unlikely that there has ever been a respondent who failed alto-gether to have any Lockean intuitions about the case of the prince and the cobbler, and had only animalist intuitions instead. But suppose for the sake of argument that there had been such a respondent. (It is important that we imagine a respondent who is untutored in the philosophical problem of personal identity, and whose intuitions have not, therefore, been altered by too much exerted theoretical effort.) By hypothesis, this respondent would find it intuitively obvious that the prince remains the prince, and the cobbler remains the cobbler, even after their consciousnesses have been switched. Furthermore, the respondent would find Locke's own account of the case somewhat mystifying and quite possibly unintelligible. To this respondent, it would be obvious that the procedure of switching consciousnesses cannot interfere with the facts of personal identity; all that the procedure would really accomplish is the perpetration of systematic delusions in two human animals about who they really are. It is important to bear in mind here that the question being raised is not whether this animalist attitude toward the situation described in Locke's thought experiment is reasonable. The question is whether there truly is anybody whose untutored intuitions are consistently and exclusively animalist—so much so that they have never for a single moment had a Lockean intuition about the condition of personal identity. Since this is an empirical question, it ought perhaps to be left open until the data are in. But it is striking that the protracted philosophical discussion of Locke—even at its most critical—has not included reports of such respondents with wholly absent Lockean intuitions.[3] Indeed, it was briefly indicated earlier, and the point will be further elaborated in section 3, that Locke's opponents have mainly opposed him on theoretical rather than intuitive grounds. Presumably, if his opponents had found that intuition was all on their side, they would have availed themselves of this fact in their arguments against him. So we are left with the very strong impression that intuitive responses to his thought experiment do provide some support for his conclusion in favor of a distinction between personal and animal identity.

In the initial phase of his discussion of the Lockean thought experimental method, Williams contributed to this impression. He began by introducing several new features into Locke's original experimental design. First, he specified that when the switch of consciousnesses takes place, it is the total psychology of each person that is transferred to the other's body. This allows the experiment to ignore (just as the present discussion is ignoring) the variations among possible psychological analyses of personal identity—for no matter what their differences, all psychological analyses agree that the preservation of total psychology suffices for the continued existence of a person. Second, Williams proposed a way of imagining the transfer of total psychology that is consistent with materialism: the brain of each person is thoroughly reprogrammed with the other's total psychology. Third, he added a condition to ensure that the respective psychologies of the two persons could be sustained in one another's bodies after the transfer, namely, that the physical characteristics of the two bodies involved be sufficiently similar so that the transfer

---

[3] It is also worth noting for the record that in thirteen years of teaching the subject of personal identity, I have never yet encountered a student who was completely lacking in Lockean intuitions.

would not induce any dramatic psychological changes. Fourth, he required that each respondent imaginatively project itself into the hypothetical situation described by the thought experiment, and respond to that situation from a first person point of view. Thus the respondent is asked to determine whom it would regard as itself after the transfer of psychology has taken place—the person with its original body, or the person with its original psychology. And finally, Williams injected prudential considerations into the experiment. He stipulated that one of the persons who results from the psychology-transfer will be awarded a significant sum of money while the other will be subjected to torture, and he instructed respondents to consult their feelings of prudential self-concern when they determine which of the resulting persons they would regard as themselves. Like Locke's appeal to the ethical dimension of responsibility, Williams's appeal to prudential considerations is significant, and will be addressed in section 4, and again in the next chapter. But the present issue simply concerns what his redesigned Lockean thought experiment directly shows, both about the condition of personal identity and about the thought experimental method itself.

To facilitate the discussion, here is a sample thought experiment of Williams's design: I am told that my total psychology is about to be transferred to my friend's body, and hers to mine, and that after the transfer has taken place, the person who will have my original body and her original psychology will be tortured, while the person who will have my original psychology and her original body will be rewarded. If, in consulting my selfish feelings, I find that I am relieved that this will be the outcome, that shows that I do not regard my identity as grounded in the life of a particular human being; I regard it rather as grounded in a purely psychological condition that can be realized in my friend's body as well as in the body that I now have. For the record, that is precisely how I do respond to the experiment: I feel prudential concern for, and identify myself as, the person who will have my original psychology and my friend's original body. Williams would not immediately quarrel with my response. In fact, he would concede that, as the experiment is presented, mine is a perfectly natural response. He even went so far as to allow that such cases could aptly be described as cases of "body-switching"—in order to keep attention fixed on the uninterrupted lines of psychological continuity with which many respondents (like myself) want to identify themselves, even in the face of changing bodily circumstances—hence Williams's initial contribution to the impression that intuition really is on Locke's side.

However, Williams went on to run a second trial of the same thought experiment that turns intuition squarely against Locke. In the second trial, the respondent is presented with only half the imagined facts of the case, namely, the facts about what will happen to one of the human beings involved. Furthermore, the facts about this human being are deliberately presented in a somewhat question-begging fashion, as facts about what will happen to the *respondent*. So in the sample experiment where I was instructed to imagine undergoing a psychology transfer (body-switch) with my friend, here is what I would be asked to imagine on the second trial: first I will undergo a proce-

dure that gives me amnesia and removes all of my other psychological characteristics; then I will undergo a second procedure that gives me someone else's
memories and psychological characteristics; and after both of these procedures have been carried out, I will be subjected to painful torture. Williams
rightly assumed that I can regard this imagined circumstance as one that could
in principle befall me. This means that I can, as this second trial of his experiment requires, imaginatively project myself into a situation where I expect
this circumstance to befall me. When I do so, I naturally imagine myself to
feel great fear and dread—*selfish* fear and dread—of the anticipated torture. I
also imagine myself to fear and dread the other anticipated changes as well,
the loss of my own memories and psychological characteristics and the acquisition of alien memories and psychological characteristics. But that makes no
odds against my ability to conceive these changes as happening to *me*, or my
ability to think that despite the massive psychological changes, *I* would still be
the one who was going to face the pain of torture. Of course when I think
these things, I am conceiving my identity in animalist terms, as tied to the life
of a particular human being, and my previous Lockean intuition about my
identity seems to have vanished entirely. Thus we get a peculiar result. Earlier, it seemed highly unlikely that any respondent to Locke's original experiment about the prince and the cobbler could be wholly without all Lockean
intuitions. Now, by the end of the second trial of Williams's redesigned
Lockean experiment, it seems just as unlikely that any respondent could be
wholly without the opposed animalist intuitions.

Once again, suppose for the sake of argument that there was such a respondent, in this case, a respondent (again, untutored in the philosophical study of
personal identity) who lacked all animalist intuitions and had only Lockean
intuitions instead. By hypothesis, this respondent would find some of the
terms of Williams's second trial unintelligible. It would be intuitively obvious
to this respondent that massive psychological change constitutes death—not
something just as bad as death or worse than death, but literally a form (the
only form for persons) of death. In consequence, the respondent could not
possibly regard the imposition of new memories and psychological characteristics, or the subsequent torture that is supposed to follow upon this imposition, as events in its own life. But that, of course, is precisely what Williams's
second trial stipulates. As before when we considered the possibility of absent
Lockean intuitions, perhaps we ought to regard it as an open empirical question whether there really are any persons in whom all animalist intuitions are
absent, and who have only Lockean intuitions instead. Such persons would
necessarily regard the following common events of human life as forms of
death: massive strokes, advanced senility, diseases and accidents that cause
severe brain damage. Furthermore, they would be incapable of dredging up
any selfish fear on their own behalf of the pain that might be suffered after
such a psychologically catastrophic event had taken place. As a result, they
would not look upon the prospect of residence in a hospice or nursing home
after such an event with the dread that many of us feel toward that prospect.
They would not regard that future circumstance as one that would be

happening to *them*; it would happen only to their human bodies. Again, it is important to bear in mind that the question being raised is not whether these Lockean attitudes are reasonable. The present question is empirical rather than normative. It is whether there actually are any persons who can honestly claim that, prior to all philosophical reflection about the problem of personal identity, they never had any animalist intuitions whatsoever. Although this is an empirical question that must officially remain open until the data are in, it is safe to wager that there are very few such persons, if any. Unless their guard has been put up by philosophical training, most persons at least some of the time readily assent to the animalist proposition that they are human beings, and would regard themselves as the same person even after massive psychological change.

In insisting that animalist intuitions about personal identity are common and natural, it was part of Williams's aim to undermine Lockean convictions. That is fair enough. However, it would be wrong to try to substitute animalist convictions in their place. The real lesson of Williams's discussion is that the Lockean thought experimental method should serve in the end to shake *all* conviction about the condition of personal identity. If at first it seemed intuitively obvious that in a transfer of psychologies I go where my psychology goes, it seemed just as obvious in a second trial that my identity remains tied to a particular human being even when there is massive psychological change. Once we acknowledge that our intuitions conflict in this way, we simply cannot suppose that the issue of personal identity is resolvable by appeal to intuition alone, as all Lockean thought experiments try to do.

It has been granted as an unconfirmed (and also unlikely) empirical possibility that there might be persons who do not themselves experience this conflict of intuitions that the rest of us experience upon going through the paces of Williams's two experimental trials. Such persons—that is, persons whose intuitions are either exclusively Lockean or exclusively animalist— might be optimistic about the prospects for a thought experimental determination of the condition of personal identity. But such a determination would be forthcoming only if we *all* had consistent intuitions, and moreover, we all had the *same* consistent intuitions. If the philosophical literature on personal identity has established anything, it has established that this is not so.[4]

The frustration with the Lockean thought experiments has been such that their very legitimacy has been called into question, and with them the legitimacy of all philosophical thought experiments.[5] However, it has not been the

---

[4] There have been attempts to refine the thought experimental method so as to minimize the chances of conflicting responses. But these efforts are unduly optimistic about the extent to which persons really do have consistent commonsense beliefs about the condition of personal identity. Peter Unger's *Identity, Consciousness and Value* (New York: Oxford University Press, 1990) offers what is perhaps the most systematic and sustained effort in this direction. But see my "Critical Notice" in the *Canadian Journal of Philosophy* 24 (1994): 119–33, for an account of why his proposed refinements of the Lockean thought experimental design do not guarantee concordant responses.

[5] See Kathleen Wilkes, *Real People: Personal Identity without Thought Experiments* (New York: Oxford University Press, 1988).

aim of this section to debunk the philosophical thought experiment. The question whether such experiments are useful, and therefore legitimate, philosophical tools cannot be answered without first making clear what their purpose is. If their sole purpose was to provide definitive solutions to philosophical problems, then their legitimacy probably should be called into doubt, for as a general rule, philosophical thought experiments have generated far more controversy than agreement. Consider, for example, Locke's inverted spectrum, Descartes's dreams and evil demon, Wittgenstein's universe of two qualitatively indistinguishable spheres, Strawson's sound world, Rawls's veil of ignorance, Putnam's twin earth and brains-in-vats, Searle's Chinese room, and Burge's arthritic Bert. Clearly, none of these thought experiments has commanded universal agreement about the philosophical issue it was meant to illuminate. Yet each experiment has nevertheless proven to be instructive—either because it introduced a new philosophical issue, or because it changed the terms in which we think about an old issue, or simply because it brought some issue into sharper relief than it had been before. Several of these merits can be claimed for the Lockean thought experiments about personal identity. Of course the issue they were meant to illuminate— namely, what is the condition of personal identity?—is not new. But the Lockean experiments have certainly introduced new ways of thinking about that issue—mainly by separating it from the metaphysical doctrine of substance dualism, and also by connecting it with two important ethical dimensions of personhood, namely, responsibility and self-concern. (Section 4 and chapter 3 will discuss the proper role of these ethical dimensions of personhood in the Lockean and neo-Lockean arguments about personal identity. And section 2 of chapter 6 will consider what the overall implications of this book's arguments are with respect to them.) Reframing the issue of personal identity in these ways has not led to a firm thought experimental conclusion about the condition of personal identity. But all the same, the Lockean experiments have proved highly instructive. They have helped to clarify and enrich the philosophical discussion of personal identity. And more importantly, they have revealed a basic conflict in our commonsense outlook: we find it natural both to affirm and to deny Locke's distinction between personal and animal identity.

So we turn now to the various strategies for coping with this conflict of common sense, which has generated the central philosophical dispute about personal identity.

2. THE CONFLICT IS NOT MERELY APPARENT

The first strategy aims to show that there really is no conflict in our commonsense beliefs about personal identity.

This would have been Locke's strategy. He certainly did not think that we actually have conflicting beliefs about personal identity. And it seems not to have occurred to him that his thought experiment about the prince and the cobbler might be inconclusive. Of course he recognized that there had been disputes of a philosophical nature about personal identity. But he chalked them up to a superficial confusion about the meanings of terms, a confusion that could easily be cleared up by carefully defining the term "person" and using it accordingly. Once the term "person" is defined as "rational being," he thought we should all be able to see that it cannot refer to a human being, but must refer to that thing we call "self"—a psychological subject whose identity is grounded in the phenomenological unity of consciousness rather than in the biological unity of a human animal. Locke did allow that we sometimes give the *appearance* of denying the distinction between personal and animal identity. We do this whenever we use the term "I," a term that is generally understood to refer to one's self, in order to refer to a human being. But he did not take this to show that we thereby deny the real distinction between the self, that is, the person, and the human animal. He took it to show rather that the term "I" is ambiguous, sometimes referring to a person, and other times referring to a human being.

If Locke had been right, then there would be no need for revision, for there would be no commonsense conflict to resolve. But he was not right. Even once we fix the meaning of the term "person" as he suggested, to mean "rational being," we are still free to deny his distinction between personal and animal identity. All we need do—and this we often do, both in common affairs and in philosophy—is suppose that a rational *being* is also a rational *animal*, the only known case of which is the *human* being. And this truly does *conflict* with a tendency that we also have, to *affirm* Locke's distinction between these things.

There is a second way of trying to show that there is only the appearance of a conflict in our commonsense beliefs about personal identity. This way, unlike Locke's way, does not require that we choose between affirming and denying his distinction. It proposes to remove the contradiction by making these affirmations and denials relative to a social context. On this relativistic view, the inconstancy of our intuitive responses to the Lockean thought experiments is not a sign that we have conflicting beliefs about personal identity; it is merely a reflection of the fact that different experiments impose, either implicitly or explicitly, different social parameters relative to which we make different determinations of personal identity.[6]

The relativistic view of personal identity does not suffer the conceptual difficulty that attends the relativistic conception of truth—that difficulty being that any statement of the relativistic conception of truth seems to presuppose the very absolute conception that it denies. The particular form of social relativity in question is no more problematic than the relativity of space-time. Just as it is logically coherent to suppose that all spatial and tem-

---

[6] A subtle and thorough exploration of the sensitivity of judgments about personal identity to social context can be found in Stephen White's "Metapsychological Relativism and the Self," *Journal of Philosophy* 86 (1989): 298–323, reprinted in his *Unity of the Self* (Cambridge: MIT Press, 1994).

poral determinations are relative to an observer, likewise, it is logically coherent to suppose that all determinations of personhood and personal identity are relative to a social context.

Some may find discomfort in the relativists' claim that persons owe their very identity to their social context. But this is not necessarily a cause for discomfort. After all, it is a plausible to suppose that persons could not achieve their personhood except through social interaction. And to grant this is precisely to grant that there are personal facts that simply cannot obtain except within social contexts. Of course to grant all this is not yet to grant the relativistic view of personal identity. It is merely to take the first step toward that view, by granting the dependence of at least some personal facts on social context. A further condition must be met if personal facts are to be relative to a social context, namely, that there be more than one such context. And even that is not a sufficient condition for the relativity of personal identity, since even if some personal facts are relative to a social context, the facts of personal identity might not be among them. But then again they might, and according to the relativist about personal identity, they are.

It might wrongly be thought that the plausible supposition that was offered above, namely, that personhood is achieved through social interaction, points to a further supposition on which the relativistic view of personal identity must founder. This further supposition is that there must be some underlying nature that is not created by the social interactions that generate personhood, but that is already there for these social interactions to do their work upon. The truth of this further supposition is clearly indicated by the following fact: we cannot devise a process of socialization by which we could transform dogs and cats into persons. We can of course treat dogs and cats as *if* they were persons, but that is quite another thing. What we cannot do is give something the right sort of nature by virtue of which it can enter into distinctively interpersonal relations. That, it seems, must already be given prior to socialization. The relativists' idea is that this underlying nature which is prior to socialization cannot qualify as a specifically *personal* nature unless and until it is pronounced so from within a particular social context. But the question naturally arises whether the process of socialization could possibly alter the facts of personal *identity*. More specifically, if it is *human* nature (as opposed, say, to feline or canine nature) that is required, why does that not imply the nonrelativistic conclusion that personal identity is just the same as human (i.e., animal) identity? The relativist about personal identity has a ready answer to this question. Although it is human nature that social forces do their work upon, there are other facts, besides the facts of human nature, that may enter into the determination of personal identity. To name just a few, there are facts concerning technology, medicine, religion, and law. All of these are social facts that clearly differ from context to context. And depending on how they differ, they may, according to the relativist, entail different answers to the question, what makes something the same *person*?

Thus the relativistic view need not make the absurd proposal that social contexts create the facts of personhood and personal identity out of nothing. The view can perfectly well allow that there is a fixed human nature out of which the facts of personhood and personal identity arise. And there is no problem about reconciling the absolute reality of human nature with the relativity of personal identity to social context.

In fact, the normative analysis of personal identity also requires a similar sort of reconciliation between the fixed reality of human nature and the alterable facts of personal identity. As the last chapter's preview made clear, the normative analysis equates the condition of personal identity with the condition in which there is a single rational point of view. It will later emerge that the analysis assumes that there is a fixed human nature that supplies the basic capacities whose exercise is necessary for the production of a rational point of view.[7] But in addition, the analysis claims that these capacities may be exercised in such a way as to give rise to rational points of view that do not coincide with the perspectives of individual human beings. They may give rise to multiple points of view, and hence multiple persons, within a single human being; and they may give rise to group points of view, and hence group persons, that encompass many human beings.

Thus the normative analysis shares the relativists' idea that a fixed human nature may give rise to variable facts of personal identity. However, at the same time, it rejects the relativists' idea that personal identity is relative to a social context.

The real problem with the relativistic position lies in the fact that it requires us to give up an aspect of our commonsense outlook that is absolutely crucial from an ethical point of view, and that will figure centrally in the proposal of the next chapter, to adopt the ethical criterion of personhood. We generally take for granted that persons are set apart from other things by the fact that they recognize themselves as persons and, moreover, that they mutually recognize one another as persons—which is to say, they mutually recognize one another as things that recognize both their own and one another's personhood. This capacity for mutual recognition among persons is essential to a whole range of distinctively interpersonal relations. For example, such mutual recognition comes into play whenever persons converse, argue, cooperate, compete, or hold one another responsible. It also comes into play in the agency-regarding relations that figure in the ethical criterion of personhood that will be proposed in the next chapter. The agents who can engage in such relations can mutually recognize one another as such, that is, as the givers and receivers of regard for agency. And it is an essential part of this mutual recognition among agents who can engage in agency-regarding relations that they mutually recognize one another as facing the same choice concerning whether and when to engage in such relations—and furthermore, they must mutually recognize that it is, for them, an ethically

---

[7] See section 3 of chapter 5 for further discussion of this point.

significant choice. Thus, according to the ethical criterion, the class of persons is the class of agents who mutually recognize one another as facing, in all of their relations, the same ethically significant choice concerning whether and when to engage in agency-regarding relations. And the troubling possibility that is raised by the relativists' position is that some persons may be barred from standing in the whole range of distinctively interpersonal relations that rest on mutual recognition, including the agency-regarding relations that figure in the ethical criterion. The persons who may be barred from such relations are of course persons who belong to different social contexts. Once the facts of personhood and personal identity are made relative to a social context, there is no guarantee that they will be recognizable across contexts. And when they are not, there simply cannot be any interpersonal relations or ethical choices of the sort that depend on mutual recognition among persons.

To raise this problem is not yet to show that the relativistic view of personal identity is either false or unworkable. But it does show that, unlike Locke's way of trying to remove the appearance of a contradiction in our beliefs about personal identity, the relativists' way is explicitly revisionist. Although relativizing personal identity to a social context does allow us to reconcile all of our apparently contradictory intuitions about the condition of personal identity, it still asks that we give something up—namely, our commonsense belief that it is in the nature of persons that they can recognize one another as persons, even across social contexts. And that is the main ground on which this book rejects the relativistic position. However, the full argument for retaining this aspect of common sense must wait until the next chapter.

For the present, let it be noted that the only merit which the relativist position can claim so far is that it releases us from having to admit that we really do have conflicting beliefs about personal identity. Given the earnestness and the intensity of the central philosophical dispute about personal identity that Locke inaugurated and failed to resolve, it is not easy to accept the relativists' verdict that there is no conflict and that everyone is right: a person both is and is not a human being, depending.

3. NEITHER SIDE OF THE CONFLICT IS INCOHERENT

Philosophers have not tended to articulate what they sometimes call the "problem" of personal identity as a problem that is generated by the fact that we have conflicting commonsense beliefs about personal identity. But in labeling it a *problem*, rather than, say, a question, they have acknowledged that there are conflicting tendencies of thought about the matter. Furthermore, most philosophical discussions of the problem that is generated by this conflict assume that it cannot be disposed of via the strategy considered in the last section, of trying to show that there is no real conflict after all. Where Locke claimed to find a mere semantical confusion, it is generally recognized that there is a genuine disagreement between the animalists and the proponents of Locke's distinction between personal and animal identity. And this disagreement is not regarded as one that can be removed by the expedient of simply relativizing all beliefs and claims about personal identity to social contexts. The disagreement must be *resolved* rather than accommodated. The second strategy proposes to do this by a process of elimination. That is, it proposes to establish a positive conclusion about the condition of personal identity by showing that all of the conflicting alternatives are incoherent.

In order to simplify the discussion, this book has chosen to concentrate on just two main alternatives: the animalist analysis and the standard psychological analysis of the neo-Lockean project. But of course no conclusion about the condition of personal identity could possibly be established by the strategy of eliminating alternatives unless all of the alternatives were on the table. And since philosophers have shown great ingenuity in producing new and ever more complicated analyses of personal identity, it is not clear how we could ever be in a position to know that all of the alternatives actually are on the table. For this reason alone, the prospects for resolving the philosophical dispute about personal identity via this second strategy are somewhat bleak. But this section will argue that it is in any case hopeless. As things stand, both of the alternatives that are already on the table in this simplified discussion are coherent.

It is well known to any student of personal identity that the coherence of the neo-Lockean alternative has often been challenged. Yet these challenges have not undermined the project of analyzing personal identity in purely psychological terms. Rather, they have led to important and exciting developments of it. To provide an exhaustive history of all of the various developments of this neo-Lockean project, and of the challenges to which those developments were so often direct responses, would be impossible in any reasonably short space.[8] What follows is a very quick review of four central and widely discussed challenges that have been raised against the project. Recounting these challenges, and rehearsing some of the standard lines of neo-Lockean response, will accomplish two things. It will rescue the neo-Lockean project from the immediate charge of obvious incoherence, and it will show that the project has at its disposal a great many resources on which to draw in responding to charges of incoherence. Accomplishing these things will not suffice to rule out the possibility that some other, more damning objections might be raised against the neo-Lockean project. But it will bring out that the

---

[8] Three anthologies include important portions of this history: Perry, *Personal Identity*; Amelie Rorty, ed., *The Identities of Persons* (Berkeley: University of California Press, 1979); and Part 2 of Daniel Kolak and Ray Martin, eds., *Self and Identity* (New York: Macmillan Publishing Co., 1991). There are also two very useful introductory books that are at once rewarding and demanding: Shoemaker and Swinburne, *Personal Identity*; and Harold Noonan, *Personal Identity* (New York: Routledge, 1989).

project has proved to be highly resilient, and cannot easily be dismissed on charges of incoherence. Once this is brought out, the section will close with a very brief discussion of what should be obvious, which is that the animalist account of personal identity is also coherent.

A. Some neo-Lockean developments of Locke's original analysis have been in direct response to an objection that was raised against him by Reid.[9] Reid reminded us that the identity relation is transitive: if a is identical with b and b is identical with c, then a must be identical with c. He also noted that the psychological relations of memory and consciousness in terms of which Locke proposed to analyze personal identity are not transitive. He therefore objected that Locke's analysis fails to preserve the logic of identity. Reid illustrated this failure with an example about a general who was flogged as a boy and who captured a standard as a young man. The example stipulates that this general can remember capturing the standard as a young man and cannot remember the boyhood flogging, though as a young man he could remember the flogging. By the lights of Locke's analysis of personal identity, the general would be identical with the young man, and the young man in turn would be identical with the boy, but the general would not be identical with the boy, and so the result would be a violation of the transitivity of identity.

Grice proposed to save Locke's analysis from Reid's objection by weakening its requirements.[10] This was a salutary move, because Locke's analysis imposes an exceedingly strong mnemonic requirement that is in any case undesirable. It requires that at every moment in a person's life, the person must be able remember every previous moment of its life. It is of course precisely this requirement that Reid's forgetful general fails to meet. But what is worse, it is a requirement that most of us fail to meet at most, if not all, points of our lives. Grice therefore proposed a memory-based analysis of personal identity with a much weaker mnemonic requirement. Rather than requiring that every moment of a person's life be remembered at *all* later moments in the person's life, his analysis requires merely that every moment in a person's life be remembered at *some* later moment in that person's life. In formal terms, this is the ancestral of the memory relation. Grice's analysis is not vulnerable to Reid's objection because, unlike the memory relation, its ancestral is a transitive relation. And for this reason, Reid's counterexample to Locke is not a counterexample to Grice: since each moment in the senile general's life (at least each that is recounted by Reid) is remembered by him at some other moment, he does meet the requirements of Grice's analysis of personal identity.

It may seem that Grice's weakened version of the memory-based analysis still imposes overly strong mnemonic requirements on personal identity. It is a consequence of his analysis that no event can belong to a person's life unless it is remembered at some other point in the person's life. And this

[9] Thomas Reid, *Essays on the Intellectual Powers of Man* (Edinburgh, 1785; reprint, Perry, *Personal Identity*).

[10] H. P. Grice, "Personal Identity," *Mind* 50 (1941): 330–50; (reprint, Perry, *Personal Identity*).

means that events that occur during sleep, anesthesia, senility, and very early infancy may fail to belong to the life of any person at all. In order to avoid this consequence, most neo-Lockeans have broadened the number and range of psychological relations that they take to constitute personal identity—their thought being that even forgotten dreams and the musings of the senile bear *some* psychological relation to the other events in a person's life.

B. Another early objection to Locke's memory-based analysis was raised by Butler.[11] Along with Reid, he emphasized that consciousness and memory are merely forms of knowledge. And both protested that Locke's attempt to analyze personal identity in terms of such knowledge wrongly conflates the object of knowledge with the knowledge itself. But furthermore, Butler maintained that the particular forms of knowledge in question, namely, consciousness and memory, actually presuppose the fact of personal identity, with the result that Locke's analysis is hopelessly circular.

Shoemaker helped to elucidate this problem of circularity by pointing out that it is a logical or conceptual truth that a person can remember only its *own* past.[12] Prima facie, the presence of this conceptual tie between personal identity and memory might make the prospects for analyzing the former in terms of the latter look promising. But Shoemaker found a problem. He noted that sometimes memories are merely apparent, that is, they purport to provide a person with knowledge of its own past, but for one reason or another fail to do so. And the problem is that we cannot make sense of the possibility of such apparent memories unless there is an independent condition of personal identity, such as the human body, that is the repository of the actual, as opposed to the merely apparent, history of a person. In short, the problem that Shoemaker has posed for memory-based analyses of personal identity is this: if memories are corrigible at all, then they presuppose another, non-mnemonic condition of personal identity. This means that at the very least, a memory-based analysis of personal identity would be incomplete. And if it pretended to be complete then it could justly be charged with circularity, for it would have had to smuggle in the independent fact of personal identity by which real memories are to be distinguished from merely apparent memories. Despite this problem, Shoemaker nevertheless claimed to find a kernel of truth in Locke's analysis of personal identity, which is that memory is an important *criterion* of personal identity, if not its sole constituent.

It was Perry who met the challenge of circularity straight on.[13] The challenge is of course to distinguish real from apparent memories without appealing directly to the concept of personal identity. This Perry proposed to do by appealing instead to the concept of a reliable causal process by which repre-

---

[11] Joseph Butler, *Analogies of Religion* (1736; reprint, Perry, *Personal Identity*).

[12] Shoemaker, "Personal Identity and Memory," in Perry, *Personal Identity*.

[13] John Perry, "Personal Identity, Memory, and the Problem of Circularity," in Perry, *Personal Identity*.

sentations of past events qualify as real memories. The reliable causal process that he actually discussed is the natural process by which a human brain retains information about the past. However, there is no reason why such a process must be confined to a single human organ or organism. Technologically based processes, such as brain reprogramming (of the sort envisaged in Lockean-style thought experiments), might also qualify as reliable causal processes that can underpin the distinction between real and apparent memory. And by appealing to such processes, Perry was able to rescue all memory-based analyses of personal identity from the charge of being strictly circular. Yet he himself did not go so far as to advocate such an analysis. Like many neo-Lockeans, he regarded the memory-based approach as far too narrow. He thus concluded his discussion of the problem of circularity with the following remark: "it is only by generalizing from the memory theory, and incorporating somehow into our account of personal identity the sort of character development, the stability of ideals and values, influence of past intentions, and the like, that we normally expect to find in humans, that the forensic and moral importance of personal identity, which Locke so rightly emphasized, can be explained."[14] Despite his reference to "humans," Perry was not actually recommending that we reject Locke's distinction between personal and animal identity. His point was rather to draw attention to the fact that there are many psychological relations besides memory that we normally regard as important in the lives of persons. In point of fact, these other psychological relations are precisely the relations that the standard neo-Lockean analyses of personal identity invoke. And there is no reason to think that the problem of circularity will arise for these psychological analyses too. But if it should arise, it can presumably be solved along the same lines that Perry proposed for memory-based analyses.

C. A third challenge has been directed not just against memory-based analyses of personal identity, but against all purely psychological analyses. Like Reid's original objection to Locke, this objection concerns the logic of identity. In addition to being transitive, the identity relation is one-one. The objection, which is often referred to as the "duplication objection," is that psychological analyses of personal identity fail to preserve the one-one character of the identity relation because psychological relations can in principle take a branching form.[15] If psychological relations can take a branching form, then two (or more) presently existing persons could all bear those relations to a

---

[14] Ibid., p. 155. Like Locke's and Williams's appeal to ethical dimensions of personhood, Perry's is also very significant. To repeat, these ethical dimensions will be addressed in section 4, and in chapters 3 and 6.

[15] A great many philosophers have raised and discussed this objection, including: David Wiggins, *Identity and Spatio-Temporal Continuity* (Oxford: Oxford University Press, 1967); Williams, "The Self and the Future"; Parfit, *Reasons and Persons*; John Perry, "Can the Self Divide?" *Journal of Philosophy* 69 (1972): 463–88; David Lewis, "Survival and Identity," in Rorty, *Identities of Persons*; Sydney Shoemaker in Shoemaker and Swinburne, *Personal Identity*; and Noonan, *Personal Identity*.

single past person.[16] And it would seem to follow from the standard psychological analyses of personal identity that both (or all) of those presently existing persons must be identical with that same past person. The one-one character of the identity relation could be preserved in such a case only if the two (or more) presently existing persons were also identical with each other. But clearly they are not. And so the one-one character of the identity relation is not preserved.

Shoemaker proposed a wonderfully simple solution to this duplication objection. He simply added a nonbranching proviso to his psychological analysis of personal identity. Thus, according to him, certain specified psychological relations suffice to constitute personal identity *provided* that they do *not* take a branching form.[17]

Parfit has endorsed this solution to the duplication objection. However, he has also noted that it has an odd implication. Given Shoemaker's nonbranching proviso, the occurrence of branching necessarily constitutes the death of the individual person. This is odd, because death by branching would hardly be like ordinary death. Some kind of life would clearly go on after branching had taken place: projects and relations could be pursued, a sense of psychological continuity preserved—only several times over. According to Parfit, these are the things that really matter to us, and that we really want in wanting to survive. So if they were to be preserved several times over, that would constitute something just as good as ordinary personal survival.[18]

This provocative claim raises two crucial questions. The first concerns the possibility that there might be a closer connection than Parfit allows between personal identity and what matters to persons. The second question is a more general one about whether and why ethical considerations (in the broad sense that comprehends most practical concerns, including what "matters" to us) should be brought to bear in the philosophical study of personal identity. Both of these questions will be addressed in the next chapter. However, the answers to them do not bear on the present task, which is merely to explain why the neo-Lockean project of analyzing personal identity in purely psychological terms is not doomed from the start by incoherence. And Parfit's sug-

---

[16] In "Persons and Their Pasts," Shoemaker pointed out that this is not strictly true of memory. If it is a logical truth that a person can remember only its *own* past, it follows that a person must be identical with any past person to whom it bears the memory relation. However, Shoemaker did not take this to obviate the duplication objection. He showed how to preserve the general possibility of branching psychological relations, by introducing the technical notion of *quasi-memory*, and companion notions such as *quasi-intention*. Unlike memory, quasi-memory does not imply the strict identity of a rememberer with the person whose past it remembers. Similarly, the notion of quasi-intention does not imply that the formulator and executor of the quasi-intention are identical. (N.B.: Although the notion of quasi-memory helps to reinstate the duplication objection, it also helps to obviate the circularity objection. The rationale for introducing the notion of quasi-memory is precisely that it does *not* presuppose the identity relation.)

[17] See Shoemaker and Swinburne, *Personal Identity*, p. 85.

[18] Parfit first put this extraordinary thesis forward in "Personal Identity," *Philosophical Review* 80 (1971): 3–27. (This article is reprinted in Perry, *Personal Identity*.)

gestion that death by branching would be as good as ordinary survival does not indicate any incoherence in Shoemaker-style analyses of personal identity that incorporate a nonbranching proviso.

Lewis has offered a quite different response to the duplication objection from Shoemaker's, and part of its aim was to preserve—against Parfit's suggestion—the idea that what matters to persons is identity after all.[19] Yet it was not part of Lewis's aim to deny that what matters to persons is psychological relatedness over time, or that psychological relations might take a branching form. His aim was rather to show that even when psychological relations do branch, that never disrupts the continued existence and identity of the persons who are constituted by those relations. Lewis accomplished this aim by analyzing the condition of personal identity as a set of appropriately interrelated person-stages (the relations in question are of course psychological relations). Since it is in the nature of sets that they can share members, it follows that distinct persons may have person-stages in common. And according to Lewis, that is what happens when psychological relations take a branching form: there are two (or more) continuant persons who have person-stages in common at some points in their existence. This means that *both* persons (or all of them if there are more than two) exist all along, even before the branching occurs. The duplication objection is thereby met, since in each person's case the one-one character of the identity relation is clearly preserved. And the connection between personal identity and what matters to us in Parfit's sense is also preserved. What matters to us is a certain kind of psychological relatedness over time, and on Lewis's analysis that always constitutes the continued identity of a person (or persons), even when psychological relations take a branching form.

Lewis's solution to the duplication objection comes with a cost that few have been willing to bear. In claiming that persons may have person-stages in common, Lewis has committed himself to the idea that persons can share mental properties and states—not merely in the sense that they can have *similar* mental properties and states (as when we both believe that the speed of light is constant), but in the sense that *individual mental episodes* can figure in the life of more than one person at once. This idea of Lewis's, that persons can have *overlapping* mental lives, violates both common sense and received philosophical opinion.

All the same, this book will offer some additional reasons, over and above the formal problem that is presented by the duplication objection, for taking Lewis's idea seriously. These reasons have to do with the possibility of group and multiple persons, and their relations to human-size persons. We might want to allow, for example, that a single episode of wanting philosophy to flourish might figure in the life and projects of a roughly human-size person who is composed of the greater part of a particular human being, and that this very same episode might also figure in the life and projects of a certain group

[19] Lewis, "Survival and Identity."

person whose composition includes a small part of that same human being (and parts of other human beings as well).[20] Of course, this sort of reason for taking Lewis's idea of overlapping persons seriously is not within the range of vision of most neo-Lockeans, since they have not acknowledged the possibility of group persons. Indeed for the most part, neo-Lockeans find Lewis's idea objectionable. Partly for this reason, few of them have adopted his analysis of personal identity, or the particular solution to the duplication objection that it affords.

D. Unlike Lewis's analysis, Shoemaker's analysis has been widely adopted by neo-Lockeans. And so it has been targeted for further criticism. In particular, it has been charged with failing to preserve the modal character of the identity relation, that is, its necessity. Like the duplication objection, this modal objection fastens on the fact that psychological relations could in principle take a branching form. Here is a simple example to illustrate why this fact is supposed to present a modal difficulty for Shoemaker's analysis of personal identity, and for all other psychological analyses that follow his in incorporating a nonbranching proviso. If I am identical with CR at the age of twenty then, given the necessity of identity, I am necessarily identical with CR at twenty. But if branching is possible, then at some point in the past, say on my twenty-first birthday, the psychological relations that constitute my identity over time might have taken a branching form. If that had happened, then it seems to follow from Shoemaker's analysis that I would not have been identical with CR at twenty. And that in turn seems to imply that my actual identity with CR at twenty is contingent rather than necessary, contingent on the fact that I did not die a death of branching at the age of twenty-one. Hence the charge that Shoemaker's analysis fails to preserve the necessity of identity.

Some have claimed that the necessity of identity can be preserved and accounted for only within a certain sort of essentialist metaphysics. Minimally, a thing's essence is its necessary nature—that without which it cannot exist and cannot be what it is. But according to those who claim that the necessity of identity presupposes essentialism, the essence of a thing also supplies the metaphysical principle of its identity, where the function of that principle is precisely to ensure the metaphysical necessity of a thing's identity by making it a metaphysical impossibility that the thing could branch.[21] And it is because Shoemaker's analysis of personal identity does not rule out branching as a metaphysical impossibility that such essentialists deem it inadequate to support the necessity of the identity relation.

Shoemaker has successfully invoked aspects of the theory of reference in order to show that his analysis can accommodate the necessity of the identity relation after all, aspects which have to do with Kripke's distinction between

[20] See section 3 of chapter 5 for further discussion of this implication of the normative analysis of personal identity.

[21] For a sustained defense of this brand of essentialism, see David Wiggins, *Sameness and Substance* (New York: Oxford University Press, 1980).

rigid and nonrigid designation.[22] It would take us too far afield to provide a detailed review of the relevant aspects of the theory of reference in this brief discussion. But here is what can be conveyed of Shoemaker's general idea without *explicitly* appealing to Kripke's distinction between rigid and nonrigid designation (though the distinction is actually implicit in what follows). Suppose that I might have branched on my twenty-first birthday. Any possible world in which this is true is a world in which I died a death of branching on my twenty-first birthday. So it is a world in which *I* do not, strictly speaking, exist in 1996. (Underscoring the term "I" in this way implicitly invokes Kripke's idea of rigid designation). By hypothesis, some of the persons who would exist in that possible world in 1996 would be psychologically related to me at twenty. But since there would be more than one of them (due to the fact of branching), none of them would be identical with *me* (i.e., the person who did not *in fact* die a death of branching on her twenty-first birthday, but who might have). Since none of these possible psychological continuants of me would be identical with me, their possibility does not entail the further possibility that *I* could have failed to be identical with *myself*. Thus their possibility—which is just to say, the possibility that I might have branched—is, after all, consistent with the necessity of my identity.

In addition to Shoemaker's Kripkean response to this modal objection against the neo-Lockean project, there is also a much more general point that ought to be registered in response to essentialist scruples about the project. The problem of reconciling the possibility of annihilation by branching with the necessity of identity is not specific to the neo-Lockean project of analyzing personal identity in purely psychological terms. It is a perfectly general problem whose solution must be perfectly general as well. (It should be mentioned that Shoemaker's solution to the problem about branching in the case of persons is generalizable.) There are after all many things in the world that can and do branch, and that therefore lack the sort of essential nature that would make their branching a metaphysical impossibility. Witness: rivers, roads, vines, amoebas, sponges, galaxies, political parties, and New York City apartments. When these things do not branch (or to be more precise, at the times before and after these things have branched), they are perfectly individual things with their own identities. Insofar as it is a modal truth that everything is necessarily identical with itself, it would seem that each of these things, that is, each individual river, road, and so forth, is necessarily identical with itself—despite the fact that it can end by branching. But if the necessity of identity can be preserved in these cases, then it should also be preservable in the case of persons when their identity is analyzed along Shoemaker's neo-Lockean lines, as consisting in nonbranching psychological relatedness over time. Furthermore, if it should turn out that the necessity of identity cannot be preserved in any of these cases, that would not show that the neo-Lockean

---

[22] Saul Kripke, *Naming and Necessity* (Cambridge: Harvard University Press, 1990); see Shoemaker and Swinburne, *Personal Identity*, pp. 116ff.

project was incoherent. For in that case, we would have to allow that there are many things in the world—namely, rivers, roads, and the like—whose identities are merely contingent due to the possibility that they can branch. And if we were to allow that some things have merely contingent identities, we could not reject any neo-Lockean analysis of personal identity merely on the ground that it entailed that persons number among them.

This brief and partial survey of the philosophical literature on personal identity has shown that the neo-Lockean project can withstand the four objections that have most often been raised against it. That is, it is possible to provide a purely psychological analysis of personal identity that preserves the transitivity of identity, and is not circular, and also preserves the one-one character of identity. And as for the necessity of identity, Shoemaker has argued persuasively that psychological analyses can preserve that too. But even if the essentialists had been right to say that they cannot, that would not undermine such analyses as incoherent. It would merely put persons on a par with the all of the other things in the world that can branch and whose identities are not—at least not by the lights of some essentialists—metaphysically necessary.

The philosophical debate about personal identity did not end with the neo-Lockean responses to these four main objections that have been reviewed here. Just as neo-Lockeans have refined their psychological analyses of personal identity in order to meet these objections, the objections themselves have also been refined in various ways so as to try to undermine the refined analyses. But these refined objections have led in turn to yet further developments of the neo-Lockean project. Indeed, the present book is intended as a stab at such a development of it. Of course, no matter how many objections have already been answered, there will always remain a possibility that other, more damning objections might yet be raised. Yet although this possibility cannot absolutely be ruled out, this section has shown that the neo-Lockean project has so far proved highly resilient. So it cannot (at least not at this time) be rejected on the ground that all purely psychological analyses of personal identity have been shown to be incoherent.

It would be downright silly to reject the animalist analysis of personal identity on grounds of incoherence. For none of the four main challenges that the neo-Lockean project has had to meet can even be raised against it: the relation of animal identity is clearly both transitive and one-one; there is certainly no circularity in saying that the identity of a person consists in the identity of a suitably endowed animal; and even the most demanding essentialists are willing to grant that animal nature provides for the metaphysical necessity of the identity relation.

Of course neither of the two alternatives on the table, the animalist or the neo-Lockean, manages to accommodate all of our commonsense beliefs about personal identity. But given that there is a basic conflict in our commonsense outlook, that is not a sign of *incoherence*. And this section has made clear that the other main charges of incoherence—all of which have been leveled specifically at the Lockean and neo-Lockean analyses—are answerable. Given that this is so, and given that the animalist analysis is so obviously coherent, the second strategy must be abandoned. There can be no realistic hope of establishing an analysis of personal identity by eliminating all of the alternatives as incoherent.

4. Seeking Positive Reasons to Embrace One Side of the Conflict

The arguments of the three preceding sections suffice to show that we must relinquish a natural philosophical goal in the study of personal identity, namely, the goal of establishing our conclusion by strict proof. Due to the conflict in our commonsense outlook, we have available premises from which to argue for two different and opposed conclusions, namely, the animalist and the neo-Lockean conclusions. And neither of these conclusions can be eliminated on grounds of incoherence. This ensures that every argument that we offer in favor of one conclusion or the other will fall short of the standard of strict proof; for whatever conclusion the argument supports, it will leave the other conclusion standing as a competing alternative. We ought not, then, to expect to attain the goal of strict proof as we try to resolve the philosophical dispute about personal identity—even if it is the natural and appropriate goal (or at any rate, a regulative ideal) of philosophy in general.

This leaves us with a general methodological difficulty about what will count as an adequate philosophical justification in the absence of strict proof. The difficulty is especially acute in connection with the problem of personal identity. We are in the position of having to establish a *revisionist* conclusion with something short of strict proof. Given that this is so, there is an even stronger sense in which our conclusion will be revisionist than there otherwise would have been had we been able to prove it, for in this circumstance, our conclusion can amount to nothing more than a *nonbinding recommendation*. Thus we will have proposed a *revision* in our beliefs, as opposed, say, to a *correction* of them. And our methodological difficulty concerns how we are to justify such a revisionist recommendation.

The third strategy of revisionist response that was outlined in the introduction to this chapter is a direct and straightforward response to this methodological difficulty. It instructs us to resolve the philosophical dispute about personal identity by seeking *positive* reasons to embrace one side over the other, and to revise our commonsense beliefs accordingly. This strategy may initially seem unsatisfying and disappointing. But it would be quite wrong to think that it is in any way illegitimate or inadequate. To think so would be to fail to take in the full significance of the preceding arguments. They have shown that we *must* settle for something less than strict proof in the study of personal identity, and there is nothing else to settle *for* except reasons that provide some sort of *positive support* for our conclusion—even though they fall short of proof.

Given the straightforwardness and simplicity of this response to the methodological difficulty, it might be wondered why it is important to underscore it. There are two quite independent reasons why it is important to do so. First, the difficulty has been wholly overlooked in the philosophical literature about personal identity—and that is the outstanding reason why the central philosophical dispute about personal identity still remains unresolved. Second, although it is easy to *say* that what we require in order to get out of the difficulty are positive reasons for embracing one side of the dispute over the other, it is quite another thing actually to *find* such reasons, and to make the case that they are *compelling*.

In order to drive home just how formidable the methodological difficulty is, let us skip ahead for a moment to the arguments of the chapter 3. The chapter will lay down an ethical criterion of personhood, from which subsequent chapters will develop a broader account of the kind 'person', and eventually derive a conclusion about personal identity. Thus the positive reasons that we seek for taking sides in the dispute about personal identity are, according to this book's argument, to be found in a substantive account of the kind 'person'. But prima facie, it would seem that reasons drawn from such an account could never be compelling. After all, just as there is a basic conflict in our commonsense beliefs about personal identity, so also there is a corresponding conflict in our beliefs about what kind of thing a person is: we believe both that a person is, and that a person is not, an animal. Clearly, no account of the kind 'person' will be adequate unless it resolves this latter conflict, either by affirming or by denying that the kind 'person' is an animal kind. And in taking such a stand, the account will directly entail a particular resolution of the dispute about personal identity. But this means that there is a real danger that we will have resolved the dispute only by *begging the question*; for certainly, the question would have been begged if our account of the kind 'person' simply began either by assuming that persons are animals or by assuming that they are not. Over and above this worry about begging the question there is a second worry, which is that we cannot in any case find *compelling* reasons to revise our beliefs about personal identity in an account of the kind 'person' if the account itself is also revisionist. The next chapter will address both of these worries—and the larger methodological difficulty to which they belong—by imposing appropriate methodological constraints on the task of devising an account of the kind 'person'.

It might, however, seem quite unnecessary to turn to a substantive account of what kind of thing a person is in order to find positive reasons for taking one side or the other in the dispute about personal identity; it might seem that we can find such reasons in more *general* considerations that do not concern the nature of persons per se. Clearly, if we could proceed in this fashion, then our methodological difficulty would be mitigated. There would certainly be no danger of begging the question in the dispute about personal identity if our reasons for taking one side or the other were drawn from considerations that have nothing to do with the nature of persons. And there is some hope that such reasons would also be compelling—or at least more compelling than reasons that were drawn from a revisionist account of the kind 'person'. Unfortunately, as the rest of the section will show, the dispute about personal identity cannot be resolved in this way; there are no highly general considerations that supply positive reasons for favoring one side of the dispute over the other. Yet given the clear advantages that such a resolution would have had, it is worth going through the motions of trying to effect one. Then, once we have assured ourselves that this cannot be done, we shall better be able to see that we cannot hope to resolve the dispute without taking into account what kind of thing a person is, and that we must face up to the methodological difficulty that this procedure lands us in.

The most highly general considerations that could conceivably be brought to bear in the dispute about personal identity would be logical in nature. But section 3 has already argued that both sides of the dispute, the neo-Lockean and the animalist, are able to meet the relevant logical requirements. Next in order of generality would be considerations of a more broadly theoretical nature. Thus if there were some important theoretical desideratum that could be met by only one side of the dispute, that might well count as a positive and non-question-begging reason to embrace that side.

The task of determining whether there is such a theoretical desideratum is somewhat complicated by the fact that there is a diversity of theoretical considerations that might conceivably be brought to bear in the matter. Persons are appropriate objects of study from the perspective of at least three distinct theoretical enterprises, namely, metaphysics, science, and ethics.[23] Of course, many philosophical treatments of personal identity have chosen to concentrate on just one of these enterprises, most often metaphysics. Yet just as persons must be given their due place in the logical and modal order that is the proper subject of metaphysics, so also they must be situated in the natural order that is investigated by science, and in the ethical order as well. And no philosophical account of the person can be regarded as complete unless it affords a comprehensive vision that situates the person in all three of these orders—the logical/modal, the natural, and the ethical—that respectively define the enterprises of metaphysics, science, and ethics. An integrated way of putting it might be to say that there is one main general theoretical desideratum that any adequate analysis of personal identity should meet: the analysis ought to afford such a *comprehensive vision of the person*, as a subject of metaphysical, scientific, and ethical investigation.

This theoretical desideratum of comprehensiveness of vision clearly qualifies as a general theoretical consideration, as opposed to a lower-level substantive consideration that might be accused of begging the question about personal identity. All that the desideratum requires is that persons be

---

[23] Theology might constitute a fourth enterprise, or it might be regarded as a particular way of combining the enterprises of metaphysics and ethics.

portrayed as having three general *sorts* of properties—logical/modal, natural, and ethical. Otherwise, it leaves the nature of persons wholly undecided. It certainly makes no mention of any specific property of persons that obviously forces the issue of personal identity in favor of either an animalist or a neo-Lockean analysis. Still, it is conceivable that only one analysis of personal identity should be able to meet it. And if only one analysis were able to meet it, that would clearly constitute a positive reason to embrace the analysis—a positive and compelling reason that does not beg the question. But unfortunately, such a reason is not forthcoming. Each side in the dispute about personal identity, the neo-Lockean and the animalist, affords a suitably comprehensive vision of the person, as an appropriate subject of metaphysical, scientific, and ethical investigation.

Some animalists have already drawn attention to the fact that their analysis affords such a comprehensive vision of the person.[24] By portraying persons as members of an animal kind (or kinds), the animalist vision automatically assigns persons a definite place in the logical and modal order of interest to metaphysicians. Since animal kinds are generally regarded as essence-conferring natural kinds, the vision supplies persons with an essential nature that, among other things, provides the metaphysical principle of their identity—thereby ensuring, in the way described in the last section, that they conform to the strictest logical and modal requirements that essentialists could ever want to place on the identity relation. The animalist vision also assigns persons a definite place in the natural order, as appropriate subjects of biological investigation. And finally, the animalist vision provides for a naturalistic account of the ethical dimensions of personhood, as grounded in animal nature. Although this naturalistic approach to ethics sometimes takes a scientistic turn (as in some versions of bioethics), it has often taken the form of a descriptive theory of human nature, after the fashion of Aristotle and Hume.

It may not immediately be evident that the neo-Lockean alternative affords an equally comprehensive vision of the person. And here, for once, the decision to simplify the central philosophical dispute about personal identity, by lumping all psychological analyses together in a single neo-Lockean project, does not serve to clarify the issues. Since different psychological analyses might afford quite different visions of the person, the question of their comprehensiveness ought really to be settled on a case-by-case basis. That the normative analysis of personal identity that will be defended in this book affords such a comprehensive vision of the person, and hence meets the main general theoretical desideratum that any analysis of personal identity should meet, is something that will be shown in the course of the book's larger argument. For now, here is a brief account of why we can expect that most neo-Lockean analyses would afford a suitably comprehensive vision of the person.

---

[24] See especially Wiggins, "Locke, Butler and the Stream of Consciousness, and Persons as a Natural Kind," in Rorty, *Identities of Persons*; see also Wilkes, *Real People*.

In general, the neo-Lockean project conceives persons as sets or series or systems of psychologically related mental items. Unlike the animalist vision of the person, this neo-Lockean vision does not portray persons as belonging to an essence-conferring natural kind. Yet this does not mean that the neo-Lockean project fails to situate persons properly in the logical and modal order. Even the most committed essentialists must grant that some things, such as clubs and cities, fail to belong to essence-conferring natural kinds. And it may well be that persons are like clubs and cities in this respect, of *not* belonging to such a kind. Indeed, that is precisely what most neo-Lockeans (starting with Locke) have all along suggested, in suggesting that persons are sets or series or systems of appropriately related mental items.

In drawing a distinction between personal and animal identity, the neo-Lockean project does of course place persons outside the normal scope of biological investigation. Yet it does not place persons outside the entire natural order investigated by science. In fact, it places persons firmly within the scope of cognitive science. Cognitive science has always taken the functionalist view of mind very seriously, and functionalism conceives psychological abilities and processes in abstraction from any particular biological category—indeed, it is notoriously indifferent to the question of how psychological functions are realized, allowing that silicon chips might realize them just as well as living cells. For this reason, functionalism in principle allows that a single continuous functionally defined process might be successively realized in different types of entities. (Think of a single act of calculation that begins in the head, proceeds to pen and paper, then resorts to a pocket calculator, and is finally completed by a computer.) Such a view of psychological processes clearly goes hand in hand with the neo-Lockean idea that the continued psychological life of a person might come apart from the life of a particular animal.[25]

Finally, the neo-Lockean project has always included ethical dimensions of personhood within its vision of the person. It was mentioned in section 1 that two such dimensions have often been associated with the Lockean thought experiments. Locke supported his conclusion that a prince may endure in a cobbler's body by arguing that the prince would bear responsibility for his past actions so long as he was aware of them as his own through consciousness, no matter what his bodily circumstance happened to be. And ever since Williams incorporated self-concern into his redesigned Lockean experiment, it has become a standard feature in neo-Lockean thought experiments about personal identity. Both of these ethical dimensions of personhood are particularly interesting from the point of view of the philosophical study of the

---

[25] For further discussion of this point see section 3 of chapter 5.

[26] There is of course a family resemblance between the sort of self-concern that *persons* manifest and the biological instinct for self-preservation that is found in most animals. Yet they are importantly different. Personal self-concern is voluntary rather than instinctual, and this can be seen from the fact that persons may choose to sacrifice their own well-being for the sake of other goods to which they attach greater value.

person. After all, both belong exclusively to persons.[26] And one of the virtues that neo-Lockeans can claim for their psychological analyses of personal identity is that they promise to *explain* these distinctive ethical dimensions of personhood.[27] In particular, it is because persons have a capacity for reflective rationality, and because they are bound to their own futures and pasts by the psychological relations of memory and anticipation, that they may bear responsibility and exercise self-concern. And it is because neo-Lockeans take these psychological facts to constitute personal identity that their analyses of personal identity can claim to explain these (and perhaps other) ethical dimensions of personhood.

Thus it is clear that the neo-Lockean project does afford a comprehensive vision of the person as belonging to the logical/modal order of metaphysics and the natural order of science and the ethical order, and so meets the main theoretical desideratum that any adequate analysis of personal identity should meet.

There is no other broad theoretical requirement, besides comprehensiveness of vision, that it would be reasonable to place on an analysis of personal identity. Since both sides in the philosophical dispute about personal identity can in principle meet it, and since both can also meet the relevant logical requirements (as section 3 has argued), we may safely conclude that highly general considerations do not supply a positive reason to embrace one side rather than the other. If we are to find such reasons, we must seek them in substantive considerations that have *specifically* to do with the nature of persons. And this means, of course, that we must return to Locke's original instruction, and approach the issue of personal identity via an account of what kind of thing a person is.

[27] An early and insightful advocation of this advantage of the neo-Lockean project, namely, that psychological analyses of personal identity help to explain important ethical dimensions of personhood, can be found in John Perry, "The Importance of Being Identical," in Rorty, *Identities of Persons*. Indeed, his insight was already in evidence in the passage quoted in subsections B, which was drawn from a much earlier paper of his.

A Revisionary Proposal

CHAPTER 2 left us with four conclusions: (1) we cannot resolve the philosophical dispute about personal identity, between the proponents and the opponents of Locke's distinction between personal and animal identity, without revising some aspect of our commonsense outlook; (2) since both sides of the dispute are coherent and well supported by common sense, we cannot strictly prove that one side or the other must be correct; (3) we must seek positive reasons to embrace one side or the other anyway; (4) we must seek these positive reasons in a substantive account of the kind 'person'.

Chapter 2 also raised and postponed two worries about the last conclusion. The first is that a substantive account of the kind 'person' will inevitably *beg the question* in the dispute about personal identity. This worry arises because such an account must take a stand on whether the kind 'person' is an animal kind, and in doing so it will directly entail a particular resolution of the dispute about personal identity. But even if such an account managed to avoid begging the question, there is a second worry, which is that the account could not possibly provide *compelling* reasons to embrace the particular side of the dispute that it supports. This second worry arises because the underlying conflict in our commonsense beliefs about whether personal identity is the same as animal identity is matched by a corresponding conflict in our beliefs about whether the kind 'person' is an animal kind. This means that any account of the kind 'person' will also necessarily be revisionist—just as any conclusion about personal identity will be. And there is a natural worry about whether, when we thus propose to justify one revision by another, we shall have produced a truly compelling justification.

In order to allay these two worries, we must begin by imposing some *methodological constraints*.

No account of the kind 'person' can get off the ground without first laying down a *substantive* assumption about the nature of persons, from which further investigation into the kind may proceed. The task of settling on this initial assumption is really the task of greatest moment in the entire book. *Everything* will eventually turn on it. The assumption will constitute the main source and justification of the more complete account of the kind 'person' that will be developed from it. And it will also serve as the ultimate justification for the book's eventual resolution of the philosophical dispute about personal identity—that is, for the normative analysis of personal identity, which countenances the possibility of group and multiple persons, and which therefore supports, while at the same time reinterpreting, Locke's distinction between personal and animal identity.

The two worries that were just raised above can be laid to rest by imposing appropriate constraints on our initial assumption. *First*, if we aim to arrive at an account of the kind 'person' that can resolve the dispute about personal identity without begging the question, then we must see to it that the account proceeds from an initial assumption about the nature of persons that does not itself beg the question. In order to do this, we must find an initial assumption about persons on which *both* parties in the dispute, the animalists and the neo-Lockeans, can agree. Only then will the assumption be invulnerable to the charge of having begged the question. But on the other hand, the agreement between the two parties should be about something sufficiently nontrivial and fertile for the purpose at hand. Since the purpose is to arrive at an account of the kind 'person' that can provide compelling reasons to embrace a particular side in the dispute, the following further constraint can be laid down: the account must proceed from an initial assumption about the nature of persons that is sufficiently *important*. The assumption must be so important that both parties to the dispute can agree that *any* adequate account of the person *ought* to preserve it. That is the only way to ensure that both parties will have a compelling reason to embrace whatever revisionist consequences follow from the assumption, both with respect to what kind of thing a person is and with respect to the condition of personal identity.

It is in order to meet the second of these methodological constraints that we will turn to ethical considerations. That is, we will begin our investigation into the kind 'person' by assuming that it is a certain *ethical kind*. This will lead us to impose a third methodological constraint, which is that our initial assumption should, in addition to being non-question-begging and important, also be completely uncontroversial from an ethical point of view.

The central task of this chapter, then, is to propose and defend an ethical assumption about the nature of persons by showing that it meets all three of these methodological constraints. In the course of showing this, the chapter will also begin to develop the broader metaphysical account of the kind 'person' that follows from this ethical assumption.

But before introducing this ethical assumption, let us first consider what the available options are. The last chapter articulated a broad theoretical desideratum that any adequate account of personhood and personal identity should meet: it should deliver a theoretically comprehensive vision of the person as an appropriate subject of study within the three distinct theoretical enterprises of metaphysics, science, and ethics. Insofar as we are committed to such comprehensiveness of vision, we have at our disposal two theoretical enterprises *besides* ethics in which to look for an initial assumption about the nature of persons. And in fact, these other two enterprises are the ones to which philosophers would most naturally turn first in any investigation into personhood and personal identity.

Let us first consider metaphysics. It is highly unlikely that this theoretical enterprise will yield up any substantive assumptions about the nature of persons, from which a more complete account of the kind 'person' might be developed. Metaphysics consists in the systematic study of the most fundamental logical and modal properties of things. And these fundamental properties leave the specific nature of persons almost completely undetermined. (Again, it had been a hope that purely metaphysical considerations might *directly* resolve the dispute about personal *identity* by exposing one side or the other as incoherent. But, as the last chapter showed, this hope has been dashed by the success of both sides in accommodating relevant logical and modal properties of the identity relation.)

It is more reasonable to expect that a specific scientific agenda might yield a substantive assumption about the nature of persons. For example, a commitment to studying persons from the perspective of evolutionary biology would naturally lead us to assume that the kind 'person' is a biological kind. But it is hard to see how this could be done without violating the first of our constraints, which is that our initial assumption must not beg the question in the dispute about whether personal identity is the same as animal identity—for what other biological kind would it be appropriate to equate the kind 'person' with than an animal kind?

The psychological sciences hold much more promise of generating an initial assumption about the nature of persons that meets the constraint of non-question-beggingness. It is possible (in fact, it is, in our time, virtually a standard and orthodox procedure) to study minds in a way that is open to, and yet does not insist upon, the biologistic perspective that would bring in train an animalist resolution of the dispute. So it should come as no surprise that the psychological sciences might provide us with some non-question-begging assumptions. It may, however, come as a surprise that the very psychological claim which served as the premise of all of Locke's arguments about personal identity should qualify as such a non-question-begging assumption. His premise was that a person is a certain kind of agent, namely, an agent who is both rational and self-conscious. And this is a substantive claim about the nature of persons that animalists can perfectly well accept. The dispute between them and Locke does not concern whether a person is a self-conscious rational agent. Their dispute concerns whether such an agent is necessarily an animal, whose condition of identity is the condition of animal identity.

This book will take for granted that Locke's psychological premise is true as well as non-question-begging. However, it will not take for granted that his premise meets the second constraint that we have imposed on our assumptions. That is, it will not take for granted that his premise is, as it stands, *important* enough to serve as the initial assumption of the present investigation. To repeat, such an assumption must be important enough to serve as the driving premise of an entire account of what kind of thing a person is, and also, as the ultimate justification for any revisionist conclusions about personal identity that follow from the account.

In order to show that an initial assumption about the nature of persons is sufficiently important—that is, so important that it can bear the entire weight of this whole investigation—here is what must be shown. Any such assumption will ascribe some property *x* to persons. What must be shown is just why it should be a matter of paramount importance to recognize the class of things which are *x* as the class of *persons*. Now of course, many philosophers (including, presumably, Locke himself) would claim that Locke's premise meets this standard of importance. They would claim that it is of paramount importance to recognize the class of self-conscious rational agents as the class of persons. However, we cannot rest with a mere stipulation that this is so. We need to know *why* it should be a matter of paramount importance to recognize this class as the class of persons.

This question is crucial because it brings out the fact that in order to explain why this is so important, it will be necessary to introduce an *ethical* assumption, over and above Locke's psychological premise. If this is not obvious now, it will be when the investigation's revisionist conclusions concerning the possibility of group and multiple persons begin to emerge. Many might be prepared to grant that there is a sense in which groups and parts of human beings might qualify as self-conscious rational agents in their own rights, and hence might satisfy a *version* of Locke's psychological premise. (Unlike Locke's version, this version would have to construe self-consciousness in nonphenomenological terms, as a capacity to reflect upon and know one's reasons for action, rather than as a direct introspective awareness of one's unity as a thinking subject, for it would seem that group agents could have only the former, and not the latter, sort of self-consciousness.) Indeed, this seems to be why we have a use for the notion of a legal person who need not be of human size. Yet even those who are prepared to grant the possibility of such group and multiple *agents* might nevertheless deny that there is any very compelling reason to recognize them specifically *as persons*. If they denied this, they would by implication be denying that Locke's initial psychological premise about persons is sufficiently important. And that is why an ethical assumption needs to be introduced, in order to bring out why it really is a matter of paramount importance that the agents who satisfy his premise (and who also have certain social capacities, as well as reflective rationality) be recognized as persons.

So of the three areas in which we have been casting about, it is not metaphysics, nor biology and psychology, but ethics that will yield an initial assumption from which to develop our overall account. In order to be comprehensive, though, the account must eventually span metaphysics and science as well, even if its starting point is an ethical assumption.

Some might object to the procedure of beginning a general investigation into the nature of persons with an ethical assumption. Perhaps such objectors are opposed to the goal of arriving at a comprehensive vision of the person as a subject of ethical, over and above metaphysical and scientific, study. To such an objector this book offers no answer except dismayed dissent; persons clearly are appropriate objects of study within *all* three of these theoretical enterprises. To such an objector, who has made such an unnuanced objection, this will no doubt sound dogmatic. If so, there is nothing to do but to acknowledge this and proceed.

But perhaps there are objectors who have a more nuanced point in mind: objectors who accept that a comprehensive vision of persons must include within it ethical considerations, but who also believe that, in the proper order of investigation, ethics must always come after metaphysics and science. They might offer the following ground for this procedural priority: there can be no evaluative differences of an ethical nature unless they rest on differences of fact, and so we had better discover what there is in the world by way of metaphysical and scientific fact before we try to pronounce on any ethical matters at all—since otherwise we shall be in danger of giving a false account of what there is in the world that is based on ethical wishful thinking. The antecedent of this recommendation is probably true. That is, ethical differences probably do supervene on differences of fact. But even if this is the case, it does not follow that we ought not to begin an investigation into the nature of persons with an ethical assumption. If we are committed to arriving at a comprehensive vision of the person (as this book is), then we are committed to making metaphysical and scientific sense of persons as well. And if our ethical assumption should make this impossible, then we shall be bound by our commitment to comprehensiveness of vision to relinquish it. So there really is no danger that we shall arrive at a false account of the facts that is based on ethical wishful thinking simply because we have begun our larger investigation into the nature of persons with an ethical assumption.

This last objection, though unconvincing for the reason just given, nevertheless instructs on how to proceed with the inquiry. By warning against a certain danger, it instructs us, as an extra safeguard against this danger, to place our third constraint on any specifically ethical assumption that we might make about the nature of persons. We can insist not only that it should not beg the question in the dispute about personal identity and that it should be sufficiently important to justify any revisionist conclusions that follow from it; also, we can require that it be *completely uncontroversial from an ethical point of view*. If our ethical assumption is completely uncontroversial from an ethical point of view, that should increase our confidence that it can be accommodated within our metaphysical and scientific theories. Moreover, it will make any revisionist conclusions which follow from it that much more compelling.

Of course, some residual objectors might endorse all three of these methodological constraints and yet doubt whether it is possible to arrive at an ethical assumption about the nature of persons that can meet them. That is, they might doubt whether any such ethical assumption can be completely non-question-begging about personal identity, and also important enough, and uncontroversial enough from an ethical point of view, to bear the entire weight of this investigation into personhood and personal identity. To such objectors the only response can be, wait and see. It may take all of the arguments of this chapter to quell your doubts.

Let us, then, turn to the matter of seeing whether ethical considerations will offer up a satisfactory initial assumption about what kind of thing a person is.

The last chapter observed that Locke himself introduced some ethical considerations into his discussion of personal identity. He claimed of the term "person" that "It is a Forensick Term appropriating Actions and their Merit; and so belongs only to intelligent Agents capable of a Law, and <u>Happiness</u> and Misery" (2.27.26). These relatively isolated words intimate a somewhat richer appreciation of how various ethical considerations might bear on the topics of personhood and personal identity than is actually manifest in the rest of Locke's discussion. The only ethical dimension of the person to which he paid much attention is responsibility in the sense of full moral accountability—that is, in the sense that justifies punishment. The mention of "a Law, and Happiness and Misery" seems meant only to bring out that punishment presupposes both an aversion to pain and an understanding of that principle (which may or may not be law in the judicial sense) in the name of which a punishment is inflicted. Clearly, to punish a subject without these dispositions would have little point. What Locke saw in addition is that punishment for a particular action presupposes first personal knowledge of that action. "For supposing a Man punish'd now, for what he had done in another Life, whereof he could be made to have no consciousness at all, what difference is there between that Punishment, and being created miserable?" (2.27.26). He went on to observe that even on the Great Day, "The Sentence shall be justified by the consciousness all Persons shall have, that they *themselves* in what Bodies soever they appear, or what Substances soever that consciousness adheres to, are the *same*, that committed those Actions and deserve that Punishment for them."

Locke regarded all of these forensic considerations as providing additional support for his analysis of personal identity in terms of sameness of consciousness. However, it would be inappropriate to adopt them as the initial assumption of the present investigation. This is not because they fail to meet our two basic constraints of being non-question-begging and important. They very likely do. The difficulty is rather that they do not satisfy the extra constraint that any specifically ethical assumption should meet, of being completely uncontroversial from an ethical point of view. Of course it is not controversial to emphasize, as Locke did, that accountability for an action generally presupposes first person knowledge of it. But all the same, his notion of accountability is bound up with the following claims, each of which has been a subject of long-standing controversy in moral philosophy: there is such a thing as desert; desert justifies retributive punishment; both desert and punishment presuppose some form of freedom and, quite possibly, a radical form of free will that is incompatible with determinism. (Although Locke himself was highly critical of the doctrine of free will, it is often held to be the sine qua non of the related claims about desert and punishment to which he was explicitly committed.)

For similar reasons, it would also be inappropriate to begin with the ethical assumption that has figured centrally in neo-Lockean work on the subject of personal identity, namely, the assumption that persons have reason to be prudentially concerned for their own future well-being. Although this might not seem to be a controversial assumption, it has bred significant controversy. This can be seen from the fact that none of the following questions have straightforward answers: in what does personal well-being consist? what is the nature and extent of our reasons for prudence? (e.g., should prudential reasons span developments in our future desires that are incommensurate with our present desires?); how ought prudential considerations to be weighed against broader ethical and moral concerns? In addition, the last chapter's discussion of Lockean-style thought experiments suggested that the subject of prudence breeds confusion as well as controversy. When neo-Lockeans injected prudential considerations into such experiments, that did not serve to clarify the issue of personal identity at all. Rather, it served to bring out that we are capable of showing prudential concern for our own future well-being regardless of what we take ourselves to be—animals or more abstractly conceived psychological subjects. As might be predicted, this indiscriminateness of our self-regarding attitudes has fueled fresh arguments about what really constitutes the proper ground of our prudential self-concern. And these arguments are another sign that the central neo-Lockean ethical assumption about prudence is truly controversial.

Here is a much weaker assumption about prudence that would not be controversial: persons are the sorts of agents who have a capacity for prudence— that is, they are agents who can in principle grasp prudential considerations, and who can also act on such considerations if they so choose. This weaker assumption manages to escape controversy simply by refusing to take a stand on any of the controversial questions raised above, concerning the proper object, grounds, and extent of prudential self-concern. Given that it meets the constraint of being uncontroversial from an ethical point of view, this weaker assumption about prudence might serve our present purposes—but only if it meets our two more basic constraints, of being non-question-begging, and sufficiently important as well. To reiterate, an assumption will meet the constraint of importance only insofar as it is a matter of paramount importance to recognize the class of things that satisfy the assumption as the class of persons. And it is not at all clear that a weak assumption about a mere capacity for prudence can meet this constraint. That is, it is not clear that it is of paramount importance to recognize the class of agents who have a capacity for prudence as the class of persons. (Consider the fact that any corporation that is capable of engaging in long-term planning thereby has a capacity for prudence; that is, it can take measures that are directed at securing its future welfare. It is not clear why this fact alone should compel us to recognize such corporations as persons.)

As chapter 6 will explain, the account of the person that this book offers has some clear implications with respect to both of the ethical dimensions of personhood which have figured so centrally in Lockean and neo-Lockean arguments, namely, accountability and self-concern. But to begin with, the book will concentrate on a quite different ethical dimension of personhood. It will begin by assuming that *persons are agents who can engage in agency-regarding relations*. That is to say, it will assume that persons can engage in the particular kind of *relation* which arises between agents when *one agent attempts to influence another, and yet aims not to hinder its agency*. And it will take this assumption as articulating a necessary and sufficient condition for falling under the kind 'person'. Thus the assumption is really a criterion of personhood, a criterion that was introduced earlier in these pages as the *ethical criterion of personhood*.

The rest of this chapter will be devoted to clarifying and defending this ethical criterion of personhood.

The defense will consist in showing that it meets all three of the methodological constraints that it must meet if it is to serve as the starting point for the present investigation, which aims to elaborate an account of the kind 'person' that will provide positive and compelling reasons for taking sides in the dispute about whether Locke was right to draw a distinction between personal and animal identity. Thus, what must be shown is that the ethical criterion (1) does not beg the question in this dispute, (2) is sufficiently important that any account of the kind 'person' ought to accommodate it, and (3) is completely uncontroversial from an ethical point of view.

The importance that will be claimed for the ethical criterion of personhood is an ethical importance. This may seem surprising and implausible, since the criterion also claims to be ethically uncontroversial. But on the other hand, the claim that the criterion is ethically uncontroversial may seem even more surprising and implausible than the claim that it is ethically important. After all, the criterion defines persons in terms of a notion—agency-regard—that many substantive ethical positions place above all others in ethical importance, including most especially Kantian and rights-based ethical theories. But, as the introduction to Part I briefly explained, the criterion is distinguished from these ethical theories by the fact that it makes no particular moral *demands* on persons with respect to agency-regard. It does not say either that persons must or even that they ought to engage in agency-regarding relations. It simply *defines* persons in terms of the ability to engage in such relations. This feature helps to ensure that the criterion, like the weaker assumption about prudence that was just considered above, manages to meet the constraint of ethical uncontroversiality. However, the latter assumption about prudence was rejected on the ground that nothing of importance hangs on recognizing all and only the agents who have the capacity for prudence specifically as persons. In contrast, something of importance does hang on recognizing all and only the agents who can engage in agency-regarding relations as persons. Doing so serves to define and identify a particular form of prejudice against persons that is distinguished by the fact that it is hypocritical as well as discriminatory. This point is connected with another, which is that the ethical criterion of personhood picks out a distinct ethical kind. Even though it does not instruct persons on the matter of whether and when they should engage in agency-regarding relations with one another, it does ensure that persons recognize that they stand in a certain distinctively interpersonal ethical relation to one another—one that they cannot escape except through hypocritical prejudice. And the ethical kind that is picked out by the ethical criterion is the kind whose members stand in this ethical relation.

None of these points—about how the ethical criterion helps to define and identify a hypocritical variety of prejudice against persons, about how this ensures that the criterion meets the constraint of importance, and about how it also manages to meet the constraint of ethical uncontroversiality—can be further elaborated without first clarifying the criterion itself. This will prove to be a lengthy and involved task that will occupy all of section 1. The criterion stipulates that persons are agents who can engage in agency-regarding relations, and that such relations arise when one agent attempts to influence another and yet aims not to hinder the other's agency. So to begin with we must clarify at least two things: what the aim not to hinder agency is, and how this agency-regarding aim can enter into and inform efforts at influence. But of course, we cannot clarify what the aim not to hinder agency is without clarifying what it is to hinder agency, and we cannot do that without saying a good deal about the nature of agency itself. In addition, we cannot clarify how the aim not to hinder agency can enter into and inform efforts at influence without examining in detail the various forms that influence among agents can take. In the course of clarifying all this, we will learn a great deal about the particular kind of agency that persons, qua agents who satisfy the ethical criterion, possess. The metaphysical insights that emerge will play a central role in the arguments of Part II in favor of the possibility of group and multiple persons.

Thus the prior clarificatory task of section 1 will actually constitute the beginning's of this book's larger account of the kind 'person'. Yet none of the claims of section 1 can be taken as claims about the nature of persons until the arguments of section 2 in defense of the ethical criterion have been given. In keeping with this aspect of the overall dialectic, section 1 will never refer to persons, but only to agents who can engage in agency-regarding relations and who therefore satisfy the ethical criterion. However, once the end of the chapter has been reached, and the ethical criterion of personhood has been fully justified, then all of the claims that section 1 makes about the nature of such agents can automatically be taken as claims about the nature of persons.

1. What Are Agency-Regarding Relations?

The expression "agency-regarding relations" is an omnibus one and hides many possible interpretations. But the present context—that is, the proposed ethical criterion of personhood and the larger argument of the book that will follow from the criterion—requires that the expression be given a very specific reading. And so it is important to be clear about how it should be read and not read.

The most familiar readings derive from Kantian and rights-based ethical theories, in which the ideas of regard and disregard for agency are substantively moral. On these readings, the idea of agency-disregard in particular is intended to carry with it the suggestion of a moral wrong, and is counted to be such a wrong by the lights of a substantive ethical position. The reading given in this book to the expression "agency-regarding relations" has no such suggestion of issuing from a substantive ethical position, or of pronouncing in a general way on the moral rightness or wrongness of agency-regard and disregard. (This is crucial if the ethical criterion of personhood is to meet the constraint of ethical uncontroversiality.)

If we set aside all substantively moral readings of the expression, then we shall have to find a more strictly metaphysical reading. And we shall naturally be led to consider first a purely causal reading. This causal reading is invited by the crudest cases of apparent disregard for agency, such as when one agent physically restrains another, as for example when one agent locks up another in order to prevent it from doing something. But we shall see that this purely causal reading is unsatisfactory. We must give a normative reading instead—in the sense of "normative" that was elucidated in the introduction to Part I, which concerns the nonethical sort of normativity that marks the domain of the rational.

Thus the reading of the expression "agency-regarding relations" that will be given in this book is intended to clear a space for understanding the expression that is precisely not purely causal and therefore normative, and yet not substantively moral and therefore metaphysical. It is a space—much needed in this subject—where the metaphysical and the normative come together, without overinterpretation from either point of view so that it slides into the purely causal or the substantively moral, respectively.

This space will be filled by a specific understanding of what agency-regarding relations are that makes essential reference to, and use of, the notion of a *rational point of view*, as that notion was defined in chapter 1. In order to arrive at this understanding, many more *intuitive* conceptions of what agency-regarding relations are will be shown to be unsatisfactory, at least as far as this book's argument is concerned. And it is necessary to arrive there in this roundabout way, because "agency" and "regard for agency" are terms in such common philosophical currency that it would be methodologically insensitive simply to plonk down, at the very outset, one's own understanding of them for the purposes of one's own argument without addressing the many intuitions that people have about them. Moreover, if we did not go over the intuitions, and show that the intuitions can actually be explained by this book's reading of the notion of an agency-regarding relation (not explained in the sense that the intuitions are shown to be true, but in the sense that it is explained why they seem intuitive), then the reading would seem facile. But finally, by proceeding in this roundabout way, and situating the reading in relation to some of our prior intuitions, the book will be able to bring to the surface a few things that our more intuitive conceptions have tended to overlook. The first is just that there is a consistent and well-motivated reading of the expression "agency-regarding relation" that is neither purely causal nor substantively moral. The rest concern what this new reading shows us about the nature of agency itself, or to be more precise, about the particular kind of agency that is possessed by the agents who satisfy the proposed ethical criterion of personhood (though some of these aspects of specifically *personal* agency will not be fully brought out until Part II).

How to Sort Out Intuitions about Regard for Agency

In the ethical criterion of personhood as stated above, the notion of an agency-regarding relation figures as a *relation that arises between agents when one agent attempts to influence another, and yet aims not to hinder its agency.* Now, people's intuitions about the notion mostly have to do with which, among cases of attempts to influence another agent, do and which do not aim to hinder the agent's agency. Here is a laundry list of cases about which most people have fairly firm intuitions: hypnosis, manipulation, lies, threats, and rational argument. Of these cases, the last seems intuitively to be regardful of agency. In contrast, all of the former seem intuitively to be disregardful of agency. And they are intuitively disregardful and regardful of agency because the former are seen intuitively as aiming to hinder agency in some way (their own particular way in each case), and the last is seen intuitively as aiming not to do so.

These are specific intuitions, then, about which cases of influence aim to hinder agency and therefore are disregardful of agency and which aim not to hinder agency and therefore are regardful of it. So let us ask: what is it about rational argument in virtue of which it incorporates an aim not to hinder agency? And what is it about hypnosis, manipulation, lies, and threats in virtue of which they do not incorporate this agency-regarding aim, and perhaps incorporate an aim to hinder agency instead?

As said earlier, the point of these questions is not necessarily to preserve all of our intuitions about particular cases. The point is rather to *use* these intuitions in order to learn a general lesson, and in order to bring out a particular notion of regard for agency that will serve the purposes of this book. In the end, it will emerge that this particular notion does not preserve *any* of the intuitions on the laundry list given above. That is, it will emerge that hypnosis, manipulation, lies, threats, and so forth, can all be agency-regarding, while rational argument can fail to be agency-regarding, and can even be agency-disregarding. Yet it should not be inferred that the point here is to criticize or undermine our intuitions about these cases. The point is really to nonarbitrarily change the subject from our intuitions about regard for agency, which are so often governed by crude metaphysical conceptions and substantive moral doctrines, to a particular notion of regard for agency that is, to repeat, neither purely causal nor substantively moral. (Though, as the Postscript will explain, there are some fresh dividends in moral philosophy too that come with this particular way of construing what regard for agency consists in, at least when persons are defined as agents who can exhibit such regard. However, everything until the Postscript will restrict its focus on the relevance of this construal to the project of resolving the central philosophical dispute about personal identity.)

Whatever the merits of our intuitions about particular cases, we cannot do philosophy casuistically with a laundry list. We must do the work of *sorting out* our intuitions—or rather, the work of sorting out the particular cases about which we have the intuitions. A start was made above, just by posing the following questions: What is it about rational argument in virtue of which it incorporates an aim not to hinder agency, and hence qualifies as agency-regarding? And what is it about hypnosis, manipulation, lies, and threats in virtue of which they incorporate the opposite aim, and hence qualify as agency-disregarding? These questions can sensibly be answered only by sorting the different items on the laundry list and seeing how they fall under more general categories of the different modes of influence that agents can wield on other agents, and then identifying which of these categories are likely to aim to hinder agency and which not. If we can make such an identification, we would have given a more philosophical statement of what an agency-regarding relation is than simply presenting a list of intuitively agency-regarding and agency-disregarding cases.

Let us begin with a very general conception—much too general—of why an effort to influence an agent would aim to hinder its agency. On this conception, an effort to influence an agent aims to hinder its agency just in case it aims to bring about a result whereby the agent does not do what it otherwise would have done. There is an unhelpful generality to this because it does not distinguish between two cases that might seem intuitively to be quite distinct in the matter of agency-regardingness. The first case is that you are about to leave the house without taking your umbrella, and I decide that it would be amusing to hypnotize you into taking it. If my effort to hypnotize you succeeds, the result will be that you do not do something that you otherwise would have done—namely, leave the house without your umbrella. And so I would intentionally have hindered your agency in the sense here being considered. In the second case, you are again about to leave the house without your umbrella. But this time I advise you to take it because rain has been forecast, and I know you dislike getting wet. Here too, if I should succeed, then the result will be that you do not do something that you otherwise would have done—namely, leave the house without your umbrella. Yet intuitively, it seems quite wrong to see the two cases on a par, that is, to see the case of friendly advice as one in which I have aimed to hinder the exercise of your agency. If anything, my advice to you seems to be aimed at fostering, and perhaps even enhancing, the exercise of your agency. Things are worse than that, in fact. This first overly general conception is inadequate not merely because it fails to distinguish these two kinds of cases, but because it makes *no distinctions at all* among the different ways in which agents can influence one another. After all, the whole point of influence is to achieve results in which agents do not do *something* which they otherwise would have done. If this were not so, then the influence would have no effect, and hence would not be *influence*.

Here is an alternative conception of what it is to aim to hinder agency that does succeed in distinguishing the cases of hypnosis and friendly advice: one agent aims to hinder another agent's agency just in case it aims to exert direct causal control over events that would otherwise remain within the other agent's own intentional control. As a result of such direct causal influence, something would happen within an agent's own domain of intentional control, and yet it would not be something that the agent intentionally *did*. And this would be due to the fact that the effort at influence somehow *bypassed* the agent's exercise of its own agency. Hypnosis clearly satisfies this second conception of what it is to aim to hinder agency, for hypnosis aims to achieve its effects through the mechanisms of hypnotic and posthypnotic suggestion, and these mechanisms clearly do bypass an agent's exercise of its own agency.[1] The case of friendly advice is quite different. It does not aim to achieve its effects by bypassing an agent's exercise of its own agency; it aims rather to achieve its effects *through* such exercise, that is, by getting another agent to *do* something intentionally.

Unlike the first conception, this second conception does not construe hindrances to agency in the most general possible terms. It makes specific reference to *how* someone is prevented from doing or not doing what it would otherwise have done or not done. In particular, it rules *out* the more *purely causal* category of modes of influence (under which the case of hypnosis falls) as intuitively agency-regarding, while it rules *in* what should intuitively be ruled in, namely the case of friendly advice. So perhaps we should conclude that the distinction between the purely causal and the not purely causal categories of modes of influence underlies the distinction between agency-regarding and agency-disregarding relations.

---

[1] This is so even if the initial hypnotic trance cannot be induced without some voluntary cooperation on the part of the agent. Once the hypnotic trance has been induced, the agent has no intentional control over whether it is susceptible to hypnotic and posthypnotic suggestion. Furthermore, when such suggestion takes effect, the result is not something that the agent intentionally does.

The second conception is not, in fact, adequate. Consider the following example. Yet again, you are about to leave the house without your umbrella. And again, I decide that it would be amusing to get you to take it. Only in this case, I happen to know that you always take your umbrella on days when your housemates take theirs. I also happen to know that there is an umbrella stand near the door which is usually full of umbrellas, except on days when your housemates have taken them. So I remove all of the umbrellas but yours from the stand with the following aim: you will notice that the other umbrellas are gone, you will infer that your housemates have taken their umbrellas, and you will decide to follow suit by taking yours. In this example, I aim to achieve my effects through your exercise of your own agency. So by the lights of the second conception, I do not aim to hinder your agency. Yet there is an intuitive sense in which this effort to influence you is an effort to hinder your agency: I aim to manipulate you into doing something that you otherwise would not have done.

It is not perhaps entirely on the surface why or how I would be aiming to hinder your agency in the example of manipulation just considered. I would, after all, be aiming to achieve my effects through your exercise of your own agency. And this distinguishes the case from other cases of more direct *causal* manipulation that would bypass your exercise of your agency, as in the cases when I hypnotize you, or bind you, or gag you, or drug you, or even tamper with your brain. Yet there is something that all of these cases (including the case of manipulation just considered) have in common, and that distinguishes them from the case of friendly advice. They all employ *nonrational*, as opposed to *rational*, means in order to achieve their effects.

There is one mechanism that is always at work in nonrational influence, namely, the exploitation of the purely causal properties of things. However there are a variety of ways in which nonrational influence can achieve its results. This variety is due to the fact that different kinds of things have different causal properties that such influence can exploit. So for example, material things can be pushed and pulled, growing things can be nourished and fertilized, sentient things can be drugged. And rational things can be manipulated in the way I manipulate you in the example above: I employ *non*rational means in order to manipulate your situation (I physically remove umbrellas from an umbrella stand), with a view to prompting you to exercise your rational capacities in a certain way (I aim to get you to infer that you have reason to take your umbrella with you today). In contrast, *rational* influence does not merely *exploit* a thing's ability to exercise its rational capacities. It involves a direct *appeal* to those capacities. Or rather, it involves a direct appeal to the rational point of view from which those capacities are exercised. Such an appeal consists in the presentation of a reason to another agent, with the aim that the agent will grasp the normative force of that reason and respond appropriately, which is to say, rationally.

Now it will seem as if we are really getting somewhere. This discussion of the limitations of the second conception has presented us with a distinction between categories of modes of influence that may serve better in defining agency-regarding relations. The distinction between rational and nonrational modes of influence may be what underlies the distinction between agency-regarding and agency-disregarding relations. Thus it suggests a third conception of what it is to aim to hinder agency: one agent aims to hinder the agency of another just in case it attempts to exert nonrational influence over it. This third conception entails that all of the cases of purely causal influence listed above, as well as manipulation, aim to hinder agency, while friendly advice does not, for friendly advice is clearly a case of rational, as opposed to nonrational, influence.

The third conception, like the others so far considered, has unwelcome consequences: lies and threats are cases of rational, as opposed to nonrational, influence, and this means that they do not qualify, on this third conception, as efforts to hinder agency. The point is perhaps clearer in the case of lies. A lie is generally offered as a *reason* for another agent to do something, namely, believe the lie.[2] But so too, a threat is generally offered as a reason for another agent to do something, namely, comply with the threat. So like lies, threats must be *addressed to* agents, from within the space of reasons. That is precisely what distinguishes threats from manipulation, as well as from the cases of more direct causal influence, such as hypnosis, binding, gagging, and drugging.

If we are to make sense of our intuitions about lies and threats, it would seem that we need to draw yet more distinctions among the different categories of modes of influence that are available to agents. In addition to the broad division we have made between the nonrational and the rational, we must also make distinctions within the rational. That is, we must determine what it is that distinguishes friendly advice, lies, and threats as falling under *different* categories of modes of influence, even though they all exploit the normative force of reasons.

Here is one account of these differences. Consider first the mode of rational influence that is exemplified by friendly advice. It is characterized by two things, which we can call the *purity* and the *openness* of the rational means that it employs. What makes an effort at influence purely rational is easy to explain: the effort must exploit nothing else but the normative force of the particular reason that it presents. What makes such an effort open as well as pure is a bit more complicated to explain. All efforts at influence are undertaken for some end. And all efforts at rational influence aim to achieve their

---

[2] Now, it is sometimes claimed that belief formation does not, or at least does not usually, involve the exercise of agency. And so, insofar as the point of a lie is to induce belief, it might seem incorrect to say that liars offer their victims reasons to *do* something. But clearly, this claim is much closer to the truth than the opposite claim to the effect that liars aim to achieve their effects through a form of direct causal control that bypasses an agent's exercise of its own agency. There is a broad notion of intentional control, whereby the liar leaves an agent in full intentional control of its beliefs and actions. After all, a liar does leave a victim with the option of reflecting upon whether it (the victim) has good reason to believe what it (the liar) says. And the success of a lie depends upon the outcome of such reflection.

ends by offering another agent a reason to do something. But when an effort at rational influence is open, the reason that it presents is explicitly presented as a reason to embrace and act for the sake of the very end for the sake of which the effort at influence was itself undertaken. Thus when, in the course of my friendly advice, I give you a reason to take your umbrella today by informing you that it will rain, my effort is *openly* rational insofar as the end that I aim to realize is the very end that I announce (or if not announce verbally, at least clearly imply in a way that I expect you to grasp) when I inform you that it will rain, namely, that you should take your umbrella with you today. And my effort is *purely* rational insofar as I aim to exploit nothing else but the normative force of this reason that I have presented to you, in the form of information that it will rain.

Consider next the mode of rational influence that is exemplified by lies. This mode is purely rational, but not openly so. It is *covert* in the following sense: it does not divulge the end for the sake of which it is undertaken. Thus suppose that I know full well that it will be gloriously sunny today. Nevertheless I tell you that it will rain. Part of what I aim to accomplish in telling you this lie is to get you to take your umbrella today. But my ultimate end is to prove to a common friend of ours how gullible you are. In such a case, I would be attempting to wield covert, rather than open, rational influence on you since I would not have disclosed to you the real end for the sake of which I was offering you a reason to take your umbrella. And in point of fact, it is in the nature of the case that I cannot realize this end and also disclose it to you. Consider what would happen if I offered you the following more open assertion instead of my lie: "It will rain today, so you had better take your umbrella; but I am telling you this only to prove to our friend how gullible you are." Such openness about my true end would clearly spoil the prospects of realizing it (unless you were stupid as well as gullible). And this is a characteristic, though not an essential, feature of lies, that is, of assertions that are not believed by their utterers. Usually, a liar lies in order to get someone else to believe what it (the liar) takes to be false. And in the normal run of things, this is an end that a liar can realize only by keeping it hidden.[3] But the important point here is not that lies are generally offered in the course of attempts at covert rational influence. The important point is that lies are instances of a much broader class of deceitful actions, all of which employ covert rational influence. It is in the nature of all deceit to *mis*represent, as well as to present, a reason for doing something. And it is in the nature of all misrepresentation to keep what it misrepresents hidden. (On this broad construal, even silence

---

[3] There are imaginable circumstances in which this may not be so. For example, we might be playing a game in which I always make double assertions of the following form: "*P*; and I am telling you this in order to get you to believe *p* even though I don't believe *p*." In each case, one half of the double assertion is a lie, and you must guess which. I win if you are wrong. It would seem that sometimes my winning might consist in the fact that I have gotten you to believe *p* even though I don't believe *p* and I have openly declared this. (However, it might be called into question whether any such declaration that was made in the context of this game could truly be open.)

can count as deceit. Suppose, for example, that I listen to the weather report every morning, and we have a long established habit whereby I always inform you if I have heard a prediction of rain. Thus given our habit, whenever I do *not* tell you that it will rain today, I thereby give you a reason *not* to take your umbrella. However, one day I am angry with you for taking me for granted. So I omit to inform you that rain was predicted, in the full hope that you get caught in a downpour without your umbrella. In this context, my omission is a deliberate misrepresentation; that is, it is an instance of covert, and hence deceitful, rational influence.)

Consider, finally, the mode of rational influence that is exemplified by threats. This mode is openly rational, but not purely so. What makes it *impure* is this: it goes beyond merely presenting an agent with a reason to do something and actually *generates* a reason that was not there before. Thus, suppose that there is a slight chance of rain today, and I want you to take your umbrella. But I also know that you do not regard a slight chance of rain as sufficient reason to take your umbrella. So I decide to get you to take your umbrella anyway, by threatening to divulge an embarrassing secret of yours if you do not take it. This is clearly an effort at rational influence, since I offer you my threat as a reason on which to act. And it is a perfectly open effort at rational influence, since I have no undisclosed motive (the entire point of my threat is to get you to take your umbrella today). Yet my threat is not an attempt at purely rational influence. By lodging my threat, I do not merely present a reason why you should take your umbrella today. I also do something to generate a reason that was not there before. The most generic way to describe this extra action that makes rational influence impure is this: it involves the production of an *incentive* that is meant to constitute the reason for action that it offers.

A great many common transactions qualify as impure rational influence in this sense, of trying to achieve ends by offering incentives to others. Such incentives would include all coercive threats to life, limb, and other attachments (including secrets, as in the present case). They would also include the more positive incentives that are offered in bribes. And they would even include all of the incentives that are offered in bargaining situations. Indeed, depending upon how hard-driven a bargain is, it can be viewed either as an effort at mutual coercion or as an effort at mutual bribery. Thus on this account, there is a single mechanism on which coercive threats, bribery, and bargaining all rely: they all attempt to achieve their ends through the actions of others by offering incentives to them, where such an incentive is not merely the presentation of a reason for action, but is also the generation of the reason in question. Yet it is common and intuitive to speak as if coercive threats involved a quite different form of influence from that which is exercised in the course of bribes and bargains. We often say that the victims of coercive threats are somehow *forced* to comply, and we do not typically say this about the recipients of bribes and bargains. However, the point of a coercive incentive is to provide its victim with sufficient *reason* to comply with the coercer's wishes. And so the "force" that is most directly at work in attempts at coercion is the normative force of the reason that is created by a coercive incentive. Again, if this were not so, then there would be no difference between coercive threats and the cases of nonrational influence that were discussed above, such as binding an agent, or drugging it, or hypnotizing it. (These remarks should not be taken as a denial of the real and important ethical differences between coercive threats on the one hand, and bribes and bargains on the other. But if this account is at all on the right track, these ethical differences do not show that these cases of influence fall under different categories of modes of influence. In all three cases it is the category of *impure rational* influence. The ethical differences between them seem to concern rather the particular values that they try to exploit, the particular circumstances in which they do so, and also, crucially, the attitudes that they manifest toward the rational points of view of others. This last point will be pivotal in understanding how and when impure rational influence can fail to be agency-regarding, in the sense being clarified here.)

Where have we gotten now in the categorization of the modes of influence under which the cases from our laundry list fall? We have seen the limitations of even the third conception of what it is to aim to hinder agency, which exploited the distinction between rational and nonrational influence. That conception was too limited because it ruled in lies and threats as aiming not to hinder agency, and hence as agency-regarding, while some intuition tells us that they do aim to hinder agency, and hence are agency-disregarding. So we further distinguished within the category of rational modes of influence by adding three further categories—open and pure, covert, impure—the idea being that only the first is agency-regarding, and that lies and threats qualify as agency-disregarding because they fall, respectively, under the second and third.

We have now arrived at a categorization that is exhaustive. Everything we saw so far on the laundry list of examples of influence falls under one or other of these categories we have traversed while considering all of the three conceptions and their limitations. Rational argument employs open and pure rational influence; manipulation employs nonrational influence; lies employ covert but pure rational influence; threats employ open but impure rational influence. And anything we *add* to our laundry list will have to be a mode of influence that is either nonrational or rational, and if rational, either open and pure, or not open, or not pure. (As an aside, it should be said that there is one last category we have not yet considered, namely, the mode of influence that is rational but neither open nor pure. By adding this category, we would arrive at a logically exhaustive list: starting with open and pure rational influence, we could derive all of the others by negation. However, there would be little point in a separate discussion of this last category, and it will not be mentioned again in this book. It simply combines the features of covert rational influence and impure rational influence. And there is nothing to say about it that will not already have been said in connection with the other two modes whose features it combines. Readers who want to construct an example of this fifth mode on their own should try to think of a case where someone has reason both to offer an incentive to another party, and also to keep the ultimate end for the sake of which this incentive is being offered covert.)

It is now time to consider what it is about these modes of influence, if anything, that might account for our intuitions about why these different cases do and do not qualify as agency-regarding. So here, then, is a fourth and seemingly final conception of what it is to aim to hinder agency that reflects this exhaustive categorization of the modes of influence: one agent aims to hinder the agency of another just in case it attempts to wield any mode of influence except open and pure rational influence. Of the cases on our laundry list, only rational argument employs open and pure rational means, and so only it qualifies as a case of influence that aims not to hinder agency, and hence is agency-regarding. And that is precisely the intuition with which we began. All of the other cases in the laundry list are intuitively agency-disregarding, and they are all cases that employ other modes of influence, modes that either are not rational, or are not openly rational, or are not purely rational.

We have thus systematically consolidated our intuitions that had surfaced only haphazardly when we simply were presented with the laundry list. And so we are now in position to ask more illuminatingly whether the consolidated intuitions are good ones for our purposes. Do they really help in clarifying the notion of an agency-regarding relation? If it turns out that finally they do not—and that is exactly how it will turn out—we will be able to see the underlying theoretical motive for putting aside our intuitions in the task of understanding agency-regarding relations, and for adopting the quite different understanding that will be proposed here.

Let us begin with the question why open and pure rational influence *seems* so clearly to be, by the light of these now systematically consolidated intuitions, a mode of influence that aims not to hinder agency, and seems therefore to be uniquely agency-regarding.

The aim in all efforts at *open* rational influence is to realize an end by getting another agent to embrace it and act for the sake of it. When the means employed are *purely* rational means, the aim is to accomplish this solely by virtue of the normative force of the reasons that are presented to the other agent, as that force holds within the other agent's own rational point of view. This means that the wielder of such influence must do nothing else, in its effort to realize its end, than to find and present reasons for action with the following property: the reasons will show why the end that it aims to realize through its effort to influence the other agent is an end that the other agent ought, from its own rational point of view, to embrace, quite independently of the effort at influence itself. This may seem paradoxical. How can an effort to influence another agent aim to achieve a result that is independent of the effort itself? The answer is simple. The independence in question is normative and not causal. Thus it might well be the case that the agent being influenced would not, as a matter of fact, embrace the influencer's end unless it were subjected to the effort at influence. And yet it might also be the case that the agent nevertheless has *reason*, from its own rational point of view, to embrace that end anyway, quite independently of the effort at influence. And this is the only condition in which open and pure rational influence is designed to succeed, namely, that an agent has reason anyway, from its own rational point of view and quite independently of the effort at influence itself, to embrace and act for the sake of the influencer's end.

This design feature of open and pure rational influence is manifest in the example from above, of friendly advice. My own end in the example is to get you to take your umbrella today. I openly offer you a reason to embrace this end, by informing you that it will rain today. And I rely on nothing else but the purely normative force that this information holds within your own rational point of view. Now, there is only one condition in which I can succeed in this effort to influence you: you must already have, from your own rational point of view, a conditional preference to take your umbrella today if it rains. If you do have this preference, then you have independent reason, from your own rational point of view, to want to know whether it will rain today. So when I supply the information that it will rain today, I am simply fulfilling a desire that you already have, quite apart from my effort to influence you, and which you ought, in any case, to fulfill by some means or other. And if you were to fulfill this desire by some other means—say, by listening to a weather report or checking a barometer—then you would be led to embrace the very end that I aim to get you to embrace through my effort to influence you, which is that you take your umbrella with you today.

Clearly, no mode of influence could possibly be designed to incorporate a higher degree of regard for another agent's own rational point of view than open and pure rational influence. A wielder of such influence must find and present reasons that suffice to show that its own end—that is, the end that it is trying to realize through its effort to influence another agent—is justified from the rational point of view of the other agent. And in order to accomplish this, a wielder of such influence must, as far as possible, suppress the differences between its own rational point of view and that of the other agent. Indeed, it must suppress these differences to such an extent that its effort to influence the other agent mimics or reproduces a rational process that the other agent would normally carry out anyway, just through the individual exercise of its own agency. As a result, if an effort at open and pure rational influence succeeds—that is, if reasons are found that do show why one's own end ought to be embraced by another agent whom one is trying to influence, and if presenting these reasons should move that agent to act so as to realize that end—then it will be, for that other agent, as if only *one* rational point of view had been involved, namely, its *own*.

If this is the philosophical basis for why it *seems* so intuitive that the category of open and pure rational influence aims not to hinder agency, if this is what makes it seem uniquely agency-regarding, then we can say something general about what notion of *agency* has been presupposed in these many pages as we considered the various cases about which we have intuitions concerning regard and disregard for agency. This will allow us in turn to give a general account of the notion of an agency-regarding relation, and thereby clarify the ethical criterion that defines persons as agents who can engage in such relations.

The point, however, is not that the intuitions with which we began actually get right what agency-regarding relations are. As stated at the outset, it will be argued that our intuitions about these matters *are in fact wrong*, at least from the point of view of the present project. So the point is rather this: We may take our intuitions in this area as standing in need of explanation. And in trying to find this explanation we shall uncover some *general lessons*—both about agency and about agency-regarding relations. But when these lessons are properly learned, we will conclude that we must *give up* our initial intuitions *even as we explain their seeming intuitiveness*.

What, then, are the general lessons about regard for agency that we have learned from this lengthy discussion? They are as follows.

Some General Lessons That Emerge from the Intuitions

The ethical criterion of personhood defines both agency-regarding relations, and ultimately personhood itself, in terms of the idea of hindering agency. This idea presupposes that all agents want to be agents, that there is a *universal goal of agency*.[4] Thus an attempt at influence that aims not to hinder agency is aimed at not hindering this universal goal. What, then, is this goal a goal toward? The uninformative answer is, of course: agency. That is why aiming not to hinder the goal is to relate to another with regard for its agency. The informative answer is built up on two basic facts about all agents.

The first basic fact is that agency is always exercised from a rational point of view. For there can be no such thing as agency unless agents have reasons on which to act, and these reasons comprise an agent's rational point of view. What is that? It is a point of view from which an agent not only acts; it is a point of view from which the agent can also reflect upon various reasons for action, and assess their relative merits. It is, in other words, a deliberative point of view from which the agent can determine what would be best to do, all things considered, in the broadest sense of "do" that comprehends all

---

[4] The presupposition is fair enough, since the only view that would deny it is a view that succumbs to an extreme form of alienation and nihilism, in which agents would find themselves without the very motives that make them agents to begin with. And this book is not at all concerned to address this view, which is really a form of skepticism about the very existence of agency.

intentional activities, including mental activities. (Section 2 of chapter 1 has already described this notion of a rational point of view in some detail; other details will continue to emerge as the argument of the book proceeds.)

The second basic fact is that every agent must have a particular domain of intentional control. For there can be no such thing as agency unless reasons are, at least some of the time, efficacious, in the sense of leading to actions (or conclusions) that are justified by them. And the domain of an agent's intentional control is simply the domain in which its reasons are, in the normal course of things, efficacious.

Both of these two basic facts of agency will be discussed and examined at greater length in Part II of the book. But even when they are stated briefly and simply as they have been stated here, they bring to light that, when you put the two of them together, there is a certain *universal goal* that any agent is bound to have. *This goal is to bring the events that fall within the agent's domain of intentional control into line with the dictates of its rational point of view, so that what it does is what it has most reason to do.* In fact, the exercise of agency is nothing else but the attempt to realize this goal, which is therefore the defining, as well as the universal, goal of agency. And when agents are reflective (which they must be if they are to stand in agency-regarding relations), they actually conceive the exercise of their agency in relation to this goal. That is, when a reflective agent exercises its agency, it knowingly aims to bring the events that fall within its domain of intentional control into line with the dictates of its rational point of view, so that what it does is a proper reflection of what it takes itself to have most reason to do.[5]

(A longish aside is necessary to preempt a misunderstanding. Strictly speaking, the phenomenon of weakness of will constitutes a counterexample to this

---

[5] This book has nothing very much to say about *unreflective* agents (if there are any) who cannot grasp the normative force of reasons. Such agents could not engage in agency-regarding relations, and hence would not satisfy the ethical criterion of personhood—and so are irrelevant to this book's project of resolving the dispute about personal identity. But it is perhaps worth registering that if there are any such unreflective agents, all of the aspects of agency just described must hold in *some* form for them. That is, they must have a rational point of view and a domain of intentional control, and their actions must be directed toward the universal goal of agency, which is to bring the latter into line with the former.

It might seem odd to suppose that an agent could have a rational point of view at all unless it was a deliberative point of view in the sense that involves reflection upon the relative merits of reasons for action. It is precisely this oddity that leads such philosophers as Descartes and Davidson to deny that there are any unreflective agents. This book will not take a stand on this matter. It will simply affirm that *if* there are unreflective agents, then they must act on reasons, and *if* unreflective agents act on reasons, then they must have rational points of view that are constituted by those reasons—even though they lack the power to deliberate. It might seem preferable to affirm that unreflective agents act on *motives* rather than reasons, and that these motives comprise the *psychological*, rather than the rational, points of view from which they act. However, the point remains that there would be no agency involved here unless motives provided something very much like a reason in the ordinary sense that holds for reflective creatures, namely, that reasons *rationalize* actions. Unless this were so, there would be no way to distinguish *agency* from the operation of the nonrational causes that govern the larger course of natural events.

last claim, since weak-willed actions are plausibly construed as deliberate failures to realize the universal goal of agency. However, this does not really undermine the claim altogether; it merely points to the need for an important qualification. Rather than claim that every exercise of agency is in fact directed at realizing the universal goal of agency, we must claim instead that every exercise of agency ought to be directed at realizing this goal, and is so directed insofar as it is fully rational. This normative version of the claim clearly holds even for the weak-willed agent. Indeed, if it did not hold, then it would be impossible to say what makes weak-willed actions irrational. The irrationality of a weak-willed action derives from the following fact: the reason for which it is undertaken is not the reason that the agent judges to be best, all things considered. But of course, this would not constitute a form of irrationality unless the weak-willed agent were actually committed to arriving at and acting upon such judgments. And in the case of reflective agents, this is the same thing as being committed to realizing the universal goal of agency. In their case, the goal of bringing the events that lie within their respective domains of intentional control into line with the dictates of their respective rational points of view just is the goal of arriving at and acting upon all-things-considered judgments. And to reiterate, without a commitment to realizing this goal, there would be nothing irrational about weak-willed actions. So the normative version of the claim above does stand, even in the case of weak-willed agents: every exercise of agency ought to be directed at realizing the universal goal of agency, and is so directed insofar as it is fully rational.)

Returning, then, to the matter of agency-regardingness, let us look at the point made just before this aside and see how it applies to attempts at influencing others and what makes them aimed at hindering or not hindering agency. An effort to influence another agent is always undertaken for the sake of some particular end. And, applying the recently made points, we can now say that, usually, it is an effort to realize this end by influencing events that fall within another agent's own domain of intentional control. (It is not as if all events within the life of an agent must be within the intentional control of the agent. But any events within its life that are relevant to the question of its agency being hindered or not must fall within its intentional control.)[6] Whenever one agent attempts to influence events that fall within

[6] It is, in fact, a difficult question whether there are events in the lives of agents that fall completely outside their own domains of intentional control. As the book proceeds it will be less and less clear that there are any such events. Even from the start it should be clear that we ought not to take a stand on this issue in advance of determining, in a quite general way, what actually does lie within an agent's domain of intentional control. And this will prove to be a vexed and difficult issue. There is a temptation to try to settle it by appeal to the idea of motor control over a particular body. But even if we took for granted, as animalists do, that the identity of an agent's body can always be unproblematically determined by biological criteria—and this book does *not* take this for granted—it is far from obvious that we ought to identify an agent's domain of intentional control with the domain of its biologically based motor control. That would discount the sort of intentional control which an agent is able to exert through the use of tools, through its knowledge of cause and effect, and through its contingent social circumstances (e.g., legally

another agent's own domain of intentional control, the question arises whether what happens through such influence accords with the other agent's own rational point of view. A lack of accord would constitute a hindrance of that agent's realization of the universal goal of agency. And any effort at influence that intentionally produced such a lack of accord would *aim* to hinder the agent's agency, and so would constitute a failure of regard for the agent's agency.

This, then, is *the most general lesson we have learned* from a discussion of the intuitions and examples, a lesson that allows us to state succinctly what regard for agency is. It is to stand in a relation toward another agent in which an attempt to influence the agent is informed by a *thoroughgoing regard for its own rational point of view*, where this means exactly what was said above: that one aims not to produce any discord between what happens within the agent's domain of intentional control and its all-things-considered judgments.

Let us now consider what this general lesson, with its explicit definition of agency-regardingness, can show us about our intuitions. Does it afford an explanation of why the category of open and pure rational influence intuitively seems to be agency-regarding, while the other categories (the nonrational, and the covert and impure rational modes) intuitively seem not to be? Since we arrived at the general lesson and definition by considering the first category, let us proceed to the others.

Take the *nonrational* category first. When an effort to influence an agent employs nonrational means, it aims to realize its end through the brute force of causation, that is, without invoking the normative force of reasons. In consequence, efforts within this mode can generally proceed, and also succeed, without any regard whatsoever for the rational point of view of the agent being influenced. And this means, of course, that such efforts may be directed at realizing ends regardless of whether those ends are in accord with the rational point of view of the agent being influenced. The example of hypnosis from above makes this very clear. My end in the example is to get you to take your umbrella with you today, and clearly, this is an end that I can realize by hypnotizing you no matter what you yourself think about it from your own rational point of view. The same holds for the other methods of nonrational

---

based control over what happens to one's body through a living will). And these forms of intentional control ought not to be discounted. Indeed, they cannot be discounted if the notion of a domain of intentional control is understood in accordance with the stipulation above, as the domain in which an agent's reasons are, in the normal course of things, efficacious. But of course, insofar as we do allow that an agent's domain of intentional control might comprehend all of the events over which it has intentional control in this extended sense, then we shall be hard-pressed to find events that clearly belong to the life of the agent and yet clearly fall outside this domain. Because animalists equate the life of an agent with the biological life of an organism, they are likely to assume that there are many such events—for example, the beating of an organism's heart or its secretion of bile. But even these events that are given by biological nature are subject to significant medical and technological control, and hence intentional control in the extended sense just explained. And in any case, not every view of what an agent or person is will equate its life with the biological life of an organism.

influence that were mentioned above, such as binding you, drugging you, and tampering with your brain.

As before, there is one case of nonrational influence that merits separate discussion, namely, the sort of manipulation that exploits a thing's rational capacities. Because this sort of manipulation exploits a thing's rational capacities, it cannot display quite the same total lack of regard for another agent's own rational point of view that is generally possible in nonrational influence. But all the same, it can be wielded in order to achieve an end even when the agent on whom it is wielded does not embrace that end. The point is confirmed by the example that was discussed above, though this is not immediately obvious. In the example, I attempt to manipulate you into taking your umbrella by removing umbrellas from an umbrella stand, my plan being that you will take the absence of umbrellas as evidence that your housemates have taken theirs, and that you will infer that you ought to follow suit and take yours. Under one description, my end in the example is simply to get you to take your umbrella. So described, it seems correct to say that I aim to realize my end precisely by getting you to embrace it and to act for the sake of it. Yet here is a more accurate description of my end: to get you to take your umbrella on a day when your housemates do not take theirs. So described, this is an end that I aim to realize without getting you to embrace it, and indeed that I aim to realize even while believing that you positively reject it. And in general, this is a possibility that nonrational influence is designed to afford. Because this is so, it is a mode of influence that is not designed to incorporate a very high degree of regard for an agent's own rational point of view.

Like the sort of manipulation that was just discussed, none of the *rational* modes of influence can ever be completely disregardful of an agent's own rational point of view. The reason why, however, is slightly different. Rational modes of influence aim to realize their ends by *offering* other agents reasons to do something. And a wielder of such influence must therefore be regardful of how the reasons that it offers to another agent would appear from—that is, what normative force they would have within—that agent's own rational point of view.

Yet when rational influence is *covert* it can, just as nonrational influence can, be used to realize ends regardless of whether those ends are in accord with the other agent's own rational point of view. The whole point of covertness is that the other agent should be gotten to act so as to realize a certain end, but without knowing that it does so. In consequence, it does not matter at all to the prospects for success what the other agent thinks about that end from its own rational point of view. And that is the sense in which covert rational influence is not designed to incorporate a very high degree of regard for another agent's own rational point of view. The example of lying that was discussed above bears this out. My end in the example is to show our common friend how gullible you are. In order to realize this end, I decide to get you to take your umbrella with you today by lying to you about the likelihood of rain. This does require some minimal regard on my part for your rational point of view. I cannot disregard whether you would be justified, by the lights of your own rational point of view, in believing my lie about the likelihood of rain, and in acting upon that belief by taking your umbrella with you today. But on the other hand, I can disregard whether you embrace my end of exposing you as gullible. If you act on the reason which I offer you as I intend that you should—that is, if you decide to take your umbrella with you today because I have told you it will rain—then you will act in such a way as to realize my end of proving you gullible, but without knowing that you are doing so. So even if you should reject my end, that ought not to stand in the way of my realizing it. And again, this is a possibility that covertness in rational influence is designed to afford, namely, that an end may be realized through another agent's actions even if the end fails to accord with that agent's own rational point of view.

Open rational influence requires a much greater degree of regard for another agent's own rational point of view than does covert rational influence. For when a reason is openly presented to another agent, it is presented as a reason to embrace and act for the sake of the very end that the wielder of influence is trying to realize by offering the reason. And this shows that open rational influence is designed in such a way that it cannot succeed in realizing its end unless that end is in fact justified from the other agent's rational point of view. In fact, it can succeed only insofar as the other agent actually embraces and acts for the sake of that end. Now given this design feature, it may seem unclear how any effort at open rational influence—even when such influence is impure, as in the case of threats—can fail to be informed by thoroughgoing regard for an agent's rational point of view.

It may seem that the point just made about open rational influence does not really hold in the *impure* case. Consider, after all, what incentives are designed to accomplish: they are designed to induce an agent to act for the sake of a certain end when the agent would otherwise have insufficient reason to do so. This shows that a wielder of open and impure rational influence does not normally aim to get another agent to embrace its end for its own sake; a wielder of such influence aims rather to get another agent to embrace its end as a means to achieving whatever benefits are bound up with the incentive that it offers. This is confirmed by the example that was given above to illustrate this mode of influence. My end in the example is to get you to take your umbrella. But I see that you are unwilling. So I set about getting you to take your umbrella anyway, by threatening to divulge a secret of yours if you do not take it. When I issue this threat, I do not intend that you will embrace this end for its own sake; I intend that you embrace it as a means to keeping your secret. (This is not to say that I would not want you to embrace my end for its own sake; it is only to say that this is not what I aim to accomplish by issuing my threat.) Now some may think that this is enough to show that I aim to realize an end through my threat that is not entirely in accord with the dictates of your own rational point of view, for initially, you are unwilling to take your umbrella, and it is only after I lodge my threat that you become willing.

But nevertheless, you do *become* willing. And moreover, that is what I intend. I intend that my threat will provide you with sufficient *reason*, from your *own* rational point of view, to embrace the end of taking your umbrella. And the fact that you embrace this end only as a *means* to keeping your secret does not make it any the less a *genuine embracement*. There is no reason to suppose that Kant's dictum does not apply here: the agent who wills the end does will the means.

So in seeking an answer to our question, we must find some way in which a wielder of influence can fail to show thoroughgoing regard for an agent's own rational point of view, other than by intending to realize an end that the agent being influenced does not embrace before being influenced. There is another, very obvious way in which a wielder of influence can fail to be regardful of another agent's rational point of view: it can proceed in its effort to influence the agent without any regard for the agent's attitude toward the effort at influence itself. And this is precisely the sort of failure of regard that open and impure rational influence is designed to afford. It is in the nature of incentives that they may work—that is, they may induce an agent to embrace and act for the sake of ends—even when the agent would prefer not to have been offered them. Here are two very common reasons why an agent might prefer not to be offered an incentive: some incentives are simply offensive and unpleasant in themselves, and some incentives are powerful enough to get an agent to act for the sake of ends of which it strongly disapproves. Very often these two reasons are connected: bodily harm is offensive and unpleasant, and that is why the threat of such harm may constitute a powerful reason to perform actions of which one strongly disapproves (e.g., helping a terrorist). But whatever may be the source of an agent's preference not to be offered an incentive, the point is that the agent might well retain this preference even while responding to the incentive. Thus in the example at hand, you might prefer not to be subjected to my threat to divulge your secret. Yet this preference need not, and should not, deter you from accepting the threat as a fact with which you must deal in a rational manner. The most rational response on your part might well be to embrace the end of taking your umbrella today. But even if you do come to embrace this end, you need never change your mind about my threat. That is, you may retain your preference not to have been offered it, even while you respond to it. And if I should lodge my threat in the face of the fact that you object to it, or even in the face of the suspicion that you might object to it, I would be proceeding in my effort to influence you with less than thoroughgoing regard for your own rational point of view. And again, it is in the nature of incentives that they may achieve their effects even in such conditions. That is why open and impure rational influence is not designed to incorporate a high degree of regard for another agent's own rational point of view.

It has now been shown how it is that our definition of regard for agency is able to explain our intuitions about all of the categories of modes of influencing other agents. What is meant by "explain" here is just that the definition captures what *underlies* their seeming intuitiveness. It does so by linking the agency-regarding aim not to hinder agency with an attitude of thoroughgoing regard for an agent's own rational point of view. En route to this definition, it was observed that no mode of influence could possibly be designed to incorporate a higher degree of such regard for another's rational point of view than open and pure rational influence. And it has just been shown that the other categories—the nonrational, and the covert and impure rational modes—are all designed to succeed even when they incorporate something less than thoroughgoing regard for another's rational point of view. And that explains why the former intuitively seems to be agency-regarding while the latter do not.

Why the Intuitions Do Not Square with the General Lesson They Taught Us

The preceding discussion has finally given us all the conceptual wherewithal and framework to show that the very intuitions, the discussion of which taught us this general lesson about how to define regard for agency, are intuitions that the general lesson and the definition will reject as unconvincing.

Let us start with the category of open and pure rational influence, which seems so intuitively to be uniquely and intrinsically agency-regarding. Even efforts within this mode of influence may fail to be *entirely* regardful of an agent's own rational point of view. The most crucial point here is simple. Like the impure case discussed above, open and pure rational influence is designed to work *even when an agent objects to being subjected to it*. And just for this reason, when an agent objects to being subjected to it, it is precisely put into question whether an attempt at such influence *is* entirely in accord with the agent's rational point of view. This means that the intuitive conception of regard for agency, and the characterization of regard for agency as we have defined it above, are noncoincident. Recall that we began this entire section by saying that there is an intuitive notion of agency-regard that is defined paradigmatically in terms of a specific and singular case on a long laundry list of cases, namely, the case of information given by a friendly adviser. The category of influence that is exemplified in the case, open and pure rational influence, is precisely what we are now saying need not always be agency-regarding as we have now defined it.

However, it is important to distinguish two kinds of objection that an agent might have to being subjected to open and pure rational influence: the reasonable and the unreasonable. It is only in the former case that an effort within this mode of influence would actually fail of thoroughgoing regard for an agent's rational point of view, and hence aim to hinder agency (or at least not aim not to). To see this, let us look at the latter case, and see why it is agency-regarding even in the face of an agent's objection. Suppose that you hate to take your umbrella. And suppose that on this ground you object to my offering you a reason to do so, in the form of information that it will rain today. Like an incentive (e.g., my threat to divulge your secret), this pure reason might well move you to take your umbrella even though you object to being presented with it. Yet this ought not to count as evidence that open and pure rational influence can successfully be wielded even when it does not incorporate thoroughgoing regard for an agent's own rational point of view. For consider why it is that the information that it will rain today should move you to take your umbrella. As has already been explained, if my effort to influence you is purely as well as openly rational, then the only condition in which I can succeed is the condition in which you already have a conditional preference to take your umbrella today if it rains. If you do have this preference, then you have independent reason to want the very information that I am giving you. And in that case, your objection to my effort is *unreasonable by your own lights*. So in making such an effort, I would actually be displaying *more* regard for your own rational point of view than you yourself would in objecting to it. Indeed, I would be displaying thoroughgoing regard for it. But this is not so when I threaten to divulge your secret in order to get you to take your umbrella. In such a case, your objection to being subjected to this threat may be entirely reasonable by the lights of your own rational point of view. And if I should proceed (and succeed) in the face of your objection, it cannot be said that I would thereby exhibit thoroughgoing regard for your own rational point of view.

Thus if open and pure rational influence can fail of thoroughgoing regard, then it must be possible that an agent can have *reasonable* objections to being subjected to such influence. In certain special circumstances this is true. Suppose, for example, that you are in a competitive setting, or an educational setting, where your goal is to work out what is best by the lights of your own rational point of view, but without the aid of anyone else's help. In such a setting you would of course have good reason to object to my influencing you in any way at all, even by open and pure rational means. And if I were to wield such influence on you in the face of your objection, I would thereby fail to exhibit thoroughgoing regard for your own rational point of view. This is so even though I would be wielding a mode of influence that is designed to incorporate as high a degree of regard as is possible in the course of an effort at influence.[7]

---

[7] It is tempting to argue that, despite these exceptions in which open and pure rational influence does not incorporate thoroughgoing regard for another agent's own rational point of view, it is nevertheless a mode of influence that is intrinsically agency-regarding. The only condition in which it aims to hinder agency (or fails to aim not to hinder agency) is the condition in which it is wielded over an agent's *reasonable* objections to being subjected to it. And such objections are hardly ever reasonable, because the mode is designed to reproduce or mimic a rational process that an agent has reason to carry out for itself anyway, as part of the normal exercise of its individual agency. So it would seem that, in general, whatever reason an agent has to exercise its own agency is also a reason why the agent should welcome efforts at open and pure rational influence. However, this is not *necessarily* so. An agent might have an overriding commitment to exercising its agency without the benefit of influence from anyone else—not just in the exceptional situations of competition and learning, but *always*. And the extent to which open and pure rational influence is agency-regarding would seem to be *contingent*, therefore, on the extent to which agents do not have, and are believed not to have, this commitment. But then it is hard to mount to an effective argument to show that this mode of influence is *intrinsically* agency-

These last remarks show that the one mode of influence that seems, intuitively, to be intrinsically regardful of agency can, at least on the present definition of agency-regardingness, fail to be regardful of agency. It is also the case that the other modes of influence, which intuitively do *not* seem to be intrinsically regardful of agency, nevertheless *can* be. That is, they are modes of influence that *can* be informed by thoroughgoing regard for another agent's own rational point of view, and therefore aimed at not hindering agency.

We have seen that there are two main ways in which efforts at influence can fail to be informed by such thoroughgoing regard: they can aim to realize a particular end by influencing another agent even though the agent does not embrace that end, and they can aim to do this even though the agent has a reasonable objection to the effort at influence itself. Let us now see why it is that efforts to influence other agents via the modes of nonrational, covert rational, and impure rational influence *need* not fail of regard in either of these ways, even though they are designed to succeed in realizing their ends when they do fail of such regard.

In the case of impure rational influence, this is not only possible, but common. Agents often aim to influence one another by offering incentives. And often, they offer incentives that are actually *welcome*. Thus suppose that instead of threatening to divulge your secret in order to get you to take your umbrella, I offered you money (or perhaps some other incentive that you value even more than money). And suppose that you not only welcomed this offer of money, but furthermore you were, in general, prepared to do *anything* for money, or at least anything that I was likely to ask of you in exchange for money. If I knew this (or even just believed it) when I attempted to influence you by offering you money, then my effort would be thoroughgoingly regardful of your own rational point of view, and hence agency-regarding. There would be nothing that I intended to achieve through my effort that did not accord, in every way, with the dictates of your own rational point of view.[8]

It may seem less plausible that efforts at nonrational and covert rational influence can likewise be thoroughgoingly regardful of another agent's own rational point of view. But this is in principle possible. Suppose, for example, that you believe that you ought to take your umbrella with you today, but you really hate to take your umbrella and you are very weak-willed. In such a case, you might be unable to realize your own goals as an agent without the intervention of my influence. But the sort of influence you need is not open and

---

regarding. (Michael Della Rocca has rightly pointed out that such an argument would have to be a transcendental argument that showed the following: the nature of agency is such that it would be irrational to have the commitment just described, to exercising one's own agency without the benefit of anyone else's influence. Yet this transcendental conclusion does not seem to be within reach, insofar as we do have to allow for the exceptions of learning and competition. If these exceptions are allowed, then it simply cannot be concluded that open and pure rational influence is *necessarily* agency-regarding.)

pure rational influence. You have already made a well-informed judgment about what it would be best to do, all things considered; you have judged that you ought to take your umbrella with you today. What you need is help in implementing this judgment via some other mode of influence. And you might be quite content if I were to wield *any* mode of influence, so long as it would bring about the desired outcome that you take your umbrella with you today. Thus within the mode of nonrational influence, you would approve of my hypnotizing you into taking your umbrella or even chaining it to your wrist. Within the mode of covert rational influence, you would not mind being brought to take your umbrella unwittingly, say, by my sneaking it into a package that I pretended I needed delivered. And within the mode of impure rational influence, you would be happy to be offered any incentives that might effectively induce you to take your umbrella. Now suppose that I knew all this. In such a case, I could certainly engage in any or all of the modes of influence that are not designed to incorporate a very high degree of regard for an agent's rational point of view, and yet my effort could be informed by an attitude of thoroughgoing regard for your own rational point of view—which is to say, my effort could be perfectly agency-regarding. My end would be to get you to take your umbrella with you today; and my means would be hypnosis, chains, lies, or threats; and I would employ these means in order to realize this end precisely because that would accord with the dictates of your own rational point of view.

These last examples are somewhat frivolous. All the same, they suffice to show that the modes of influence that are not designed to incorporate a very high degree of regard for another agent's own rational point of view can in principle do so. Because this is true, these modes of influence may sometimes

---

[8] The mere fact that you generally welcome monetary incentives does not ensure that every effort to influence you via such incentives will be regardful of your agency. There might be ends that you would prefer not to help realize by accepting monetary incentives. You might, for example, have a very strong preference never to help realize the ends of the tobacco industry in any way. And this might well lead you to object to being offered monetary incentives in order to help realize those ends. Suppose that I knew this. Suppose that I also knew that your need for money was very great—so great that you would accept money in exchange for working for the tobacco industry. And suppose finally that I offered you money in exchange for such work. In these circumstances, my effort to influence you via monetary incentives would fail to be agency-regarding, despite the fact that you generally welcome such incentives.

Robert Adams has suggested to me that there is a convention surrounding monetary transactions, under which agents are released from all responsibility for the ends that the other participants in such transactions might aim to realize through them. Given this convention, it is arguable that an agent who in desperation accepts money in exchange for helping to realize ends of which it disapproves would not bear responsibility for realizing those ends; only the wielder of influence would. But even if that is true, the existence of the convention in question cannot ensure that all monetary transactions are agency-regarding in the sense defined by the ethical criterion of personhood. The convention does not entail that individuals cannot object to being offered monetary incentives in exchange for helping to realize certain ends. And whenever monetary incentives are offered in the face of such objections, they fail to be informed by thoroughgoing regard for an agent's rational point of view—and so fail to satisfy the present definition of regard for agency.

be welcomed by an agent. In fact, it might even be a failure of rationality to fail to seek them out—especially when an agent has difficulty in executing its own all-things-considered best judgments, either as a result of weakness of will or as a result of some other incapacity. In such circumstances, an agent has reason to seek help through therapy and training. Although we do not usually emphasize this, training and therapy often employ modes of influence that are not designed to incorporate a very high degree of regard for an agent's own rational point of view, that is, that are not designed to be agency-regarding. (Imagine a personal trainer who actually advertises this fact: "I will do whatever it takes to get you into shape. I will use physical force, hypnosis, drugs, deception, bribes, and threats. All you have to do is put yourself in my hands.") By the lights of the ethical criterion of personhood this does not, by itself, entail that therapists and trainers have a failure of regard for the agency of others. If their efforts are informed by an attitude of thoroughgoing regard for their clients' own rational points of view, then their efforts qualify as agency-regarding.

The definition of agency-regarding relations we have formulated has shown that there is an extremely wide variety of interactions which may qualify as agency-regarding, including even such apparently agency-hindering activities as hypnosis, lies, and threats. Many of these were on the laundry list of examples that we intuitively counted as agency-disregarding. So once again (this time from a different direction and with different cases) we have shown the noncoincidence of our intuitive conceptions of regard and disregard for agency and the definition that we have formulated.

Summarizing Conclusion

The subject of regard for agency is a subject where it is difficult to separate our metaphysical and our moral responses. This section has tried to take seriously the idea that our intuitive parsing of cases, into agency-regarding and agency-disregarding relations, is not *primarily* a moral matter, and deserves to be studied from a cleanly metaphysical perspective. It deserves to be so studied because, even if we do not always think that any particular action that aims to hinder agency is bad, or that aims not to hinder agency is good, our intuitions are much more clear and consensual on a metaphysical (rather than moral) matter, namely, which particular cases of influence do and do not aim to hinder agency. So, for instance, there is a strong intuition that manipulation, lies, and threats all aim to hinder agency. And yet there is no consensus that they are always wrong. Indeed, by the lights of certain egoists and consequentialists, they are perhaps not even prima facie wrong. (Our metaphysical and moral intuitions might be closer together in the case of rational argument. It is intuitive not only that it aims not to hinder agency, but also, perhaps few will find it unintuitive that it is morally acceptable.)

The guiding thought in this section has been that we might be able to make something of our intuitions about the particular cases in metaphysical terms—that is, that our intuitions about cases latch on to real distinctions among the different ways in which agents can treat one another; that some categories of modes of influence aim to hinder agency, while one does not; that all of this can be explained without marshaling in any substantive moral doctrines.

For this reason, we studied in detail the various categories of modes of influence with a view to arriving at such a metaphysical understanding of regard for agency and of the agency-regarding aim not to hinder agency. At the end of this study, it was found that a purely causal conception of what it is to hinder agency was quite inadequate to provide such an understanding. Instead, we arrived at a metaphysical understanding of the idea of the aim not to hinder agency, which was defined in terms of a *normative* relation that an effort to influence an agent can bear to the agent's own goal as an agent, namely, the universal goal of agency, which is to bring the events that fall within one's own domain of intentional control into line with the dictates of one's own rational point of view. (This was what we earlier called the "general lesson" to be derived from a study of the particular cases and our intuitions about them.) This normative relation consists in thoroughgoing regard for the agent's rational point of view. When such regard is in place, a wielder of influence intends to bring about no changes within another agent's domain of intentional control unless they are in complete accord with the agent's own rational point of view, that is, unless they are consistent with that agent's realization of the universal goal of agency. In that case, the wielder of influence can be said to be regardful of the agent's agency. It follows from this definition that none of the categories of modes of influence is intrinsically agency-regarding or intrinsically agency-disregarding. This is because agents may reasonably take differing attitudes toward being subjected to these modes of influence on particular occasions, and that bears crucially on the question whether particular efforts within the modes qualify as agency-regarding or not.

Of course, the resulting definition of regard for agency, which translates the aim not to hinder agency into regard for an agent's rational point of view, could have been plonked down at the outset, without considering our intuitions about cases. And it would even have been possible to give a metaphysical rationale for the plonked-down definition without going through the cases. Indeed it would have been possible to give the very *same* rationale that we arrived at by going through the cases (the one making essential reference to a rational point of view) without going through them. That rationale can be explained simply by spelling out some of the basic facts of agency that were set out above, and without drawing on any details from particular cases and our intuitions about them.

However, had we proceeded in that more expeditious way, then some of our intuitions about cases would have posed a serious obstacle to accepting this rationale as a sufficient reason for adopting the definition. For some of our intuitions are driven by our moral views, and the moral advantages of the definition are not immediately apparent, and will not be until the next section (and in a sense, they will not be fully in view until the Postscript). After all, if we were to try to equate morally good ways of treating agents with agency-regarding relations as they have here been defined, then we would arrive at a rather unappealing, and indeed facile-seeming, moral conclusion, which is that it would be morally acceptable to do just about anything to an agent, so long as the agent itself thought it was acceptable.

But, the goal here has not been to find a way to define regard for agency that would yield such a moral equation. The goal has been rather to make something of our intuitions about cases, to see why they *intuitively* seem to be so intrinsically regardful and disregardful of agency in a sense that does not require us to equate regard for agency with any kind of moral goodness. Because the definition *explains* these intuitions, even while undermining them, the definition cannot itself be undermined *by* them.

To the extent that this has all been achieved, it can be claimed that the space that we had promised to clear, which is metaphysical and normative without being purely causal or substantively moral, now stands occupied by the definition we have arrived at, of an agency-regarding relation.

With this definition, the notion of an agency-regarding relation has been clarified. Those who think that regard and disregard for agency are essentially to be thought of and explained in moral terms, and who think that the cases of influence we have been considering sort out along moral lines, may of course continue to do so. Our discussion has not refuted them so much as offered them a nonarbitrary change of subject, whereby these notions can be understood along more metaphysical, even if normative, lines. This nonarbitrariness will be fortified in the next section, and indeed in the rest of the book, when the notion of agency-regarding relations, which we have so far only clarified, is shown to have some real *advantages* once we define it in the way we have. In the next section, we will see how it provides both for the ethical uncontroversiality and, surprisingly, also for the ethical importance of the ethical criterion of personhood. And in Part II of the book, we will see that the definition also points to some important metaphysical insights about the nature of specifically personal agency, and about the nature of in*tra*- as well as in*ter*personal relations. These metaphysical insights will play a central role in the arguments for the possibility of group and multiple persons.

2. The Ethical Criterion Meets All Three Constraints

Having clarified the particular notion of an agency-regarding relation that figures in the ethical criterion, let us see why it makes sense to adopt it—why it makes sense to suppose that something is a person just in case it is an agent who can engage in agency-regarding relations.

First, we must remember the purpose of the ethical criterion. It is meant to serve as an initial assumption about the nature of persons, from which a substantive account of what kind of thing a person is can be developed, an account that will provide positive and compelling reasons for taking one side or the other in the central philosophical dispute about personal identity, between the animalists and the neo-Lockeans. In order to fulfill this purpose, the ethical criterion must, as stated earlier, meet three methodological constraints: (1) it must not beg the question in the dispute; (2) it must be sufficiently important; (3) it must be ethically uncontroversial. If the ethical criterion meets the first and last of these constraints, then both parties to the dispute *can* accept it; and if it meets the second constraint, then they *ought* to.

The Ethical Criterion Does Not Beg the Question

When the ethical criterion of personhood was first introduced in this chapter, it was briefly noted that it constitutes a revisionary proposal. The criterion stipulates that nothing is a person unless it can engage in agency-regarding relations. It stipulates further that such relations arise when one agent attempts to influence another and yet aims not to hinder its agency. And the last section construed this agency-regarding aim in terms of thoroughgoing regard for another agent's own rational point of view. This means that we cannot adopt the ethical criterion unless we are prepared to give up the commonsense belief that all human beings are persons. For clearly, some human beings cannot engage in agency-regarding relations.

The reasons why some human beings cannot engage in agency-regarding relations are various. But they are all quite obvious. Some human beings cannot engage in them because they cannot act intentionally at all. This would seem to be true of human beings who are very severely brain damaged and/or irretrievably comatose. But of course there are human beings who can act intentionally, and who nevertheless lack the capacity to engage in agency-regarding relations. Usually, such human beings simply lack the conceptual sophistication to form attitudes of regard for another agent's rational point of view, as is true of all human infants. But autistic human beings seem to lack a capacity that even infants possess, which is the capacity to engage in any significant social relations at all. Thus by the lights of the ethical criterion of personhood, none of these human beings qualifies as a person.

Neo-Lockeans should not find this revisionist implication of the ethical criterion objectionable. By drawing a distinction between personal and animal identity, they have already forsaken the commonsense belief that equates the class of persons with the class of human beings. In contrast, many animalists are committed to preserving this belief. Insofar as they are committed to preserving it, they must oppose the adoption of the ethical criterion that asks us to give it up.

The question therefore arises whether the ethical criterion is somehow at odds with the animalist view of personhood and personal identity, indeed so much so that adopting the criterion would amount to begging the question against an animalist resolution of the dispute about personal identity. The answer to this question is that the ethical criterion is not at all at odds with the animalist view, and it certainly does not beg the question one way or the other in the dispute between the animalists and the neo-Lockeans concerning the condition of personal identity.

This is a subtle issue. Recall that the whole point of adopting the ethical criterion of personhood is that it should serve as the starting point for a larger investigation into the kind 'person' whose outcome will, eventually, provide a positive reason to embrace one side or the other in the dispute about personal identity. It might well be wondered how the ethical criterion can serve this role without implicitly stacking the deck against one side in the dispute, thereby begging the question against that side, at least implicitly. In response, it must be remembered that this investigation has relinquished the goal of showing that either side in the dispute represents an absolutely incoherent, and therefore untenable, position. The goal is rather to find positive reasons to embrace just one side, even though both sides are coherent. And the goal is to draw such positive reasons for resolving the dispute from a substantive account of what kind of thing a person is. *Relative to this goal*, the ethical criterion can *avoid begging the question* so long as the following is true: it would be reasonable for animalists and neo-Lockeans alike to try to develop their respective accounts of what kind of thing a person is by starting with the premise that a person is the kind of thing that satisfies the ethical criterion.

In order to establish that this is indeed true, all we need do is identify the immediate metaphysical presuppositions of the ethical criterion, and then determine whether they constitute claims about the nature of persons that both animalists and neo-Lockeans could reasonably embrace and take as a starting point for an investigation into the kind 'person'.

What metaphysical presuppositions, then, did the last section uncover? That is, what did it show about the nature of the things that satisfy the ethical criterion—the agents who can engage in agency-regarding relations? It showed first and foremost that they are *rational* agents, in the minimal sense that they act on reasons. This means that each must have its own rational point of view and its own domain of intentional control, and each must be committed to realizing the universal goal of agency, which is to bring what happens within its domain of intentional control into line with the dictates of its rational point of view. The last section also showed that these agents must be *social* and *reflective*. Otherwise they would lack the cognitive and conceptual resources with which to frame the attitudes of regard for another agent's rational point of view that underlie the aim not to hinder agency. Finally, the section showed that the ability to frame such attitudes of regard goes hand in hand with the ability to wield *rational influence* on one another; for these are agents who can identify the intentional episodes that figure in another agent's rational point of view and who can appreciate how these episodes constitute reasons for action—which is just to say, they can appreciate the normative force of reasons. And when such agents come to knowledge of one another's rational points of view, they must also come to a mutual recognition of one another as agents who thus grasp the normative force of reasons. This social knowledge puts them in a position to influence one another by presenting one another with reasons for action.

Obviously, a good deal more could be said, and needs to be said, about the nature of such agents who satisfy the ethical criterion, and about the capacities that distinguish them. A good deal more will be said about them in Part II of the book. But the question now before us is whether there is any reason why neo-Lockeans or animalists ought not to assume that there are agents who have these capacities, and that something is a person just in case it is such an agent.

It should be absolutely clear that it would be reasonable for neo-Lockeans to assume this. But the more crucial point is that it would also be reasonable for animalists to assume this—for, once having made the assumption that persons are agents who have all of the capacities just described, animalists would then be free to try to show that the only kind of thing that can possess these capacities is a *suitably endowed animal*. Indeed, if the ethical criterion were adopted as a criterion of personhood, and if it were then followed by a successful argument to this effect, that would constitute an extremely power-ful and compelling reason to embrace an animalist resolution of the philo-sophical dispute about personal identity. And the important point is, there would be nothing question-begging about this way of resolving the dispute. Likewise, no question will have been begged when this book argues from the ethical criterion to a conclusion in favor of Locke's distinction instead. That conclusion will be the outcome of a sustained investigation into what kind of thing actually *does* have the capacities by virtue of which it can enter into agency-regarding relations and, hence, satisfy the ethical criterion of personhood.

Having thus established that the ethical criterion of personhood succeeds in meeting the constraint of not begging the question in the dispute about personal identity, there remains the question whether the criterion is, never-theless, somehow compromised by its deliberately revisionist character. Undoubtedly, the book's ultimate conclusion, concerning the possibility of multiple and group persons, is revisionist in the extreme. Yet the immediate revision that is entailed by the ethical criterion of personhood is not at all ex-treme. On the contrary, the ethical criterion requires only a very minor, and even superficial, revision of our commonsense outlook. It does not, in and of itself, undermine any of the distinctions to which common sense is wedded. Nor does it create any new distinction that common sense does not already recognize. In fact, the distinction on which the ethical criterion fastens, namely, the distinction between those things that can and those that cannot engage in agency-regarding relations, is *never denied* by common sense. And this is so even when common sense contradicts the ethical criterion by equating the class of persons with the class of human beings; even when common sense recognizes all human beings as persons, it also recognizes that some human beings cannot engage in agency-regarding relations (for the various and obvious reasons that were recounted at the start of the section).

Now, since the class of persons, as it is defined by the ethical criterion of personhood, is already recognized by common sense, it might be inferred that the immediate revisionist thrust of the criterion is primarily linguistic or verbal. After all, the criterion does not seem to ask us to do more than change our practice of applying the term "person" to all human beings, by confining its application to those agents who can engage in agency-regarding relations. However, the point of the ethical criterion is not merely to find an appropriate term for the class of things that satisfy it. The point is rather to find an appropriate starting point for a serious investigation into the kind of thing about which animalists and neo-Lockeans have a serious philosophical dispute concerning the condition of its identity—namely, the person.

To sum up then, the ethical criterion for what kind of thing a person is begs no questions in our dispute. Or to put it differently, the initial assumption that a person is the kind of thing who can engage in agency-regarding relations (i.e., the assumption that is formulated by the ethical criterion) does not beg any questions against Locke and his followers nor against Locke's animalist opponents. There is absolutely no temptation to think that it begs the question against Locke and neo-Lockeans. Against the animalist there might be an initial appearance of begging the question, because it allows that some human beings may not be persons. But this appearance is illusory. It is always open to animalists to accept the ethical criterion of personhood, and so to allow that not all human beings are persons, while at the same time arguing that the only things that can satisfy the ethical criterion are human beings (or perhaps, more broadly, members of *some* animal species—human or otherwise—whose normal members are suitably endowed with the requisite rational, reflective, and social capacities by virtue of which they satisfy the ethical criterion).

The Ethical Criterion Is Ethically Uncontroversial

Let us be clear about what it means to say that the ethical criterion of personhood is completely uncontroversial from an ethical point of view. It means that the criterion can be accepted without resolving any of the major controversies of ethical theory. This will be shown in two stages.

The first stage will show that all of the participants in these controversies can in principle embrace the ethical criterion of personhood without giving up their respective ethical positions. In order to show this it will not be necessary, nor of course will it be possible, to catalogue all of the conceivable ethical positions. All that will be required is to consider a representative group of diverse positions that spans a sufficiently wide spectrum of the possible positions. Here is such a group: egoism, utilitarianism, virtue ethics, Kantian ethics, theories of rights. We shall see that all of these ethical positions can in principle accept the ethical criterion of personhood. But more importantly, we shall also find that the conclusion about these positions is generalizable. In other words, there is nothing to bar a proponent of *any* substantive ethical position from embracing the ethical criterion of personhood, with the single exception of nihilism—if indeed nihilism should be counted as an ethical position.

The second stage will address a rather more specific difficulty that confronts the task of establishing the ethical uncontroversiality of the ethical criterion. Kantians and rights-theorists have a long history of making something like the idea of regard for agency central to their ethical theories. Since regard for agency is also central to the ethical criterion, there might be a challenge coming from someone who wishes to say that the criterion is at least as controversial as the Kantian and rights-theoretic positions. But of course, those positions have a very specific ethical agenda, which is to establish that persons necessarily stand under some sort of obligation with respect to regard for agency. And to be committed to this agenda is really to be committed to the idea that regard for agency has a preeminent status among the ethically significant values, and indeed among all values—something that is expressly denied by egoists, utilitarians, and virtue theorists, and therefore something that is most controversial. Thus the ethical criterion could not, in the end, retain its claim to ethical uncontroversiality if it carried a commitment to the shared ethical agenda of Kantians and rights-theorists. So after the general argument for the uncontroversiality of the criterion has been presented, it will be crucial to establish that the criterion does not implicitly carry the controversial commitments of these ethical theories. The point will be that Kantians and rights-theorists employ a very different notion of agency-regard than the one that is employed in the ethical criterion. This point is continuous with the discussion of section 1. The declared aim there was to elaborate a *metaphysical* conception of agency-regard that on the one hand incorporates some normative elements, so as not to fall in with an overly crude causal picture of agency, and yet on the other hand does not fall in with any substantive ethical position either, in which agency-regard would be conceived as moral duty or obligation—as in the Kantian and rights-based accounts of agency-regard, from which the present metaphysical account needs to be sharply distinguished.

But the question arises: how can the so-called ethical criterion of personhood introduce issues of ethical significance at all—and hence earn its title—if it is based on such a metaphysical conception of agency-regard that does not rely on any substantive ethical position? The answer to this question, in capsule form, is as follows: What goes along with the ability to engage in agency-regarding relations is a *choice* concerning whether and when to engage in such relations, and this choice is always *ethically significant* in the broadest sense of "ethical significance" that has to do with what *demarcates* the entire domain of the ethical—that is, the whole domain of issues to which all substantive ethical positions, and indeed all ethical reflection, refer. But before introducing this *ethics-demarcating* consideration, we must consider more carefully the nature of the choice concerning agency-regard. Then we can see how the ethics-demarcating consideration confers ethical significance on the choice, and why it is possible to acknowledge this ethical significance without taking a stand on any of the main controversies of ethical theory.

In order to understand the nature of the choice concerning agency-regard that is faced by the agents who satisfy the ethical criterion of personhood, three surrounding points must be noted.

First, there is an epistemic requirement on personhood: *persons must be capable of social knowledge*. Insofar as persons are agents who can engage in agency-regarding relations, they are agents who can frame attitudes of regard for the rational points of view of other agents. And these agency-regarding attitudes necessarily incorporate social knowledge of other agents, their rational points of view, and the intentional episodes that comprise those points of view.

It might be objected that this epistemic requirement on personhood is overstated, because there is an unresolved skeptical problem concerning knowledge of other minds. Those who take such skepticism seriously might want to substitute an appropriately modified version of the epistemic requirement, according to which persons must be capable of possessing social *beliefs*, as opposed to full-blown social knowledge. All of the arguments to come in this book, both in defense of the ethical criterion of personhood and concerning the criterion's wider metaphysical implications, can be recast so as to reflect this modified epistemic requirement. Whenever these arguments refer to the social knowledge that persons have of other agents, a reference can be substituted to their (well-confirmed) *beliefs* about others. Readers who take skepticism about our knowledge of other minds seriously are now instructed to make these substitutions and qualifications as they proceed through the rest of the book.[9]

Second, another point surrounding the ethical criterion follows from the first: insofar as they do achieve social knowledge, *persons face an unavoidable choice concerning whether and when to engage in agency-regarding relations*. Insofar as they do achieve social knowledge of other agents, persons are in a position to assess whether and to what extent any actions that they contemplate undertaking would influence other agents, as well as whether and to what extent the intended results of such influence would hinder another agent's agency by failing to accord with the dictates of the agent's own rational point

[9] It is perhaps conceivable that someone might take such skepticism so seriously as to lose its capacity to form social beliefs altogether. But that is no objection to the modified epistemic requirement on personhood. If the agent really did lose its capacity to form social beliefs, it would thereby have lost its capacity to engage in agency-regarding relations, and it would no longer satisfy the ethical criterion of personhood.

of view. In other words, their social knowledge automatically puts persons in a position to assess whether any actions that they contemplate undertaking would give rise to agency-regarding relations. Of course, this does not mean that persons will necessarily arrive at a preference to engage in such relations, nor even, as far as this point is concerned, that they ought to have such a preference. They might be quite indifferent to whether they exhibit regard for the agency of others, they might even prefer never to do so, and they might be justified in these attitudes. But whatever attitude persons do adopt in the matter, they will have made a *choice* concerning whether and when to engage in agency-regarding relations. And it is a choice that they cannot avoid, so long as they do achieve social knowledge.

Third, finally, there is the point that *it* matters *to agents whether persons engage in agency-regarding relations with them, and furthermore, persons know this*. It matters to agents whether they exercise their agency or not. By extension, it must also matter to them whether anything hinders the exercise of their agency, including, of course, efforts on the part of persons to influence them. Furthermore, insofar as persons generally succeed in realizing their aims, it must matter to agents whether the persons who influence them aim to hinder the exercise of their agency, or aim not to. That is, it must matter to them whether other persons engage in agency-regarding relations with them.

There is a complicating issue here that is worth noting. It must be admitted that if there are agents who are not themselves persons because they cannot themselves engage in agency-regarding relations, the sense in which it matters to them whether others are regardful of their agency is somewhat attenuated. Either such agents lack the requisite social knowledge that is a necessary condition for being able to engage in agency-regarding relations, or they lack the underlying social and reflective capacities that make such knowledge possible. If it is the knowledge that they lack, then they will fail to apprehend the difference between being hindered by the course of natural events and being intentionally hindered by a person. If it is the underlying capacities that they lack, then they may fail even to have a conception of agency, let alone apprehend whether persons aim to hinder the exercise of their agency. In either case, they will lack some ingredient that is essential to their recognizing just how and why it matters to them whether persons engage in agency-regarding relations with them.[10] In contrast, agents who can engage in agency-regarding relations—that is, agents who qualify as persons by the lights of the ethical criterion—*do* recognize this. They have the requisite reflective capacities by virtue of which they can explicitly conceive themselves as committed to realizing the universal goal of agency, and hence as caring whether they realize this goal or not. And they have the requisite social capacities by virtue of which

[10] It may seem absurd to affirm that something can matter to an agent even though the agent lacks the conceptual sophistication to recognize that, or indeed how, it matters. Anyone who finds it absurd will probably want to agree with Davidson and Descartes that there are no unreflective agents. This book has no stake in showing them to be wrong. It merely wants to acknowledge that

they can apprehend, and also care, whether or not other agents intentionally aim to hinder their realization of this goal. Thus the sense in which it matters to *persons* whether others engage in agency-regarding relations with them is not at all attenuated. In fact, its mattering to them is something that they cannot fail to recognize. And given their social knowledge, its mattering to other agents who are not persons (insofar as there are any such) is also something that persons cannot fail to recognize.

These three points surrounding the ethical criterion of personhood suffice to ensure that the choice concerning agency-regard is always, for the agents who face it, an ethically significant choice. Why is this so? The reason lies in the ethics-demarcating consideration that was mentioned above. It concerns (*a*) the *occasion* for and (*b*) the *topic* of all specifically ethical reflection.

Insofar as the world presents us with any occasion at all for ethical reflection, that occasion is surely given by the existence of things who have points of view from which things matter to them; for if that does not provide an—or rather the—occasion for ethical reflection, then nothing does. And so it is for persons in the sense defined by the ethical criterion of personhood: the choice concerning whether and when to engage in agency-regarding relations with other agents presents an occasion for ethical reflection, simply because they recognize that the outcome of the choice matters to the agents whom it affects.

So far, nothing has been said that should bar a proponent of any substantive ethical position from embracing the ethical criterion of personhood, and the particular ethical significance that it claims to capture, for insofar as persons do acknowledge that the choice they face with respect to agency-regard is an ethically significant choice, they are nevertheless free to rank such regard in any way they like with respect to other ethically significant values (and indeed with respect to all values). So to return to the ethical positions that were listed at the outset: egoists are free to rank self-interest higher than regard for agency; utilitarians are likewise free to rank the greatest overall happiness higher than such regard; proponents of virtue ethics are free to rank the various virtues higher than such regard; and of course Kantians and rights-theorists are free to hold agency-regard in the high esteem they generally do (though as we shall see, they conceive agency-regard quite differently than the ethical criterion does). All that the ethical criterion entails is that something of ethical *significance* occurs when we make these rankings, insofar as the rankings have implications for the choice we face concerning whether and when we should engage in agency-regarding relations. And this is not some-

---

many find plausibility in the idea that unreflective animals with limited social capacities, such as dogs and cats, are agents. And one of the uncomfortable concomitants of this idea is that such agents lack the conceptual sophistication to recognize a great many of the things that matter to them. What is the sense in which such things *do* matter to them? Presumably, it is just this: they experience gratification and/or frustration in connection with such things.

thing that the holder of *any* substantive ethical position need deny. Thus we have a perfectly general ground for concluding that the ethical criterion does stand above all ethical controversy: the criterion is consistent with any and every ranking of agency-regard with respect to other ethically significant values.

However, we might wonder whether the ethical significance of the choice concerning agency-regard really *must* be acknowledged from within all of the various ethical positions that have now been shown to be compatible with it. There is good reason why it should be. In order to see why, we must turn our attention to the second part of the ethics-demarcating consideration that was raised above—that is, we must turn our attention to the topic of, as opposed to the occasion for, all specifically ethical reflection.

Let us approach that topic obliquely, by first considering what it would mean to *deny* that the ethical criterion introduces any issues of ethical significance. It would mean denying that anything of ethical significance occurs when persons make a choice concerning whether to engage in agency-regarding relations. Now, it might be thought that if an ethical position does not attach any intrinsic ethical importance to agency-regard, then it already does deny this. So for example, it might be thought that when egoists pronounce it right to show disregard for agency insofar as it serves self-interest to do so, they are really saying that nothing of ethical significance occurs when they choose against regard for agency—and similarly when proponents of any other ethical position pronounce it right or permissible to make that choice. However, when we pursue this thought to its logical conclusion, we shall find that we can no longer make sense of ethical disagreement and controversy. The thought implies that there are as many kinds of ethical significance as there are ethical positions: egoism would yield a notion of ethical significance that arises only insofar as one's self-interest is affected; and utilitarianism, virtue ethics, Kantian ethics, and rights-theory would all yield their own notions of ethical significance as well, as arising only in connection with the greatest overall happiness, the virtues, respect for persons, and rights, respectively. And so we lose our grip on the idea that these different ethical positions are all trying to address the same topic, about which they are making different and competing claims.

In order to make sense of this idea—which is of course the idea of ethical disagreement and controversy—we need a more general notion of ethical significance that does not presuppose the truth of any particular ethical position, and that can, therefore, be recognized by all positions. The occasion for all ethical reflection, as it was described above, provides just such a general notion of ethical significance: ethical significance arises insofar as there are subjects with points of view from which things matter to them. And this general notion of ethical significance sets a general topic for all ethical reflection, which is: what, among all of the things that have ethical significance because they matter from some point of view or other, is ethically more important than what?

It is possible to see each and every substantive ethical position as addressed to this general topic. That is, it is possible to see them all as setting priorities of ethical importance among the various things that can lay claim to our ethical attention and consideration, because they matter to someone (or something). Some of the most familiar and often discussed positions rely on very simple formulas in order to determine their particular priorities, as in the egoistic priority of self-interest, the utilitarian priority of the greatest happiness, and the Kantian priority of respect. But there is no reason why a considered ethical position should not set a whole range of ethical priorities, and no reason why these priorities should not depend on highly contextual considerations. In fact, some versions of virtue ethics probably do set priorities in this multidimensional and contextual way. And in the limiting case, we can imagine a position that does not provide any general formula at all for determining ethical priorities, contextual or otherwise; it would merely instruct us to set whatever priorities we like whenever we like. Yet even this noncommittal position would amount to a substantive ethical position. Like all other such positions, it takes a specific stand on the general topic that is addressed in all specifically ethical reflection, for it does manage to say *something* about what, among all the things that occasion such reflection, is ethically more important than what—namely, whatever we decide, on the spot, to be more important.

It is hard to conceive a substantive ethical position that cannot be portrayed as addressing this general topic of ethical reflection. And the advantage of portraying all ethical positions in this way is, by now, obvious. Doing so allows us to see how the different positions can conflict with one another, how they can generate the sorts of ethical controversy that there are. So it is fair to say that there is a single consideration—the idea that there are subjects with points of view from which things matter to them—that demarcates the whole domain of the ethical. This single consideration is able to provide both the occasion for and the topic of all specifically ethical reflection. And this is so no matter what theoretical—or, for that matter, anti-theoretical—outcome might emerge from such reflection.[11]

So to return, finally, to the issue at hand, concerning the ethical uncontroversiality of the ethical criterion of personhood. There is a broad sense of "ethical significance" that refers to anything that falls under the ethics-demarcating consideration that was just outlined above—to anything, that is, that can be seen to matter from some point of view or other. In this broad sense,

---

[11] Bernard Williams has offered an alternative account of the topic of ethical reflection. He reserves the term "ethics" for the very personal project of reflection that is initiated by the Socratic question, how shall I live? (See chapter 1 of his *Ethics and the Limits of Philosophy* [London: Fontana Press, 1985].) And for him, the important contrast is between this personal project and the project of moral theory, which aspires to establish objective and universal rules of moral conduct. According to him, the more personal project may retain its interest and importance even if the project of moral theory should fail—and according to him, that project already has failed.

However, Williams's way of characterizing ethical reflection leaves out something crucial, which is that whenever a reflective agent does ask his Socratic question—how shall *I* live?—then unless the agent is a solipsist, another question inevitably arises for it, namely, how shall I live

the ethical criterion of personhood does introduce an issue of ethical significance. The agents who satisfy the criterion all face a choice concerning whether and when to engage in agency-regarding relations. They cannot avoid this choice. And also, they cannot fail to see that the choice is ethically significant in the broad sense—for they cannot fail to see that the outcome of the choice will matter to the agents who are affected by it. We have since seen that there is no reason for the proponent of any considered ethical position to deny that such mattering has ethical significance, because everyone is free to rank regard for agency anywhere they like on the scale of ethical importance. But furthermore, there is good reason for the proponents of every considered ethical position to acknowledge that *mattering*, in the sense in which it matters to agents whether others manifest regard for their agency, has ethical significance. By doing so, they can see themselves as addressing a common topic about which they can have meaningful disagreement. So, far from generating ethical controversy, the sort of ethical significance that the ethical criterion of personhood claims to capture is the kind of significance that makes such controversy intelligible to begin with.

Before concluding that the ethical criterion of personhood stands completely above all ethical controversy, let us proceed to the second stage of our argument. This second stage will establish that the ethical criterion is not implicitly in league with Kantians and rights-theorists, whose shared ethical agenda is to establish some sort of obligation in connection with regard for agency. Clearly, the ethical criterion would lose its claim to uncontroversiality if it shared, or even participated in, that agenda.

Let us take the Kantian position first. The Kantian is very likely to claim that the ethical criterion of personhood provides the basic premises from which the categorical imperative can be derived. Any agent who can engage in agency-regarding relations must be able to reason about the rational points of view of other agents. And any agent who can perform such a feat has the

---

among others? And in point of fact, most philosophical work in the field we normally call "ethics" is addressed to this latter question. Furthermore, this latter question implicitly invokes the general notion of ethical significance that is being employed here, for the "others" to whom the question refers are precisely others with points of view from which things matter to them. And the realm of all such things that matter from some point of view provides a common topic for all nonsolipsistic ethical reflection—the topic being, what is more important than what within this realm? And this topic is *always* the focus of ethical reflection, *both* when such reflection aspires to moral theory in the sense that Williams rejects *and* when such reflection confines itself to the more personal projects that he urges in the place of moral theorizing.

The purpose of these remarks has not been to suggest that Williams actually offers his Socratic question in a solipsistic spirit. It is rather to bring out the main virtue of the alternative account of ethical reflection being offered here. The virtue is that it helps us to make sense of the possibility of ethical controversy by allowing us to see that all ethical reflection is really addressed to the same topic. And ethical controversy in this sense comprehends not only all of the controversies of moral or ethical theory, but even Williams's own anti-theory position.

conceptual resources to think *impersonally* about what might hold from any arbitrary rational point of view, and to think *universally* about what can simultaneously hold from all rational points of view. It is, of course, precisely these conceptual resources—namely, a grasp of the impersonal and universal aspects of rationality—that constitute the premises for Kant's derivation of the categorical imperative. However, the fact that the ethical criterion secures Kant's premises shows no more than that it is in principle compatible with the Kantian position, for there is no reason why the ethical criterion would have to be relinquished if the Kantian arguments that proceed from these premises should prove to be invalid and their conclusions wrong. And this is entirely in keeping with the criterion's claim to uncontroversiality: it neither rules the Kantian position in nor rules it out.

All the same, it might not seem appropriate to try to remain neutral with respect to the Kantian ethical position. Either the arguments in favor of the position are valid or they are not. And so insofar as the ethical criterion does supply the main premises for those arguments, it might seem not only appropriate, but perhaps even mandatory, to assess those arguments. Indeed, if the arguments are valid, then it might be suggested that that would actually increase the interest of the ethical criterion. However, it would *not* increase the interest of the ethical criterion for the present investigation. The point of proposing the criterion is most definitely *not* to launch any arguments for controversial ethical positions—Kantian or otherwise. It is rather to lodge an initial assumption about what kind of thing a person is that even *non*-Kantians have reason to embrace.

In order to help dispel any lingering suspicion that the ethical criterion might nevertheless carry an implicit commitment to the Kantian position, it is worth noting that the particular notion of an agency-regarding relation in terms of which the ethical criterion defines personhood is, in any case, quite distinct from the Kantian conception of regard for agency. As Kantians conceive it, such regard can be manifested only by obeying the dictates of the categorical imperative. And it is possible to engage in agency-regarding relations without doing this.

Consider, for example, Kant's first formulation of the categorical imperative. It appeals to the idea of a universalizable reason—that is, a reason that could be the basis of successful action even if it were adopted and acted upon by everyone. In the Kantian view, to restrict oneself to such universalizable reasons is to exhibit respect for persons. And the specific focus of this respect is of course their agency (though Kantians generally prefer the stronger language of "autonomy"). This focus gives rise to a sort of generalized regard for agency that simultaneously comprehends the rational points of view of all persons. In contrast, agency-regarding relations need not involve such generalized or universal regard. All that such relations require is regard for the individual rational points of view of the particular persons (and other agents) whom one is trying to influence. Thus suppose that you had a certain end which you could realize by acting upon some reason that was not universalizable in the sense just explained. If I were to inform you that this is so, I could well be engaging in an effort to influence you that was thoroughgoingly regardful of your own rational point of view. In that case, I would be engaging in an agency-regarding relation in the sense defined by the ethical criterion. But presumably, it is not consistent with the Kantian requirement of acting only upon universalizable reasons to offer nonuniversalizable reasons to others.

The other formulation of Kant's categorical imperative that is most often discussed is the injunction to treat other persons as ends in themselves, and never merely as means. In this case, the ethical criterion might seem to come very close to the Kantian view. Although the criterion allows that persons always pursue their own ends when they influence one another, the criterion also specifies that agency-regarding relations arise only when persons' efforts to influence one another aim not to hinder their agency. And this does seem to preclude treating others *merely* as means. However, at least on one interpretation, the Kantian imperative incorporates a much stronger notion of regard for agency than that which is supplied by the ethical criterion. Suppose that I were to undertake to influence you in the following spirit: I aim to achieve a certain end by persuading you, through open and pure rational means, to embrace it and act for the sake of it; but I employ these means in a completely pragmatic spirit, simply because I think they will work; if they do not work, I intend to issue a threat in order to achieve my ends; and I intend to issue this threat even though I know full well that you will object to being subjected to it. By the lights of the ethical criterion, this background intention to threaten you is a conditional intention to hinder your agency. However, the presence of this conditional intention does not entail that my actual effort to persuade you by open and pure rational means aims to hinder your agency. This effort aims *not* to hinder your agency so long as the following is true: there is nothing that I intend to achieve *through this effort* that I do not also intend to be in complete accord with the dictates of your own rational point of view. And this is true. Yet it seems that I would not be treating you as an end in yourself in the sense that some Kantians seem to have in mind. In their view, actions satisfy the requirements of the categorical imperative only if they are performed *for the sake of* satisfying it. Thus it would not be enough that my effort to influence you by open and pure rational means would *accord* with the requirements of the categorical imperative. That must be *why* I engage in that effort—rather than, say, threaten you. But in the present example, my attitude is unblushingly pragmatic. I aim to wield open and pure rational influence on you because I think it will work, and not because I will thereby treat you as an end in yourself. And the ethical criterion allows, while the Kantian view does not, that such a case still qualifies as agency-regarding. In that sense it is much weaker, less substantial, and for that reason less controversial, ethically speaking, than the Kantian position.

It is not quite as straightforward a task to dissociate the ethical criterion from theories of rights. Of course, it should be clear that it is not the *purpose* of the criterion to establish any rights (or correlative duties) in connection with agency-regarding relations. Yet there is no real consensus about what qualifies as a right. Nor is there any one generic way to derive or establish the existence of rights. So it is impossible to say with absolute confidence that the ethical criterion fastens on a set of agency-regarding relations to which rights (and correlative duties) could not possibly attach. However, it is possible to say what the implications would be if rights did attach to that set. It will emerge that these are not implications that rights-theorists ought to welcome. This should suffice to dispel any suspicion that the ethical criterion carries an implicit commitment to their ethical agenda.

Initially, there might seem to be a real affinity between the ethical criterion and a certain generic model of rights. On this generic model, each person has a domain of sovereign control in which other persons must not intrude or interfere without the person's consent; to do so would be to violate the person's rights. Now, there is a strong structural resemblance between this model of rights and the ethical criterion's notion of an agency-regarding relation, as that notion was clarified in section 1. We saw there that each person has a domain of intentional control. And if other persons influence events in that domain without thoroughgoing regard for the person's own rational point of view, then they aim to hinder the person's agency, that is, they fail to engage in agency-regarding relations. Suppose, just for the sake of argument, that the two domains in question, of sovereign control and intentional control, were one and the same. Suppose further that the role of a person's consent within rights-theory was to ensure that no influence take place within this domain unless it was thoroughgoingly regardful of the person's own rational point of view. Given these suppositions, it would seem that the ethical criterion had gathered all of the components that go into this generic model of rights, but simply left out the glue of duties and obligations that attend rights.

However, a theory of rights that was based on the ethical criterion's definition of agency-regarding relations would impose unreasonable moral demands. Persons would have a right not to be subjected to *any* efforts at influence unless those efforts were intended to accord in every way with their own rational points of view. Correlatively, persons would have a duty never to influence others, except insofar as their efforts were governed by this same agency-regarding intention, that is, except insofar as their efforts were informed by thoroughgoing regard for the rational points of view of the persons they aimed to influence. But consider the following conditions: (1) due to contingent circumstances beyond one's control, there is no way to pursue *any* of one's own ends without deliberately running the risk of hindering the agency of others; (2) due to contingent circumstances beyond one's control, other persons pursue evil courses of action, and are deeply committed to doing so. Now consider what a duty to engage in agency-regarding relations would amount to in these conditions. In condition (1), one would have a duty not to pursue one's own ends at all. In condition (2), one would have a duty not to interfere with the evil pursuits of other persons, unless those persons should happen to welcome such interference—but of course that is an attitude that they would be extremely unlikely to take in condition (2), in which by hypothesis they are deeply committed to their evil pursuits. Clearly, it is neither a plausible nor reasonable aim of any theory of rights to establish such duties.

In point of fact, rights-theorists often allow that there is a sphere of "legitimate" interests that a person has a right to pursue even if such pursuit should, unavoidably, hinder the agency of others. Likewise, rights-theorists generally allow that it is permissible to hinder the agency of evil persons; pursuing evil is simply not a right on most accounts of rights. The ethical criterion has no stake in showing that these allowances are unreasonable. On the contrary. It simply wants to register that, in making these allowances, rights-theorists are allowing that rights and duties do not attach tout court to agency-regarding relations. The plain fact is, then, that the class of actions that rights theorists are going to count as rights-respecting and rights-violating is not the same class of actions that are aimed at regarding agency and aimed at disregarding it, in the sense embodied in the ethical criterion of personhood.

In conclusion, then, the ethical criterion carries no commitment, either explicit or implicit, to the controversial ethical agenda that is shared by Kantians and rights-theorists. It does not by itself establish any obligations with respect to agency-regarding relations, as it defines them. Nor do Kantians and rights-theorists establish any obligations with respect to such relations. Kantian obligations are bound up with the categorical imperative, and it is possible to engage in agency-regarding relations without living up to the requirements of that imperative. And it would be unreasonable for rights-theorists to insist that rights and duties attach tout court to agency-regarding relations.

The upshot of these more detailed points about these two particular ethical positions goes along with the general point that was established in the first stage of our argument, namely, that the ethical criterion does not carry with it any *substantive* ethical commitments of the sort that would arouse ethical controversy. The only ethical significance that has been claimed to follow from the ethical criterion is the following: persons face a choice concerning whether and when to engage in agency-regarding relations, and they must view this choice as an occasion for ethical reflection simply because its outcome *matters* to those whom it affects. But no *substantive* ethical commitments follow upon this claim. It places no restrictions at all upon how agency-regard should be ranked in ethical importance relative to all of the other ethically significant values. In consequence, the ethical criterion is compatible with every considered ethical position, with the single exception of nihilism, which either denies that anything ever matters to anyone (or anything) or denies that such mattering has ethical significance.

The Ethical Criterion Is Important

Why is it important to adopt the ethical criterion of personhood? To ask this question is to ask why it is important that the agents who satisfy the ethical criterion—that is, the agents who can engage in agency-regarding relations—be recognized specifically *as persons*.

In order to answer this question, we must first see what reasons there are, from the point of view of common sense and ordinary practice, to recognize the agents who satisfy the ethical criterion as persons. Then we will be in a better position to see why it is important to recognize them as persons, and also why it is not similarly important to recognize any other agents (or things) as persons. It has already been claimed that this importance lies in the fact that it helps to define, and also to expose, a very pernicious form of *prejudice* against persons, a form of prejudice that consists in a *hypocritical* denial of their personhood.

The general reasons for recognizing the agents who can engage in agency-regarding relations, and who therefore satisfy the ethical criterion, *as persons* are not at all obscure. Indeed, a cursory review of some of the distinguishing facts about such agents that have so far emerged will quickly bring these reasons to light.

First of all, it has emerged that agents who can engage in agency-regarding relations must be rational, reflective and social. Second, it has emerged that they are capable of wielding rational (as well as nonrational) modes of influence on one another. Third, it has emerged that they are agents who recognize that they stand in an ethical relation to other agents, because the choice they face concerning whether and when to engage in agency-regarding relations is an ethically significant choice.

We clearly do tend to regard each of these facts as a fact that distinguishes persons. While other, less sophisticated agents might have some minimal degree of rationality and sociality, we are inclined to think that no agents but persons combine these traits with significant reflective capacities. Likewise, we generally suppose that only persons, and no other agents, are capable of wielding rational modes of influence. And we also presume that persons alone are capable of specifically ethical reflection.

But having noted our general willingness to regard these three facts as facts that distinguish persons, it is also worth considering what, if anything, they have in common. That might point to a single underlying trait that gives rise to all, or at least many, of the facts that we normally take to distinguish persons. The most promising candidate is the relation of *mutual recognition*. Clearly, the agents who can engage in agency-regarding relations are agents who mutually recognize one another as such. And furthermore, such mutual recognition enters into all three of the distinguishing facts about persons that were mentioned above. It is, after all, the natural outcome of persons' rational, reflective, and social capacities. It also plays a pivotal role in all rational influence, in which one person explicitly addresses another person *as* a rational, reflective, and social being. And finally, the ethical relation that persons bear to all agents is a relation that persons mutually recognize themselves to bear to one another—that is, they mutually recognize one another as agents who not only occasion, but also face, the same ethical choice concerning whether and when to engage in agency-regarding relations.

Let us consider more closely, then, what the relation of mutual recognition amounts to, insofar as it arises among the agents who can engage in agency-regarding relations, and who therefore satisfy the ethical criterion. This mutual recognition involves an abstract apprehension on the part of such agents of their common nature, a nature that includes the very rational, reflective, and social capacities which are necessary for engaging in agency-regarding relations. There are two respects in which this apprehension of a common nature is abstract. First, it is universal: such agents conceive themselves as members of a class that includes *all* relevantly similar agents. Second, it does not require concrete epistemic relations to all members of the class; that is, it is not the case that the agents who can engage in agency-regarding relations have particular, identifying knowledge of all other such agents. It is a peculiar feature of this abstract apprehension on the part of such agents, of their common nature, that it actually incorporates what it apprehends. In order that an agent conceive itself as belonging to the class of agents who can engage in agency-regarding relations, it must actually exercise the very capacities that it thereby conceives itself to have—capacities for rationality, reflection, and sociality. This is more clearly true in the case of rational and reflective capacities. In order to conceive oneself as a member of a class of agents who are rational and reflective, one must certainly exercise one's rational and reflective capacities. But this self-conception also includes a kind of sociality. It requires, after all, that one conceive oneself as a member of a class of similar agents *who also* conceive themselves, and one another, as members of the same class.

Ordinarily, we do not think that anything but a person is capable of these feats of abstraction that give rise to relations of mutual recognition among the agents who satisfy the ethical criterion of personhood. That is, we ordinarily think of these relations as distinctively interpersonal relations. And this thought may be reinforced by examining how such abstract mutual recognition among agents enters into and transforms their concrete relations and interactions.

To begin with, it should be clear that when agents stand in this abstract relation of mutual recognition, this enters into their concrete epistemic relations; for when they achieve social knowledge of one another—that is, of their rational points of view and the intentional episodes that comprise them—they achieve mutual knowledge of one another as agents who have, and also apprehend that they have, a common nature as agents who are rational, reflective, and social. If this were not so, then mutual knowledge among such agents would not afford the possibility of rational influence among them. If they are to engage in such influence, they must recognize one another as agents who have the requisite rational and reflective capacities to grasp the normative force of reasons, and they must also recognize one another as agents who have the requisite social capacities to get reasons across to one another. Yet rational influence among agents requires much more than this combination of concrete mutual knowledge of one another's rational points of view and abstract mutual recognition of their common nature. In the course of rational influence, agents must *engage* one another's rational points of view and *exhort* one another to *exercise* the capacities that they have in common.

Just as we ordinarily think of mutual recognition as a distinctively interpersonal relation, we also think of the sort of *mutual engagement* that rational influence involves as a distinctively interpersonal relation. In fact, it is natural to say that when agents wield rational, as opposed to nonrational, influence on one another, they thereby treat one another *as persons*, as opposed to mere things. This manner of description will seem especially appropriate if we consider some specific activities that have not yet been discussed, but that will figure prominently in the arguments of Part II. All of these activities involve rational influence, and in addition, each involves its own distinctive form of mutual engagement. But the important point for now is that they are all activities in which agents treat one another specifically as persons.

The first set of activities that deserve separate mention are joint activities. These are cooperative activities in which many agents pursue common interests together, by coordinating their deliberations and actions, rather than pursue their individual interests separately. In order to coordinate their efforts, the participants in such joint activities must form and carry out their intentions in light of, and indeed in response to, their mutual knowledge of one another. The second set of activities involves verbal communication in the sense explored by Paul Grice in his seminal papers on meaning.[12] Such verbal communication is not distinguished by any formal or grammatical properties that are associated with the concept of a language. It is distinguished rather by the use of certain "communication-intentions" that presuppose and exploit mutual recognition among agents. (It will emerge in chapter 4 that the Gricean account affords an explanation of the distinctive ethical dimension of communication, namely, sincerity and insincerity.) A third set of activities is justificatory activities, in which agents ask one another to present and defend the reasons on which they have acted or are proposing to act. These justificatory activities are embedded in all of our practices surrounding accountability and responsibility in the sense that interested Locke, that is, in

---

[12] See Paul Grice, *Studies in the Way of Words* (Cambridge: Harvard University Press, essays 5, 6, 14, and 18.

the sense that presupposes desert and aims to justify reward and punishment. But even if there is no such thing as desert and even if reward and punishment cannot be justified, these justificatory activities provide for an interesting sort of *rational* accountability. They are activities in which agents hold one another to account *for their reasons* (this sort of rational accountability will be discussed in chapter 6).

All of these activities are ones that we generally regard as belonging exclusively to the province of persons. We would find it exceedingly odd if someone claimed to have entered into a cooperative arrangement with a nonperson, or to have been insincere toward a nonperson, or to have held a nonperson rationally accountable for its reasons and actions. And a large part of what distinguishes these activities is the fact that they involve just the sort of mutual engagement among agents that characterizes all efforts at rational influence. This mutual engagement rests in part upon the more abstract mutual recognition of a common nature as rational, reflective, and social beings. And both the engagement and the recognition do qualify, by most lights, as distinctively interpersonal relations. Because the agents who satisfy the ethical criterion are capable of such relations, it would seem that there is little to stand in the way of recognizing them as persons, and much to recommend it.

However, it is one thing to establish that there is some reason to recognize the agents who satisfy the ethical criterion as persons; it is quite another to establish that it is *important* to so recognize them, and *only* them. After all, it was declared at the outset of this chapter that Locke's own psychological premise about persons is true, namely, that persons are reflective rational agents. And yet it was conceded that this does not suffice to establish that it is important to recognize all and only such agents as persons. It was also announced that this is where ethical considerations must be brought to bear in our initial assumptions about the nature of persons. The question is, how and why do ethical considerations make a difference?

This question would be easier to answer if the ethical criterion of personhood carried certain sorts of substantive ethical commitments—if, in particular, it served to establish an obligation to engage in agency-regarding relations. An obligation is the sort of thing that only a person can bear. In consequence, it would be impossible to recognize any obligation without at the same time recognizing the personhood of the agents who bear it. And so, presuming that it would be important to recognize any obligation that might be borne by the agents who satisfy the ethical criterion, it would also be important to recognize the personhood of those agents. Similar remarks apply to the objects of obligations: insofar as certain obligations are borne only toward persons, then insofar as it is important for agents to recognize their obligations toward other agents, it will also be important for them to recognize the personhood of other agents. But of course it was shown above that the ethical criterion does not serve to establish an obligation to engage in agency-regarding relations. That was the point of distancing it from Kantian and rights-based ethical theories. And from the perspective of the book's larger argument, it is not at all desirable that the criterion should establish any such obligations; for in that case, the importance of the ethical criterion would come at the cost of ethical controversiality, and the ethical criterion could not provide a satisfactory basis on which to resolve the philosophical dispute about personal identity.

Putting an appeal to obligations aside, let us consider whether a chain of reasoning echoing the points about the significant consequences of mutual recognition can be produced in connection with the uncontroversial ethical significance that the ethical criterion of personhood does carry, namely, that the agents who satisfy it face a choice concerning whether and when to engage in agency-regarding relations, and they must view this choice as an occasion for ethical reflection because its outcome matters to those whom it affects. Is it important that this ethical choice be recognized? And insofar as this is important, is it also important to recognize the personhood of the agents who face the choice? Finally, is it important to recognize the personhood of these agents insofar as they occasion the choice, as well as face it?

At first sight, it may seem implausible that an affirmative answer should be given to any of these questions. With respect to the first question, since because of its uncontroversiality the ethical criterion carries no commitment to any particular outcome of the choice concerning whether and when to engage in agency-regarding relations, it is hard to see why it is important that the choice itself be recognized. And if it is not important that the choice itself be recognized, it is hard to see why it is important to recognize the personhood of the agents who face the choice. Furthermore, this book has assumed all along (for the sake of argument) that the choice might be occasioned by agents who are not persons. So insofar as it is important to recognize the objects of this choice, it would seem important to recognize their status as *agents*, rather than their status as persons. Despite all these points, an affirmative answer is plausible. It will soon emerge that when the choice *is* occasioned by persons, it is very important to recognize this. Moreover, the refusal to do so constitutes a form of prejudice against persons. And the reason why it is important to recognize the agents who satisfy the ethical criterion of personhood as persons lies precisely in the importance of exposing this particular form of prejudice against persons.

First, what difference does it make when the choice concerning whether and when to engage in agency-regarding relations is occasioned by agents who are persons in the sense defined by the ethical criterion, that is, when it is occasioned by agents who can themselves engage in agency-regarding relations? It has already been made clear that such agents present a whole range of practical possibilities that are open only to persons, because they involve a sort of mutual engagement with one another that rests on a mutual recognition of one another as persons. So in facing the choice concerning whether and when to engage in agency-regarding relations with such agents, one must address all of these practical possibilities of engaging with them as persons. Furthermore, one must also consider their preferences concerning these possibilities. And sometimes, their preferences will consist in active *demands* for certain sorts of mutual engagement. Now, the ethical criterion of personhood does not entail that the preferences and demands of such agents must be satisfied and met. But it does entail that the failure to do so is a failure to engage in agency-regarding relations with them. It also entails that this failure is a deliberate one based on a choice. And the choice is an ethically significant choice to boot, because it matters to the agents who can be engaged with as persons whether their preferences concerning such engagement are satisfied.

Sometimes, agents wish to retreat from such engagement with other agents as persons, but without facing up to the fact that they have thereby made and carried out an ethically significant choice. They do this by denying that the agents who occasion the choice really are persons. By denying this, they manage also to deny that these agents have any preferences in favor of being engaged with as persons. Indeed, they manage to deny that such engagement is even possible.

However, such denials are almost always hypocritical. In coming to social knowledge of an agent, one will as a matter of course come across evidence concerning whether it is a person in the sense defined by the ethical criterion. If an agent is a person in this sense, it will have the rational, reflective, and social capacities that are necessary for engaging in agency-regarding relations. And the agent's actions (and also the intentional episodes that give rise to its actions) will reflect the exercise of these capacities. For example, such an agent is very likely to engage in activities that rest on mutual recognition among persons, such as verbal communication. This is not to say that one can never have genuine doubts about whether one is confronted by another person. But usually, such doubts are warranted because *all* signs of agency are missing, as occurs in cases of injury or some other incapacity. But whenever there is definite evidence of agency, then if the sophisticated practical capacities that distinguish persons are in place, there will be evidence of them as well. The one plausible exception would be a case where an agent set about to hide its status as a person through deliberate deception. However, such deception is truly exceptional. Persons generally want to be recognized as persons and to be engaged with as persons. And the point of a hypocritical denial of their personhood is to retreat from such engagement while pretending that no choice has been made and that nothing of ethical significance has happened.

Such a hypocritical denial of personhood constitutes a pernicious form of prejudice against persons. There are, of course, many things that we are prepared to label as prejudice against persons. All involve unreasonable discrimination. And often, this discrimination takes the form of oppression and/or exploitation. But when prejudice is *un*hypocritical, it recognizes all persons as such, and *then* goes on to oppress or exploit or somehow discriminate against some of them anyway—perhaps out of naked self-interest or for some other declared purpose. Now, to say that such prejudice is unhypocritical is not to say that it is ever justified or justifiable; it is merely to say that the perpetrators of such prejudice have at least *faced* the choice that arises for all persons according to our criterion, concerning whether and when to engage in agency-regarding relations with other persons, and acknowledged its ethical significance. This involves acknowledging, as opposed to denying, all of the following: that the victims of their prejudice are *persons*: that these persons have *preferences* (almost always negative) about being subjected to prejudicial treatment; that it *matters* to these persons whether these preferences are satisfied. But however wrong and hurtful such unhypocritical prejudice may be, it is not nearly so pernicious as the hypocritical variety, for the latter does not even allow for the admission that it is a form of prejudice at all.

Some may doubt whether persons ever really do go in for the hypocritical variety of prejudice. But it would seem to be a clear matter of historical record that such prejudice has been perpetrated. In fact, the rhetoric of some discrimination against groups of persons has explicitly included a denial of their personhood, or at least of their "full" personhood (where it is allowed that they might have some of the distinguishing capacities of persons, but in such diminished degree that they cannot really be engaged with as persons). The two most obvious examples from fairly recent memory concern the discriminatory treatment of women and of slaves in the American South. In both cases, it was denied that the members of these groups were full persons. And this denial did not merely consist in a withholding of a certain political status as property owners and citizens. It was declared that the members of these groups were *unfit* for that political status because they were not full persons in a prior, metaphysical sense. Yet there was never any genuine doubt that the members of these groups could be engaged with as persons in the sense here being discussed. Nor was there any real doubt that the members of these groups both possessed and exercised the same basic capacities that distinguished their oppressors as persons, and in the light of which their oppressors claimed the rights to property and citizenship. This was of course denied by their oppressors. But if the denial had been sincere, there would have been no need to insist that education be withheld from the members of these groups, and certainly, there would have been no need to pass laws against educating them—any more than there was need to pass laws withholding education from others about whom the denial would have been sincere, such as dogs and chimps. Thus the hypocrisy of the denial of personhood in these historical cases is abundantly clear. It consists in actions that betray a recognition of the suitability for mutual engagement with certain agents *as* persons, while at the same time refusing to allow that these agents *are* persons.[13]

[13] It may, perhaps, be doubted whether these cases of prejudice really were *hypocritical*, insofar as they were bound up with rather elaborate supporting rationalizations that tried to argue for the essential difference and inferiority of women and slaves. But the presence of such rationalizations does not necessarily show the presence of *sincerity*—however loudly they may have been expressed. The loudness, after all, might signal desperation rather than conviction. To be above the

Ironically, the motives for such hypocrisy tend to be strongest among those who have very substantial ethical commitments concerning how persons ought to be treated, for example, among those who hold that persons are bearers of rights and obligations. In their case, the burdens of recognizing the personhood of others are very great. And the point and aim of their hypocrisy is to retreat from these burdens without acknowledging that they are, by the lights of their own ethical position, very wrong to do so, and indeed without acknowledging that anything of ethical significance has happened at all.

This last point raises a natural question. The importance that has been claimed here for the ethical criterion of personhood clearly lies in ethical considerations, since its dividend is that it helps to define and expose a particular form of prejudice against persons. And so it might be wondered, and asked, whether the importance of the ethical criterion is really visible *only* from the perspective of those positions that attach great ethical importance to the category of the person. If that were so, then the ethical criterion would lose its claim to ethical uncontroversiality, which is supposed to rest on the fact that its ethical significance is visible from the perspective of *every* substantive ethical position, and not just those that make the category of the person central to their accounts of the right and the good.

Before trying to answer this question, let us it raise it in a more particular form. Neither egoism nor utilitarianism makes the category of the person central to its account of the right and the good. Indeed, each of these positions (at least in their extreme forms) would license *any* treatment of persons, so long as it contributed to their version of the good (self-interest and the greatest happiness, respectively). Thus each of these positions might well license a fair amount of disregard for the agency of persons. But moreover, it seems that each might also license the practice of hypocritical prejudice against persons. Imagine, for instance, that some utilitarians and egoists found it psychologically difficult to disregard the agency of other persons, even though their ethical positions required it. If hypocritical prejudice against persons would help egoists and utilitarians to overcome their difficulty, then it seems that their positions would not only license it, but actually recommend it. So it might be asked, in particular, is it really important that egoists and utilitarians embrace the ethical criterion of personhood,

---

charge of hypocrisy would require that one display a sufficient willingness to subject these rationalizations to serious critical scrutiny. And it is important that such willingness to engage in critical scrutiny should *not* be confused with a willingness to engage in public debates where rhetorical and political points stand to be gained.

There is a somewhat harder question about these historical cases, which concerns the extent to which the perpetrators of prejudice against women and slaves might have engaged in a certain amount of self-deception—and whether by that route they might have achieved a kind of sincerity in their denials of the personhood of women and slaves. Perhaps we shall never know whether that was historically true. But the truth on that score does not really affect the *main* point here. If one has to resort to self-deception in order to deny another's personhood, that shows just how hard it is to achieve a sincere rather than a hypocritical denial of it. I thank Catherine Wilson for pressing me on these points.

since the importance of doing so lies in exposing a form of prejudice against persons that may not even be wrong by their lights?

The key to answering this question lies in the *ethics-demarcating* consideration that was made earlier, in the course of proving the ethical criterion's ethical uncontroversiality. This consideration helped to clarify the common aim of all substantive ethical positions, which is to set priorities of ethical importance among all of the things that occasion ethical reflection because they matter from some point of view or other. Now, in each and every case, when one adopts a particular ethical position with a particular set of ethical priorities, one will have made a *general choice* with respect to *persons* and *regard for their agency*; one will have decided to show regard for the agency of persons on each future occasion that the issue of regard for their agency arises only insofar as such regard is dictated by one's ethical priorities. And when one adopts a particular ethical position and thereby makes a general choice of this sort, one has no stake in denying that its deliverances will *matter* to the persons affected by it. On the contrary, one has a stake in *recognizing* that this matters, for it is precisely by virtue of this mattering that the position one has adopted, and the general choice that goes with it, belong to *ethics*. But it is impossible to recognize all this without recognizing the personhood of those who are affected by the choice—that is, without relying upon the ethical criterion of personhood.

This point is particularly clear in connection with the utilitarian perspective that equates moral goodness with whatever contributes to the greatest overall happiness. What matters to things who have points of view will bear directly on their happiness. And in the case of persons, it matters to them what we choose concerning regard for their agency and engagement with them as persons. Thus no calculation about how to maximize utility could possibly discount this—which means no such calculation could be properly carried out if it proceeded from a hypocritical denial of anyone's personhood. But even egoists ought not to proceed in their ethical calculations from such a position of hypocritical prejudice. Of course, egoism allows that it may be right to act *as if* there were no other things to whom things matter, including other persons. But to repeat, what makes egoism an *ethical* position is precisely that it allows that something of *ethical moment* occurs when this happens because the outcome matters to those who are affected—including, of course, persons. And it simply is not possible to acknowledge the way in which this matters to persons while at the same time hypocritically denying that they are persons.

When, then, of the observation above, that such hypocritical prejudice against persons might nevertheless be deemed permissible and right within the egoistic and utilitarian positions, insofar as that made it easier for some to live up to their ethical requirements? It should be clear that the ethical criterion of personhood ought not to try to rule this out entirely, given its claim to ethical uncontroversiality; for ruling it out would amount to a substantive ethical commitment to the categorical wrongness of hypocritical prejudice against persons, and such a commitment might well arouse ethical controversy. But note, on the other hand, how limited the grounds for such hypocritical prejudice are, even within these two positions that do not attach any specific ethical importance to the category of the person. These grounds arise only when egoists and utilitarians lack the courage of their ethical convictions—that is, when their moral sentiments and dispositions are in *favor* of a kind of interpersonal engagement that would be agency-regardful while their ethical positions counsel them *against* it. And moreover, there is also the crucial point that they could not actually *arrive* at their positions from the *starting point* of such hypocritical prejudice. Suppose one were trying to convince *oneself* of the egoistic or utilitarian viewpoint. One could not possibly *justify* either of these theories without confronting all of the ethical issues about which the theories have something to say, at least in a general way. These issues include all of the issues demarcated above, as providing the occasion for and topic of *all* ethical reflection—and they include not only agency-regard in general, but also the particular ways in which such regard matters specifically to *persons*, as defined by the ethical criterion of personhood. And to repeat, it is not possible to confront these ethically significant issues from an attitude of hypocritical prejudice against persons whose function is precisely to avoid confronting them.

So to conclude. The claim of this discussion has been that the importance of the ethical criterion of personhood lies in the fact that it helps to define and expose a particular form of prejudice against persons, which takes the form of a hypocritical denial of their personhood. The criterion accomplishes this by placing significant epistemic constraints on personhood: persons not only stand in an abstract relation of mutual recognition, but also, they stand in concrete epistemic relations to other persons. Again, this does not mean that every person has particular, identifying knowledge of every other person. It does not even mean that persons are guaranteed to recognize one another as persons whenever they encounter one another, since there can sometimes be honest doubts and mistakes. But all the same, to the extent that persons *can* engage in agency-regarding relations with other persons, they will be capable of achieving social knowledge of other persons (or at least sincere and well-confirmed beliefs). And this social knowledge lands persons with an unavoidable choice whose ethical significance they cannot deny, unless they are nihilists. In general, this choice concerns whether and when to engage in agency-regarding relations with other agents. But when the choice is occasioned by agents who can themselves engage in agency-regarding relations, it is also a choice concerning whether and when to engage with these other agents specifically as *persons*. Thus, the ethical criterion defines persons in such a way that the following is true: something *is* a person if and only if it can be engaged with *as* a person. And in so defining persons, it insists that they acknowledge the distinctive practical and ethical relations in which they stand: persons face a *choice* that only they can occasion or face, concerning whether and when to engage with one another *as persons*; and this choice places them in a distinctively interpersonal ethical relation with one another, by virtue of the unique link between this choice and the possibility of committing or avoiding a unique form of hypocritical rather than straightforwardly discriminatory prejudice. To acknowledge all of this is to acknowledge that the ethical criterion does indeed portray persons as comprising a distinct ethical kind.

This argument, unlike other forms of recent philosophical argument that move from premises about human capacities for language and communication to substantive ethical theories, is far more modest. The importance of the ethical criterion does not lie in the fact that it insists upon any system of rights for persons, nor even any particular treatment of persons—*except* that persons acknowledge the distinctive practical possibilities that they present to one another, and the ethical significance of these possibilities. Again, to refuse to acknowledge this is to be guilty of a pernicious form of hypocrisy and prejudice. But to be guilty of such a thing is not to transgress the moral imperatives and principles yielded by any existing substantive position within ethical theory.[14] So the ethical significance of the concept of the person presented in this chapter is not aspiring to substance in that sense. Nevertheless it is rightly seen as "ethical," since being guilty of hypocritical prejudice is clearly at odds with the general project of ethical reflection, insofar as such prejudice refuses to acknowledge something (namely, the personhood of another) that is properly demarcated as belonging to the domain of the ethical—the domain, that is, that provides both the occasion for and the topic of all specifically ethical reflection. Thus, the point of the ethical criterion is truly ethical, and yet modestly so in not aspiring to move from ethics-demarcation to a substantive ethical position.

Modest though the ethical criterion of personhood is at this stage, since it entails no substantive ethical commitments, it will turn out in the rest of this book that it is the beginning of and the basis for some highly revisionist conclusions concerning the condition of personal identity.

[14] Stronger and more substantively and controversially ethical conclusions than the one drawn here, from noticing the inconsistency in denying personhood to someone while rationally engaging in interpersonal relations with it, may be found in such philosophers as Gewirth and Habermas. See Alan Gewirth, *Reason and Morality* (Chicago: University of Chicago Press, 1978); and Jurgen Habermas, *The Theory of Communicative Action* (Boston: Beacon Press, 1989).

Personal Identity:

The Body Practic

Introduction to Part II

THE GOAL of the second part of the book is to deliver what was promised at the outset, namely, a new interpretation and a new defense of Locke's distinction between personal and animal identity, via a new, normative analysis of personal identity, which equates the condition of personal identity with the condition that gives rise to a normative commitment to overall rational unity—or in other words, the condition in which there is a single rational point of view which is governed by that normative commitment.

In a preliminary way, chapter 1 has already explained why the normative analysis brings with it a new interpretation of Locke's distinction. Locke equated the condition of personal identity with the condition in which there is a single phenomenologically unified point of view, and then went on to argue that this condition need not coincide with the condition in which there is a single animal. And in making this argument, he *took for granted* that a phenomenological point of view is a also a rational point of view. In contrast, the normative analysis distinguishes the rational point of view of a person from the phenomenological point of view of a conscious subject, linking the condition of personal identity only to the former and not to the latter. The distinction between these two kinds of point of view is best understood through two possibilities that will be explored in chapters 4 and 5, respectively: the possibility that there could be group persons who are composed of many human beings, and the possibility that there could be multiple persons who simultaneously coexist within a single human being. These are cases in which the boundaries of an individual person's rational point of view do not coincide with the boundaries of any one phenomenologically unified point of view. They are also cases in which a person's rational point of view is not circumscribed by the life of a single animal. And it is these two possibilities that show why this book's account of personhood and personal identity supports Locke's distinction, while at the same time forcing a new interpretation of it.

This means that it is possible to preserve a version of Locke's distinction even if his specific arguments and conclusions about personal identity should fail. And if he was arguing for a real empirical possibility (and not just a bare conceptual possibility), his arguments would fail if further empirical research were to reveal that the phenomenological unity of consciousness has a neurophysiological basis in the normal functioning of an individual animal's brain and nervous system. In that case, a single consciousness could not be transferred from one animal to another as he supposed in his thought experiment about the prince and the cobbler. Whether Locke's supposition is right is a matter about which this book has already declared its agnostic position. And further discussion of this and related issues can be found in section 3 of chapter 5. It will emerge there that the sort of possibility which is being claimed here in connection with group and multiple persons is not similarly vulnerable to refutation by future advances in cognitive science. What is being affirmed is a *practical* possibility, and we persons are in a position to affirm now, without waiting for scientific confirmation, that this is a genuine practical possibility for us, on the basis of what we already know about our actual rational and practical abilities. This is one—but not the only—advantage that the present approach claims over Locke.

The arguments to come for the possibility of group and multiple persons are not really separable from the arguments for the normative analysis of personal identity itself. Likewise, the arguments for that analysis of personal *identity* are not really separable from the related arguments to come about what *kind* of thing a person is. And this is to be expected, given the arguments of Part I. What is needed is a basis on which to resolve the central philosophical dispute about personal identity that Locke inaugurated, but failed to resolve, about whether personal identity is the same as animal identity. Chapter 2 showed that both sides of the dispute can claim support from common sense, and neither side can be rejected on grounds of incoherence. What is needed, then, is a positive reason to embrace one side anyway, where in accepting this reason, and the particular resolution of the dispute that it supports, we shall have embraced a particular *revision* of our commonsense outlook about persons and personal identity. Chapter 2 also showed that there are no *general* theoretical considerations ("general" in the sense that they do not make any substantive claims about the nature of persons) that supply such a reason. So we have no choice but to descend to substantive considerations, and seek our reason for resolving the dispute about personal identity in an account of what kind of thing a person is.

All of the related arguments to come—about what kind of thing a person is, the condition of personal identity, and the possibility of group and multiple persons—will proceed from the assumption of the ethical criterion of personhood, according to which something is a person just in case it is an agent who can engage in agency-regarding relations. Chapter 3 urged that this assumption (and, of course, whatever revisionist consequences follow upon it) be accepted on ethical grounds. That indeed is what makes it an *ethical* criterion of personhood. We have seen that its particular ethical importance lies in the fact that it helps to define and expose a pernicious form of prejudice against persons, which consists in a hypocritical denial of their personhood. However, the claim is *not* that the exposure of this form of prejudice brings in train a commitment to any particular ethical theory (by the lights of which it gets exposed as a moral wrong); the claim is rather that it reveals a distinctive ethical relation in which persons necessarily stand, no matter what their other substantive ethical commitments might be, and this distinctively interpersonal ethical relation can (and ought to be) acknowledged from the standpoint of every substantive ethical position. Because this is so, it is possible both to accept the ethical criterion of personhood and to acknowledge its importance without taking a stand on any of the major controversies in ethics. And this is crucial, since the ethical criterion is supposed to supply a positive reason to revise our commonsense beliefs about persons, and the reason it supplies will not be compelling unless it stands above all ethical controversy. But the most crucial point of all about the ethical criterion is this: the ethical significance that it carries is not only both ethically important and ethically uncontroversial; this ethical significance attaches to persons in such a way that it can be taken as a criterial and defining point of departure for a metaphysical account of personhood. Thus the criterion is ethical, but distinctively so in being in the service of this sort of *metaphysical* enterprise.

The metaphysical account of the kind 'person' already began to unfold in Part I. In order to clarify and defend the ethical criterion of personhood from which the account is to proceed, it was necessary to identify several of its immediate and obvious metaphysical implications—namely, that persons are rational, reflective, and social agents, and that they are capable of wielding specifically rational modes of influence on one another, in which they engage one another specifically as persons. This second part of the book will work out some of the less immediate and less obvious metaphysical consequences of the ethical criterion, which concern the possibility of group and multiple persons, the normative analysis of personal identity, and the sense in which a person's rational point of view is a first person point of view.

Although the arguments of Part II will assume the ethical criterion of personhood, they will not focus directly on the notion that figures most centrally in it, of an agency-regarding relation. The arguments will be much more directly concerned with an important *conceptual point* that was emphasized in chapter 1—namely, that there is a conceptual tie between personal identity and the normative ideal of overall rational unity, a conceptual tie that consists in the fact that the ideal defines what it is for an individual person to be fully rational. It follows from this conceptual point that if persons are committed to being rational, then they must be committed to achieving overall rational unity within their rational points of view.

The ethical criterion of personhood does not merely respect and accommodate this conceptual point; it positively depends upon it. In fact, nothing could be clearer than the following implication of the ethical criterion: there is one person wherever there is one agent who has its own rational point of view, and who is committed to achieving overall rational unity within it. Since this implication will play a pivotal role in the arguments to come about group and multiple persons, it is worth pausing to provide a proper derivation of it, and also a proper assessment of its larger significance for the account of the kind 'person' that follows from the ethical criterion.

Why is it that persons in the sense defined by the ethical criterion—that is, agents who can engage in agency-regarding relations—must have a normative commitment to achieving overall rational unity within their rational points of view? In order to engage in such relations, persons must aim not to hinder one another's agency. And in order to have this aim, they must intend that their efforts to influence others will accord, in every way, with the dictates of their respective rational points of view. These dictates are given by a person's all-things-considered judgments. And overall rational unity is nothing else than the state that a person achieves when it arrives at and acts upon all-things-considered judgments in a rationally optimal manner. In fact, to form and implement such judgments at all is already to be committed to achieving such unity. It should be clear, then, that *the whole enterprise of agency-regarding relations presupposes that each person has a commitment to achieving overall rational unity within its own rational point of view*. And that is as it should be, given the conceptual point that such unity is a normative ideal that defines what it is for an individual person to be fully rational.

What, then, is the larger significance of this implication of the ethical criterion of personhood? We have already seen that the agents who can engage in agency-regarding relations, and who therefore satisfy the criterion, can also engage in rational modes of influence. And we have seen that this is connected with the ethical importance of the criterion, which is to help define and expose a particular form of prejudice against persons that consists in a hypocritical denial of their personhood. Such hypocrisy arises whenever we deny an agent's status as a person while at the same time engaging in distinctively interpersonal relations with it. And typically, the interpersonal engagements that belie our hypocritical denial of an agent's personhood all rest on rational influence. Indeed, the *best evidence* that we can have that something is a person, in the sense defined by the ethical criterion of personhood, is precisely that it is *susceptible to rational influence*. And as it turns out, this evidence of an agent's *personhood* is, eo ipso, evidence of the agent's *normative commitment to achieving overall rational unity within its rational point of view*, for that commitment plays an essential role in all rational influence. Here is why. When one person aims to influence another by offering a reason, it leaves it up to the other person whether to accept the reason or not. And to leave this up to another person in this way is, implicitly, to have the following intention: that the other person will accept the reason because it judges that it would be best, considering all things within its own rational point of view, to do so. Which is just to say, the other person is intended to accept the reason because doing so will help it to realize its commitment to achieving overall rational unity. Furthermore, that is the *guise* in which reasons must be offered to a person in the course of rational influence, namely, as serving the person's own commitment to overall rational unity. This is, perhaps, more obvious in certain cases of open and pure rational influence, especially those that involve internal criticism. The explicit aim of internal criticism is to bring out how it would be a failure of rationality *not* to accept the reasons that the criticism offers. And such a failure would, of course, be a failure to live up to one's own commitment to overall rational unity. Thus, internal criticism actually makes a direct and explicit *appeal* to a person's commitment to overall rational unity. But in fact, *all* efforts at rational influence must make such an appeal, at least implicitly. And this is so even when they employ the covert and impure means that are employed, respectively, for instance, in lies and threats. When one presents a lie or a threat, one must portray the effect at which one aims—usually, believing the lie or complying with the threat—as something that is best, all things considered, from the victim's own rational point of view. And this shows that even lies and threats are implicitly presented as serving a person's commitment to overall rational unity.[1]

These reflections on the commitment to overall rational unity serve to bring out that something satisfies the ethical criterion of personhood just in case the following *three-part condition* holds. It is an agent who:

a. has a rational point of view

b. is committed to achieving overall rational unity within its rational point of view

c. is therefore susceptible to rational modes of influence, along with all of the forms of interpersonal engagement that rest on such influence.

This three-part condition points to an obvious strategy for establishing the possibility of group and multiple persons. All that needs to be shown is that *groups* of human beings and *parts* of human beings could in principle have the commitment to overall rational unity that characterizes the individual point of view of an individual person, and that makes possible the distinctively interpersonal relations that rest on rational influence. If this were to happen, then it would indeed be an act of hypocrisy and prejudice to deny the personhood of these groups and parts of human beings—that is, of these group and multiple persons.

Chapter 4 will apply this strategy to the case of groups of human beings. Once it has established the possibility that such groups might indeed qualify as individual persons in their own rights, it will go on to identify a structure of rational relations and practical commitments that is a sufficient condition

[1] This claim about rational influence has been harmlessly overstated in much the way that parallel claims about intentional action often are. The parallel claims posit an explicit intention underlying each intentional act. But of course we are not always aware of forming explicit intentions when we act, and this entitles us to doubt whether intentions are necessary for intentional action. Likewise, when we offer reasons to another person, we are not always aware of having an intention to serve that person's commitment to overall rational unity. And this should make us doubt whether these specific intentions are necessary for rational influence. The response to both doubts is the same. In general, if persons have acted intentionally, they can tell you after the fact what they had intended—and this is so even if it did not seem to them that they formed an explicit intention beforehand. And in particular, when persons engage in rational influence, they will be able to tell you that they had intended to get another person to embrace the reason which they offered in the course of such influence. But this intention would be unintelligible if it were not also an intention that the other person should judge it best, all things considered, to embrace the reason on offer—or in other words, that embracing the reason would indeed serve the person's commitment to achieving overall rational unity. Thus the fact that we often lack phenomenological evidence of such complex and articulate intentions does not at all speak against the point that our efforts at rational influence are nevertheless guided by an understanding, and an aim, that can be cashed out only in terms of such intentions.

of personal identity. Whenever this structure is in place, it constitutes an agent who recognizes a *reason* to achieve overall rational unity within the structure, that is, within itself. In consequence, the structure ensures the existence of a rational agent who is committed to achieving precisely the sort of overall rational unity that defines individual rationality. And the point is, even when the structure is realized in a group of human beings, it ensures the existence of a single person.

This structure of rational relations and practical commitments is, of course, the analysans of the normative analysis of personal identity. Being the analysans, the claim is to both a necessary and a sufficient condition of personal identity. But the arguments of chapter 4 serve to establish only that the structure is a sufficient condition. Chapter 5 will take up the question of whether the structure is also necessary. Its verdict is yes, on the ground that alternative conditions of personal identity, such as animal identity and the phenomenological unity of consciousness, can fail to give rise to a normative commitment to overall rational unity, and so can fail to give rise to individual rational points of view—which is to say, they can fail to give rise to individual agents who satisfy the ethical criterion of personhood. This will be demonstrated by showing that a single human being with a single unified consciousness could be the site of multiple persons, each of which has a normative commitment to achieving overall rational unity just within its own distinct rational point of view. The important point about such multiple persons is this: they are not rationally required to regard either their cohabitation in the same human body or their shared consciousness as a reason to achieve overall rational unity together. That is why these persons have separate rational points of view, rather than a single rational point of view in common. It is also why conditions such as animal identity and the phenomenological unity of consciousness fail to be the condition of identity for things that satisfy the ethical criterion of personhood, that is, why they fail to be the condition of personal identity. That condition must ensure that when persons recognize their own identity, they will also recognize a reason to achieve overall rational unity within themselves. And the only condition that ensures this is the particular structure of rational relations and practical commitments that constitutes the identity of a group person who is composed of many human beings. Thus the structure is a necessary as well as a sufficient condition of personal identity, and it holds in the cases of multiple and human-size persons as well as in the case of group persons.

The arguments of chapters 4 and 5 will together constitute the main body of the book's argument for the normative analysis of personal identity. But they will also be very much occupied with developing and extending the account of the kind 'person' that was begun in chapter 3, and that will be further developed and extended through to the very end of the book.

The particular contribution that chapter 4 will make to the account of the kind 'person' concerns a very distinctive kind of activity that only persons are

capable of carrying out because it requires a deliberate and reflectively mediated coordination of effort. Such coordination is at work both in joint activities that are carried out by groups of persons and in long-term activities that
are carried out by individual persons. It will emerge that these two sorts of
activities manifest the very same rational structure. Because this is so, the
difference between a group *of* human-size persons who engage in joint activities together and a *group person* who comprises many human beings is simply
a matter of degree.

The argument for the possibility of group persons who are composed of
many human beings will draw on various analogies between intra- and interpersonal relations that emerge when we think of such relations in *abstraction*
from how they might be realized in human beings. But eventually, the question must be addressed, what is the precise nature of the relation between
persons and the human beings of which they are composed? This question
will be addressed at the end of chapter 5, after the case has been made for the
possibility of multiple persons as well as group persons, and for the necessity
as well as the sufficiency of the condition of personal identity that the normative analysis puts forward. Some other, more general, questions about the
metaphysics of personhood will be addressed at that point as well.

On the question of the relation of persons to human beings: this book has
more than once declared its agnostic stance about whether the phenomenological unity of consciousness might have a neurophysiological basis in the
normal functioning of an animal. Taking an agnostic stance on this issue requires taking an agnostic stance on a closely related issue, namely, whether
there could be a functionalist reduction of mental events, states, and properties. After all, if the phenomenological unity of consciousness might have a
neurophysiological basis, so too might other aspects of mind and mindedness,
and perhaps even all aspects—in which case the project of functionalist reduction would fail. Thus as far as this book is concerned, it might be impossible
to have an agent who satisfies the ethical criterion of personhood composed
of nonorganic materials. Of course, if such an agent *were* to exist it would,
according to the arguments of the previous chapter, be an act of prejudice to
withhold the status of 'person' from it. Yet the possibility of such an artificial
person is not one on which this book insists. It insists only on the possibility
that multiple and group persons might be generated out of human materials.
And it insists that this could happen through the normal exercise of certain
rational and practical capacities that are part of the natural endowment of
human beings. Thus the relation between persons and human beings is as
follows: it is in the nature of human beings to exercise their rational and
practical capacities in such a way as to generate persons, and persons are rational agents whose lives are never, strictly speaking, biological lives. The
unity of a person's rational and practical life, and hence the identity of a person, is given by a structure of rational relations and practical commitments
that in some cases might take up more, and in some cases less, than a whole
human life. In fact, no person ever takes up the resources of a whole human

life, for the lives of the human-size persons we know never begin at conception nor at birth, and sometimes they do not last until biological death.

With respect to some more general metaphysical questions: It will emerge that the normative analysis of personal identity is a reductionist analysis in one sense articulated by Parfit: persons are *nothing but* certain sorts of episodes standing in certain sorts of relations. The normative analysis also shares an important consequence of reductionism: the facts that ground personal identity are not all-or-nothing, but obtain rather in degrees. However, the normative analysis takes this consequence much farther than Parfit does. Whereas he applies it only to personal identity *over* time, the normative analysis applies it to personal identity *at* a time as well. Thus the normative analysis entails that the boundaries between persons can be vague, not only over time, but also at a particular moment in time. In fact, what the normative analysis most centrally challenges is the idea that the roughly human-size persons who *actually* exist are both whole within themselves and also completely separate from one another, for the degrees of rational unity that they are committed to achieving typically involve less, and yet also more, than the life of the particular human being with whom they most closely associate themselves. The Postscript will briefly explore some of the ethical implications of this fact.

But before these ethical implications can be taken up, there is one important metaphysical issue that deserves separate discussion in a separate chapter. It concerns the first person singular mode of thought in its various aspects: the basis of first person reference, the distinctive motivational role of first person attitudes, the authority of first person knowledge, and the self-oriented ethical attitudes of accountability and self-concern. Chapter 1 observed that Locke drew a connection for which he did not expressly argue, between personal identity and a first person point of view. This book does argue for such a connection, by arguing for a connection between personal identity and a rational point of view. But that argument cannot be regarded as complete unless and until it establishes that such a rational point of view is, indeed, a first person point of view. There is a sense in which it *must* be a first person point of view. It is, after all, a point of view from which the deliberations of an individual person proceed. And deliberation always takes a first personal form, since it is always addressed to the question, what ought *I* to think and do? All the same, doubts might be raised concerning whether the book's *specific* account of a rational point of view can do justice to the first person character of deliberation, given that it countenances the possibility of group and multiple persons, and in doing so divorces the rational point of view of a person from both the phenomenological point of view of a conscious subject and the bodily point of view of an animal. And there are current positions on the subject that would have it that such a divorce would leave one without the wherewithal to capture the first person point of view. Chapter 6 will argue the first person relation that a person bears to itself and its own thoughts can be adequately characterized as a purely *normative* relation, rather than as a phenomenologically or biologically based relation. This provides for the genuinely first personal character of a rational point of view, even when such a point of view is possessed by a group person who has many human bodies and who lacks a unified consciousness, and even when it is possessed by a multiple person who shares its human body and its consciousness with others. This normative relation also provides a rational basis for a kind of personal accountability and self-concern.

Chapter 2 laid it down as a desideratum for any account of the kind 'person' that it should provide a comprehensive vision of the person as a suitable object within all three of the theoretical enterprises that might appropriately take persons as objects of study, namely, metaphysics, science, and ethics. The focus of this book, and especially of this second part of the book, is metaphysics. Yet the book cannot be accused of failing to address the ethical dimensions of personhood, since it bases its metaphysical account of the person on an ethical assumption. And some of the broader ethical implications of the account will be addressed in the Postscript. That leaves just science, in particular, empirical psychology. This book will inevitably have to make some psychological assumptions. But it will keep these assumptions to a bare minimum. It will assume nothing more than that human beings possess some very basic rational and practical capacities, capacities that are recognized in every account of human and personal nature. Otherwise, the book is determined to be open-minded about all the issues of empirical psychology, including especially the mind-body issue that some philosophers have tried to settle a priori. To be open-minded about the deliverances of empirical psychology does not, however, entail being open-minded or agnostic about the philosophical account of identity that is offered in this book. In chapter 5, the reasons will be given why such agnosticism is entailed for *Locke*'s specific conclusions but *not* the account on offer here.

Quite apart from comprehensiveness of vision, what the book wants most of all from its account of the kind 'person' is a positive reason to embrace one side or the other in the central philosophical dispute about personal identity. With the normative analysis of personal identity, the account will provide clear and strong support for Locke's side, though not for his specific arguments and conclusions about personal identity.

A Sufficient Condition for Personal Identity

THE ARGUMENTS of this chapter and the next will take for granted some of the more obvious metaphysical implications of the ethical criterion of personhood that emerged in chapter 3 and that were reviewed in the Introduction to this second part of the book. These implications are: each person has its own rational point of view; each person has a normative commitment to achieving overall rational unity within its rational point of view; each person is, in consequence, susceptible to rational modes of influence, and is capable of the distinctively interpersonal forms of engagement that rest on such influence; insofar as something actually manifests this commitment to overall rational unity by responding to rational influence, it would be an act of hypocrisy and prejudice to deny its personhood.

Section 1 will establish the possibility of group persons by showing that groups of human beings can together have, and also manifest, the normative commitment to overall rational unity that characterizes individual persons. The argument for this conclusion will rest in part on the following claim: the *solitary activities* that would be carried out by an individual *group person* would not differ in kind, but only in degree, from the sorts of *joint activities* that are carried out by groups *of* human beings—specifically, they would differ in the degree of rational unity that they involved.

Section 2 will consider an important objection to the argument of section 1, which focuses on this last claim. According to the objection, the paradigm case of an individual person is an individual of human size. And the sort of agency that would be exercised by group persons (were they possible and actual) would differ in *kind*, and not merely degree, from the sort of individual agency that is exercised by human-size persons. The objection alleges two such differences of kind: first, a group person would be unable to exert the same sort of direct intentional control over its various actions that individual human-size persons exert over theirs; second, the human constituents of a group person would have to communicate with one another in order to act together as one, whereas the objection claims that this is not so in the case of individual human-size persons. In responding to this line of objection, section 2 will argue that very often, these two points of difference do not hold. When individual human-size persons form long-term intentions in the context of a long-term activity, they do not thereby exert direct intentional control over their future actions. Moreover, these long-term intentions have exactly the same structure and point as Gricean communication intentions that one person directs toward another.

The upshot of this response to the objection against group persons is to bring to the surface some striking analogies between intra- and interpersonal relations. These analogies directly challenge the idea that the metaphysical boundaries between persons are always sharp and clear. Section 3 of the next chapter will discuss this challenge to the metaphysical separateness of persons in much greater detail. And the last pages of the book (more specifically, the last section of the last chapter and the Postscript) will show how the failure of metaphysical separateness of persons is reflected in some of their ethical relations.

Section 3 of this chapter will assess the implications of the arguments of sections 1 and 2 for the issue of personal identity, providing the first careful statement of the normative analysis of personal identity. However, this chapter makes only two claims on behalf of the normative analysis: that it puts forward a sufficient condition of personal identity, and that groups of human beings could in principle satisfy it.

1. The Case for Group Persons

The argument for the possibility of group persons will draw on certain features of joint activities, that is, activities that groups *of* persons carry out together for the sake of common ends. The first step of the argument must be to establish that persons, in the sense that is defined by the ethical criterion, are the sorts of agents who can engage in joint activities.

Given the ethical criterion, persons are by definition agents who can engage in agency-regarding relations. And given this definition, persons are by nature agents who can engage in rational influence. Both of these abilities, to engage in agency-regarding relations and in rational influence, rest on an extraordinary capacity of persons, namely, the capacity that persons have to *project* themselves into another's rational point of view, and thereby to view reasons and actions from perspectives other than their own. Now, it is important to notice that *this same* capacity also underlies the capacity that persons have to exercise their agency together, in joint activities.

In Chapter 3, this capacity for projection was explicitly mentioned only once and passingly, in the course of describing the nature of open and pure rational influence. But in fact, such projection is necessary whenever persons contemplate engaging in any form of rational influence. Rational influence always proceeds by trying to find and present reasons that another person will find compelling in the light of its own rational point of view. And this cannot be accomplished, or even attempted, except by projecting oneself into the other person's rational point of view, and considering reasons from that person's perspective rather than one's own. Obviously, this does not mean that one must actually abandon the perspective of one's own rational point of view. Quite the contrary. Persons necessarily undertake efforts at rational influence in order to realize ends of their own. Indeed, that is why efforts at rational influence can fail to be agency-regarding: the influencer may be up to something that makes sense from its own rational point of view, but that does not entirely accord with the rational point of view of the person being influenced. However, even when rational influence is agency-regarding, and hence aims at complete accord with another person's own rational point of view, it does not involve abandoning one's own rational point of view. What it involves, rather, is a kind of self-restraint. In order to be regardful of the agency of others, one must refrain from acting on one's own ends if acting on those ends will influence others in ways that fail to accord with their own rational points of view. But even when one exercises such self-restraint, one must, of course, act on one's *own* ends, on the basis of all-things-considered judgments that reflect one's *own* rational point of view. Thus, in order to engage in agency-regarding relations, persons must view their ends and actions *both* from their own *and* from others' rational points of view. And the same is true of all efforts at rational influence. The only difference is that efforts at rational influence need not be agency-regarding, and when they are not, they do not involve the same kind of self-restraint that agency-regarding relations involve.

If projective capacities are, in this way, essentially involved in regard for agency, are they involved in the same way in joint activities? No. Though the capacities involved are the same, the role they play is slightly different. In joint activities groups of persons deliberate and act together for the sake of common ends. And unlike agency-regarding relations and rational influence, these activities do not require that persons project themselves all the way in to another person's own rational point of view so as to take up that person's perspective. These activities require rather that persons project themselves into a rational space that is generated by the ends which they hold in common—a space where their distinct rational points of view overlap. When persons project themselves into this common rational space, they can reason and act together from the perspective of their common ends. The point about projection, as it applies to and holds of joint activities, leads thus into this point about a *perspective of common ends*.

This use of the term "perspective" might seem metaphorical. But "metaphorical" would be the wrong description to put on one's discomfort. Rather what is true, as will soon emerge, is that there is a difference only of degree between the shared perspective of a group of human-size persons who engage in joint activities and the single rational point of view of an individual group person who comprises many human beings. More specifically, the difference between them consists in the *degree of rational unity* that they demand. In the latter case it is overall rational unity, and in the former case, it is something less than that, in greater or less degree.

Let us see why this is so by considering a simple example of a joint activity. Imagine that there are two human-size undergraduates who set about to solve a complex philosophical problem together. Imagine further that they together mount a single argument of just the sort that an individual agent might produce on its own. There are various ways of imagining this, but think of it this way: one undergraduate works out the consequences of what the other has just said at a given stage, and then contributes the next stage in a cooperative constructive conversation, whereas a single student would have had to cogitate this by itself in an interior monologue or train of thought.

In the context of their joint endeavor, there is an intuitive sense in which it is *as if* the two undergraduates had only one rational point of view, for by hypothesis, they deliberate and act together just as one agent might act on its own. Because this is so, some of the details provided in chapter 1 concerning what a rational point of view is actually apply—albeit in diminished form—to this case of a joint endeavor carried out by two agents.

Recall that a rational point of view is a point of view from which an agent deliberates. Recall also that the function of deliberation is to arrive at all-things-considered judgments about what to think and do that reflect the whole rational point of view from which the deliberation proceeds. And finally, recall that this function of deliberation is realized through various rational activities that, when they are carried out in a rationally optimal manner, yield a state of overall rational unity within that point of view—and that this state of overall rational unity is a normative ideal that defines what it is for an individual person to be fully rational. Here is the list of such rational activities that was supplied in chapter 1: resolving contradictions and other conflicts among one's beliefs and other psychological attitudes; accepting the implications (both logical and evidential) of one's attitudes; ranking one's preferences; identifying opportunities for action; assessing the probable consequences of performing the actions that are open to one; determining what means are available for achieving one's ends; evaluating one's ends; reassessing the relative preferability of one's ends in light of both the available means to achieving them and the probable consequences of acting upon them.

It would, of course, be obviously wrong to suppose that the two undergraduates must together achieve overall rational unity simply in order to solve a philosophical problem together in the way described above. But nevertheless, they must achieve a certain *degree* of rational unity. And they must do this by carrying out together some of the very same rational activities by which an individual agent would achieve overall rational unity within its rational point of view. They must, for example, settle on a *means* to their common end. Presumably, settling this would involve the following: determining what argumentative strategies are available for solving their philosophical problem; selecting just one argumentative strategy; deciding how to implement that strategy together, by dividing and coordinating their labor. In addition to settling on a means to their common end, the two undergraduates would also have to *resolve* certain *conflicts* among their attitudes. For no matter what argumentative strategy they chose to employ, and no matter how they chose to implement it, they could not get anywhere in their joint endeavor unless they *agreed* on the premises from which their argument was to proceed. And of course, they would also have to arrive at a shared conception of what those premises *imply*. By doing all of these things, the two undergraduates would achieve a significant degree of rational unity between them. And insofar as they are committed to the joint endeavor of solving a philosophical problem together, they must also be committed to achieving this degree of rational unity between them.

Again, it is obvious that this degree of rational unity would fall short of overall rational unity, for the two undergraduates could easily succeed in their joint endeavor while remaining in conflict about a great many things. In fact, even their reasons for engaging in the endeavor itself might generate conflict between them. Thus suppose that one of them is earnestly curious while the other is a slacker. The earnestly curious one wants to know the solution to the problem for its own sake. And its reasons for engaging in a joint endeavor in order to solve the problem derive from a desire to hasten the process so as to satisfy its curiosity all the more quickly. In contrast, the slacker simply wants to fulfill a philosophy course requirement with minimal effort, and calculates that the joint endeavor will cut its work in half. Insofar as the two undergraduates do have different reasons for engaging in their joint endeavor, certain new information ought to, and generally will, affect them quite differently. In particular, if they learned that the slacker's course requirement were canceled, the slacker would lose all interest in the joint endeavor. But the earnestly curious undergraduate would remain as keen as ever. And this would, of course, put them into direct conflict about the value of their joint endeavor. Yet there would be no particular normative pressure to *resolve* this conflict, at least not any pressure to which *both* of the undergraduates would be responsive. The earnestly curious undergraduate would see no reason to agree with the slacker to drop the joint endeavor, and the slacker would see no reason to agree with the curious one to continue it. The fact that the two undergraduates do not recognize any normative pressure to resolve this conflict between them is a symptom of the fact that they are distinct agents. Being distinct, they recognize that the normative ideal of overall rational unity requires them to resolve conflicts and, more generally, to achieve overall rational unity, only within their *own* rational points of view. They are not rationally required to achieve overall rational unity together.

Nevertheless, it is clear that a group of human-size persons, such as the two undergraduates in this example, can achieve a significant *degree* of rational unity among them. And what is more, the members of such a group can have good reason to achieve such unity together, insofar as they have a shared practical commitment to a joint endeavor whose success depends on it. In such a case, the group's commitment to carrying out a joint endeavor would entail a further commitment to achieving whatever degree of rational unity the endeavor requires.

It is easy to see that different joint endeavors would entail commitments to different degrees of rational unity. For example, a marriage generally requires much more rational unity between its partners than a string quartet requires among its members. And this raises the question of whether there *could* be a joint endeavor that required its human participants to achieve *overall* rational unity. In that case, if a group of human beings were committed to carrying out that joint endeavor, then the group would also be committed to achieving the very sort of overall rational unity that is characteristic of a single rational point of view, and that defines what it is for an individual person to be fully rational.

There is no logical or metaphysical reason why there could not be such a joint endeavor that required a plurality of human beings to achieve overall rational unity together. Though the marriages we know do not achieve such rational unity, we can without any incoherence imagine something like a marital arrangement approximating the ideal of such rational unity. It would be an arrangement in which the partners agreed always to pool all of their information, and always to deliberate jointly from that common pool of information, and always to exert their practical energies together. If two human beings were together committed to such a marital arrangement, they would also have to be committed to achieving overall rational unity between them. And this is a sufficient reason for concluding that such human beings would together constitute one individual person with one rational point of view. Not only is it the case that the sort of overall rational unity to which this pair of human beings would be committed defines what it is for an individual person to be rational; but precisely because this commitment would be in place, the pair could be addressed and rationally engaged *as* an individual person with a single rational point of view. Hence all efforts at rational influence, such as persuading them, or even for that matter lying to or threatening them, could be addressed to the pair that constitutes the single person who has a unified rational point of view. And indeed that is the *only* sort of rational engagement that would be possible in the case. For insofar as the couple did live up to its commitment to overall rational unity, it would not be possible to engage just one of its human constituents separately. One might try to do so. But one could never elicit a response that reflected just one constituent's attitudes. One could only elicit a response that was the outcome of a joint deliberation on the part of both constituents, a response that was, in other words, a reflection of their common rational point of view. Given the arguments of the last chapter, it would, therefore, be an act of hypocrisy, and indeed of metaphysical prejudice, to deny that this couple was a person—a single but dual-bodied (in the sense of animal bodies) person.

2. Intra- and Interpersonal Relations

The argument presented so far raises at least as many questions as it answers. And many of these unanswered questions must be postponed until after the case for multiple persons has been added to the case for group persons, and the normative analysis has been put forward as both a necessary and a sufficient condition of personal identity.

In particular, the following, very pressing issues must be postponed:

1. It seems that a group of human beings could never constitute an individual person, because the constituent human beings would inevitably retain their own distinct rational points of view. And it seems that this would be so even if they were committed to achieving *together* the sort of overall rational unity that defines individual rationality, and indeed, even if they actually achieved such unity.

2. The argument for the possibility of group persons rests on the assumption that such a group's commitment to overall rational unity is the same commitment that an individual person has when it is committed to being fully rational. Yet this assumption is open to doubt. Intuitively, it would seem that the requirements of rationality cannot be hypothetical imperatives that take the form "Be rational *if* that serves your ends." Such a hypothetical imperative would seem to presuppose that a basic commitment to rationality was already in place. But that is precisely how a group person's commitment to overall rational unity seems to have been portrayed in the last section. It was portrayed as a *conditional* commitment to achieve overall rational unity—not for its own sake, or even in order to be rational, but rather as a *means* to realizing particular ends (such as the ideal marital arrangement that was described above) that could not be realized without it. Thus it would seem that a group's commitment to overall rational unity is really quite different from the normative commitment that an individual person has to being rational.

These two issues are not unrelated. It is natural to suppose the following: a hypothetical imperative to achieve overall rational unity within a group of human beings must be addressed to rational beings whose commitment to rationality is unconditional; these rational beings are the human beings who constitute the group; the unity of the group could not possibly undermine the distinctness of these human beings and their separate rational points of view. Chapter 5 will make clear why this supposition is not true.

For now, it should be noted that these issues do not, as they have just been set out, amount to a very effective objection against the possibility of group persons. It follows from the ethical criterion of personhood that *any* agent who is capable of rational influence and other sorts of personal engagement qualifies as a person. And in order to so qualify, it suffices that the agent both have and manifest a commitment to overall rational unity. Furthermore, this suffices no matter what *grounds* this commitment (i.e., whether it is in the service of other practical commitments or whether it is unconditional) and no matter *how* the agent might be constituted (i.e., no matter whether it is constituted by one human being or many, or even whether it is an artificial agent created out of nonorganic materials, if such robotic persons are possible).

But there is another objection that deserves to be aired and addressed here, to answer which will require raising, at some considerable length, some complex and interesting issues about intra- and interpersonal relations that are central to the overall account of personhood and personal identity being offered in this book.

This objection notes that the argument for the possibility of group persons rests on the claim that there is a difference only of degree between the shared perspective from which a group of human-size persons exercise their agency together, and the rational point of view from which a single group person is supposed to exercise its individual agency—the difference being a difference in the degree of rational unity that they demand. The objection argues that even if this claim is true, it does not by itself suffice to establish that a group of human beings could ever qualify as an individual *agent*, and hence person, in its own right, since nothing has yet been said about *how* such a group manages to *act*. The objection takes the paradigm case of an individual person to be an individual human-size person. And it alleges that there are two crucial differences between the agency of human-size persons and the sort of agency that a so-called group person would exercise, and these two differences would spoil the claims of any group of human beings to being a genuinely individual person in its own right. First, a group of human beings could never have the sort of direct intentional control over its actions that individual human-size persons have over theirs. Second, the human constituents of group persons must communicate in order to act together, whereas an individual human-size person need not.

This line of objection is helped of course, by the very line of argument that was presented in the previous section for the possibility of group persons. The argument explicitly claims that the agency of individual group persons would resemble the sort of joint agency that is exercised by many distinct persons together. And the point of the objection is to underscore certain differences between such joint agency and case of individual human-size agency that the objection takes to be paradigmatic.

It will emerge in the end that both parts of this objection can be handled in one stroke, because both of the differences that the objection alleges to hold between the agency of a group person and the agency of a human-size person rest on a misguided picture of the particular kind of agency that persons—qua agents who can engage in agency-regarding relations—possess. This misguided picture of personal agency overlooks some important analogies between intra- and interpersonal relations. These analogies bear not only on the answer to the present objection against the possibility of group persons; they also have a wider metaphysical import for the issue of personal identity and, in consequence, an ethical import for personal relations.

In considering the nature of *personal* agency, it is important *not* to take the bodily movements of animals as the paradigmatic cases of intentional action. That would lead to an inappropriate conflation of intentional control with motor control. This conflation is inappropriate, because the domain of a *person's* intentional control is determined by quite other capacities than motor capacities. Indeed it is largely determined by the reflective and social capacities that are distinctive to persons and that make agency-regarding relations possible. By virtue of these capacities, persons can engage in *coordinated activities*. Such activities include the sorts of joint activities that were described in the last section, in which many persons exercise their agency together for the sake of common ends. But they also include *long-term* activities that are carried out over time by individual persons. The key to answering the objection under discussion lies in seeing what these two sorts of activities have in common. It will emerge that persons who engage in long-term activities need not, and generally cannot, exert direct intentional control over their own future actions. And the objector would presumably not want to extend the objection so as to deny that a single long-term activity can be the project of a single person. It will also emerge that the long-term intentions of persons who engage in long-term activities have the same structure and point as Gricean communication intentions that one person has to others. It ought not to be inferred from this that long-term activities are the work of many persons rather than one, or that long-term intentions are inter- rather than intrapersonal phenomena. It ought to be concluded rather that the difference between intra- and interpersonal relations is far less obvious, and much harder to pin down, than might have been assumed. So it is no objection against the individuality of group persons who are composed of many human beings that their agency resembles the sort of joint agency that distinct persons can exercise together. This is also true of the agency of individual human-size persons.

Let us first examine the nature of long-term activities, and then go on to compare them with joint activities. What makes such activities long-term is not merely that they take up a significant period of time. That could be claimed even for the activities of geese when they fly south for the summer. The sorts of long-term activities of which persons are capable are self-consciously planned and embarked upon.[1] And they are *coordinated activities* in the following sense: they involve more than one component action; these component actions are conceived essentially as contributions to the larger long-term

---

[1] A long-term activity need not be planned in its entirety before implementation; indeed, the plan can be quite vague. That is, one might leave most detailed decisions about what the later stages or steps should be until near the time of action. Nevertheless, for something to count as a long-term activity, it must be undertaken with *some* conception of a future course of action in the light of which one's present contribution to it makes sense. See Michael Bratman, *Intention, Plans and Practical Reason* (Cambridge: Harvard University Press, 1987) for a discussion of the importance of plans to understanding intention, and also for an elaboration of this point about how plans need not be worked out entirely in advance.

activity; and these component actions would have no (or very little) point for the person who performs them unless the whole activity could be completed. Although this description of long-term activities could apply perfectly well to activities that take up a few minutes or an hour or a day, it is more revealing to consider activities that would take months or years.

Several psychological conditions must be in place when a person engages in a long-term activity. First, the person must deem some envisaged outcome to be so valuable that it is worth devoting a great deal of time and energy to achieving it. Second, the person must be able to remember its past and anticipate its future, so that it can keep track of where it is in the long-term activity. Third, the person's psychological attitudes must be relatively stable over time; this must be true of many of its beliefs about the world, and many of its general values, and also, of course, its commitment to the long-term activity itself. Fourth, the person must be in a position to take it for granted that all three of the preceding psychological conditions hold. If this fourth condition did not hold, the person would be in no position either to plan the activity or to carry it out. In making the plan, the person must believe that at each planned stage, it will remember the plan, it will know (or believe) what it needs to know (or believe) in order to do what comes next, and it will still want to carry out the plan. These same beliefs must figure in the implementation of the plan as well. For each component action of a long-term activity has no (or little) value except in relation to the overarching goal of carrying out the entire activity, and so at each stage (but the last), a person has no reason to continue unless it anticipates that at each stage yet to come it will remember the plan, it will know what to do next, and it will still want to do it.

Like long-term activities, *joint* activities must be self-consciously planned and embarked upon. Furthermore, they are coordinated activities in exactly the same sense that long-term activities are: they involve more than one component action; the component actions are conceived essentially as contributions to the larger joint activity; and these component actions would have no (or very little) point for the persons who perform them unless the whole activity could be completed. The difference, of course, is that in joint activities these component actions are contributed by distinct persons.

Such joint activities depend on psychosocial conditions that perfectly parallel the psychological conditions on which long-term activities depend. First, all of the participants in the activity must deem some envisaged end to be so valuable that it is worth devoting substantial efforts by all of them to achieve it. Second, the participants must have mutual knowledge of one another's thoughts and actions, so that they can keep track of how all of their individual actions contribute to the larger joint activity. Third, the participants must have many shared attitudes, including beliefs about the world, general values, and a common commitment to the joint endeavor. Fourth, the participants must be in a position to take for granted that all of these psychosocial conditions hold. Otherwise, they would be in no position to plan the activity or to carry it out.

Now, the objection being considered against the possibility of group persons insists on two crucial differences between individual and joint agency: first, the participants in joint activities cannot exert direct intentional control over one another's actions, whereas individual persons do exert direct intentional control over their own actions; second, the participants in joint activities must communicate in order to act together, whereas an individual person need not communicate with itself in order to act. There may be exceptions to both of these claims about joint agency. But for the sake of argument, we can grant the objection's contention that both claims are true. Even if they are true, that does not entail an *essential* difference between individual and joint agency. This is because persons who carry out long-term activities also lack direct intentional control over the component actions of such activities; and long-term intentions have the same function as Gricean communication intentions.

Let us begin by considering what the function of long-term intentions might be, without regard for whether and how they might resemble communication intentions. If I were to embark on a long-term activity, I would have to take for granted a great deal about my future attitudes, dispositions, and actions. In particular, I would have to take for granted that I will continue to pursue the long-term activity in the future, and that I will have the right sorts of memories, anticipations, beliefs, and desires that would enable me to do so. However, I ought not to suppose that my decision to *begin* such a long-term activity would settle the matter of what I will actually do in the future. That would be to regard my future self as a sort of automaton set in motion by my present intentions, a mere vehicle by which my present choices are to be carried out. In other words, it would amount to a denial of my future agency. To acknowledge my future agency is to acknowledge that the choice to complete what I start now belongs to the future.[2] That we do acknowledge our future agency when planning long-term activities is evident in our recognition of the following possibilities: in the time that intervenes between commencing a long-term activity and the (planned) future steps, new information might make the activity seem inappropriate and unfeasible, or we might change our minds about its worth. Neither of these banal and familiar possibilities makes sense except on the assumption that our future choices and actions are not, strictly speaking, determined by the long-term intentions that go into planning long-term activities. *And this shows that the formation of long-term intentions neither accomplishes nor presupposes any form of direct intentional control over the future actions that are thereby intended.*

This point brings out a hitherto unemphasized reason to think that our relations to our future selves are very much like our relations to other people. My forming a long-term intention now no more determines what I shall do in the future than my forming an intention of any sort determines what an-

---

[2] See Isaac Levi, *Hard Choices* (New York: Cambridge University Press, 1985) for a rich discussion of this aspect of agency and its implications for rational choice.

other person will do. At best I can decide what I shall do now in the light of what I believe about what I will decide in the future—just as I can decide on a course of action in the light of what I believe about what other persons will do, as I do whenever I engage in joint activities.

This last observation entails a somewhat surprising conclusion. A person might successfully carry out a long-term activity without *ever* forming any long-term *intentions* at all. The person could get along instead with memories, anticipations, and beliefs; these would suffice to allow the person to judge, at each moment in the long-term activity, what it would be best to do in the light of its remembered past contributions to the activity and its anticipated future contributions to it. And if it be protested that this is not enough, because a person needs to have some form of intentional control over what it will do in the future, there are two obvious and satisfactory rejoinders. First, we have just seen that the assumption of such temporally extended intentional control is mistaken; it wrongly denies the sense in which our future choices and actions belong to the future and cannot be determined in the present. Of course there is a sense in which we can *preempt* our future choices and actions. That is what Ulysses did when he tied himself to the mast in order to prevent himself from later heeding the Sirens' call. But this sort of case does not support the contention of the objection, which is that long-term activities depend upon a kind of temporally extended intentional control, through which one's present intentions directly control one's future actions. When Ulysses formed his present intention to disregard the Sirens in the future, the only action he thereby directly controlled was his present action of tying himself to the mast. By doing this he did not exert a form of intentional control that extends to his future actions; rather, he hindered the future exercise of his agency.[3] The second rejoinder to the protest is much simpler. Persons who cooperate with one another do not exert direct intentional control over one another's actions. Since this lack of interpersonal control does not make joint activities impossible, there is no reason to suppose that the lack of intrapersonal control over time should make long-term activities possible.

It is beginning to look as if there is no role at all for long-term intentions to play in the lives of persons. Whatever their function might be, such intentions do not—because they cannot—allow persons to exert direct intentional control over their future actions. Furthermore, whatever the function of long-term intentions might turn out to be, we can make sense of the possibility of long-term activities without supposing that they involve such intentions It would suffice for a long-term activity that a person can coordinate over time the various component actions that constitute the long-term activity. And it would suffice for such coordination that a person's present intentions to make present contributions to the long-term activity be formed in the light of two

---

[3] For a discussion of the rationality of this and related cases, see Jon Elster, *Ulysses and the Sirens: Studies in Rationality and Irrationality* (New York: Cambridge University Press, 1979). See also Parfit, *Reasons and Persons*.

sets of interrelated memories and anticipations: present memories of what it had done in the past in the light of anticipations then of what it would do later; and present anticipations of what it will do in the future in the light of memories then of what it had done earlier. Thus there is no essential role for long-term intentions to play, in contradistinction to these elaborate forms of anticipation informed by memory. But nevertheless, we shall see that long-term intentions do have a function in the psychological economy of persons (even though they are not essential to long-term activities). This function brings out an even deeper parallel between individual and joint agency than has so far emerged, for long-term intentions are structurally identical to the communication intentions in terms of which Grice analyzed speaker occasion meaning.[4]

It might be wondered, why fasten on Grice's analysis of speaker occasion meaning, given the following difficulties: (*a*) a great many convincing counterexamples have been presented to his analysis,[5] and (*b*) there are alternative accounts of meaning that can claim as many merits as his. These two difficulties are not unconnected. Many of the counterexamples to Grice's analysis exploit aspects of meaning that do not enter into his analysis—such as the idea that meaning involves the use of a *language* with a grammatical structure, and perhaps a truth-based semantical structure. Grice of course had much to say about both of these aspects of meaning; yet he did not incorporate them into his analysis of speaker occasion meaning. And so the question remains, why fasten on that analysis? The reason is this: despite the fact that the analysis fails to account for everything that we are prepared to include under the label "meaning," the analysis does successfully capture the distinctively *interpersonal* character of meaning and communication by portraying meaning as something that arises in the course of an effort by one person to influence another. We shall see that the sort of interpersonal influence that is attempted in Gricean communication is a very specific form of rational influence, and whenever it is in play, there is scope for certain ethical relations that are characteristic of interpersonal communication, namely, sincerity and insincerity. The interpersonal emphasis of Grice's analysis makes it especially germane to the present discussion. The larger objection against the possibility of group persons that is presently under discussion aims to exploit what it takes to be essential differences between the sort of joint agency that the agency of such a group person would resemble and the sort of individual agency that is exercised by human-size persons. One of these differences is that joint agency rests on communication, whereas the individual agency of a human-size person does not. By introducing Grice's analysis of speaker occasion meaning, we actually help to strengthen the objection— precisely because the analysis explicitly portrays communication as an interpersonal phenomenon. And furthermore, what the analysis most notoriously

---

[4] Grice, *Studies in the Way of Words*.

[5] For a thorough discussion of these counterexamples and Grice's prospects of handling them, see Stephen Schiffer, *Meaning* (New York: Oxford University Press, 1972).

leaves out—namely, the idea of a language with a formal structure—is not, in and of itself, an essentially interpersonal phenomenon. So for present purposes, it is safe to ignore the alternative accounts of meaning which focus on that idea.[6]

According to Grice's analysis of speaker occasion meaning, when a speaker means something by an utterance, the following three conditions must be met:

1. The speaker must intend to elicit a response in an audience.

2. The speaker must intend that the audience recognize the first intention, to elicit the response.

3. The speaker must intend that the realization of the second intention—that is, the audience's recognition of the first intention—be the reason for the audience's response.

These three conditions have not been stated here exactly as Grice stated them. Moreover, they deliberately omit one of the essential ingredients of his analysis of meaning, which is the speaker's utterance. (In his analysis, the first intention is *to produce an utterance* with the intention of getting an audience to do something.) But the omission is harmless. The point here concerns the *structure* of the intentions involved, and not the overt behavioral action that they accompany. As the following reconstruction makes clear, the very same structure is also implicit in long-term intentions:

1. As someone engaged in long-term planning, I form intentions about what actions I will take in the future. So by forming these intentions, *I intend to elicit a response in my future self*.

2. These intentions are formed with the anticipation that they will later be remembered. Or, if I anticipate forgetting, I must find a way of reminding myself of what they are. That is, *I intend that I will later recognize—either through memory or some other means—my earlier intention about what I am to do in the future*.

3. Insofar as I acknowledge my future agency, I ought not to regard my present intentions as settling, in the sense of directly causing, my future actions. But nevertheless, these intentions can still be efficacious in the following sense: my

---

[6] In particular, it is safe to ignore the two most influential accounts of the formal properties of language, namely, Chomsky's idea of a universal grammar that is shared by all of the natural languages that human beings can master, and Frege's model of sentence-meanings as truth-conditions that are functions of word-meanings. Chomsky explicitly claims that there is no essential connection between any given formal structure and the activity of interpersonal communication. In fact, he goes so far as to claim that the function of his universal grammar might just as well have been to run the digestive system as to provide the form of human communication (see his *Language and Problems of Knowledge* [Cambridge: MIT Press, 1988]). Perhaps no such flamboyant claim could be made with respect to truth-based structures of meaning (as opposed to Chomsky's syntax). But all the same, it is not at all clear why the presence of meaning in a truth-conditional sense should by itself entail the presence of interpersonal communication, rather than intentional phenomena of some intrapersonal variety. So it is not clear how an account of meaning that focuses on truth-conditions could help the objection presently under consideration, against the possibility of group persons.

later knowledge of them will lead me to carry them out. Insofar as I form long-term intentions bearing this in mind, *I intend that my later recognition of my present intentions will be my reason to do then what I now intend.*

This reconstruction of long-term intentions might seem implausible on the following ground: when I form a long-term intention, it is simply an intention to *do* something in the future; and when I execute my intention, I perform the requisite action *simply because* I formed the intention to do so, and *not* because I later *recognized* that intention. However, to take this view of long-term intentions is really to revert to the picture we have already set aside as unworkable, in which such intentions are supposed to involve a form of direct intentional control that extends from the present into the future. If that picture were correct, there would indeed be no need to recognize our long-term intentions before acting upon them; in forming them we would already have made it the case that they would later be executed, no matter what our later states of mind happened to be. To give up on this picture is to allow that our present intentions cannot determine our future actions—at least not without undermining our future agency, as Ulysses did by tying himself to the mast. Thus we must allow that our future choices and actions belong to the future. And we need to find some other way of making sense of the idea that we can execute long-term intentions that is consistent with this fact. The analogy with Gricean communication intentions provides just that; it provides a sense in which a person can execute its long-term intentions even though they do not actually determine its future actions: when the person later recognizes the intentions, it can take them as reasons for action when the occasion for action actually arises.

The point of this discussion of Grice was not to cast doubt on whether persons have the ability to form and carry out long-term intentions. The point was simply to show that the sort of agency that individual persons exercise in long-term activities does not differ in any essential way from the sort of joint agency that persons exercise together, even though the latter may depend upon communication in Grice's sense. Showing this suffices to foil the objection against the possibility of group persons that claims that their agency would have the properties of joint *rather than* individual agency. The response is that the agency of group persons is like joint agency, but joint agency is like individual agency.

But perhaps the objection can be pressed a bit harder. Even granting the parallels that have been drawn here between Gricean communication intentions and long-term intentions, there are also some important differences between them—differences which an objector might claim do, after all, show that groups of human beings cannot really exercise their agency together as one individual. There are two differences in particular that deserve scrutiny. The first concerns the ethical dimension of interpersonal communication, which seems to be entirely missing from long-term intentions: speakers can be sincere or insincere with their audiences, but there is no scope for sincerity or insincerity in the formation and execution of an individual person's long-term intentions. The second difference concerns a practical dimension that is often claimed for long-term intentions and that seems to be missing from communication: when persons form long-term intentions, it seems that they thereby undertake a commitment to do something in the future, whereas although speakers who form Gricean intentions intend to get their audiences to do something, it seems that they do not thereby undertake a commitment to their audiences' doing anything.[7] The question, then, is whether these differences might serve to bring out an *essential* difference between joint and individual agency—a difference that would also hold between the sort of agency that a group person would manifest and the sort of agency that individual human-size persons manifest, thereby successfully challenging a group person's claim to individuality.

Although Grice himself did not bring this out, his analysis of speaker occasion meaning actually explains the possibility of sincerity and insincerity. Let us see why this is so, and then consider how it bears on the question before us—in particular, whether it makes for an important disanalogy between Gricean communication intentions on which joint agency often depends and the long-term intentions of individual persons.

Grice's primary aim was to analyze a phenomenon that he called "nonnatural meaning." This is the sort of meaning that we have in mind when we say that someone *meant* something by saying (or doing) something. He distinguished this sort of nonnatural meaning from a sort of meaning that does not require a speaker at all. This latter sort of natural meaning can be found anywhere there are causal relations and regularities: smoke means fire, clouds mean rain. In drawing this distinction between natural and nonnatural meaning, Grice was not suggesting that nonnatural meaning is somehow outside the natural order. He merely wanted to draw attention to an important difference between a certain sort of verbal communication, and sundry other intentional acts and unintended natural meanings that we might find in the world. And he analyzed this sort of verbal communication in terms of the complex structure of communication intentions that was described above, as being parallel to the long-term intentions of individuals. So let us see why it is that when these intentions figure in interpersonal communication, they go hand in hand with the possibility of sincerity and insincerity.

The matter can best be approached by first seeing how Gricean communication fits the characteristic pattern of rational influence. Grice often summarized his threefold analysis of meaning in terms of a single intention, to induce a response in an audience by *means* of a recognition of that intention.

---

[7] This is not to say that one person cannot ever, in any sense, commit another person to doing something. In fact, there are social conventions that explicitly give some persons the authority to commit other persons to doing something. The army gives generals the authority to commit their troops to carrying out military actions. And in Pakistan, parents can pay their debts by committing their children to knotting carpets.

And he often emphasized the *causal* aspect of this means—that the recognition of the intention is intended to *result* in a certain response on the part of an audience. However, he also made clear that the mechanism by which this effect is supposed to be achieved is the *normative* force of a *reason*, for he made clear that the audience's recognition of the intention is intended to be part of the audience's *reason* for responding as intended. Thus Gricean communicators are engaged in a mode of rational influence. And we have seen that rational influence always appeals, either explicitly or implicitly, to a person's commitment to overall rational unity. However, we shall see that Gricean communicators make a rather more complicated sort of appeal to this commitment than generally occurs in rational influence.

In order to understand the special complexity of this appeal, it is necessary to examine more carefully the particular sort of reason that a Gricean communicator offers to an audience. The reason is peculiar. It is a reason for the audience to do something (in the broad sense of "do" that covers mental acts such as forming beliefs, as well as overt bodily acts). Yet no substantive justification or demonstration is provided that would show *why* this something is worth doing. The mere intention that the thing be done is all the reason that is offered. For Grice, this is the crucial element that distinguishes instances of nonnatural meaning from communicative interactions that exploit natural meanings. He illustrated the distinction by contrasting photographs and drawings. If I were to present you with a photograph with the intention that you come to believe something, I would intend that you believe it on the basis of the photographic evidence rather than on the basis of your recognition of my intention that you should. Whereas if I were to draw you a picture in order to induce the same belief in you, your recognition of my intention to induce that belief would really be all the reason that you would have been given. Only the second case involves nonnatural meaning, and so counts as a genuine case of *saying* something, as opposed to *showing* you something by exploiting natural meanings. (Grice gave us a distinction between saying and showing that is quite different from Wittgenstein's.)

Thus the reason that is provided with a Gricean communication intention is thin—it is not substantive. But the question remains, exactly how does such a communication intention appeal to the audience's own commitment to achieving overall rational unity within its rational point of view? The answer to this question can be found by seeing exactly how the framer of such an intention can expect to achieve the audience's compliance. It is not hard to see that, in general, an audience ought not to comply with a Gricean communication intention unless it has reason to believe that there is some further justification for doing the thing intended, over and above the fact that the speaker intends it. And this is something that speakers are bound to know when they frame such intentions. That is, a framer of a Gricean communication intention is bound to know that its effort ought not to succeed unless its audience has reason to believe that the response intended has some warrant, over and above the fact that it is intended by the speaker; it must be worth doing in some more substantial sense. Moreover, an audience is bound to know that a speaker knows this. Because this is so, a Gricean communication intention really amounts to a sort of *declaration* that there is good reason— over and above the fact of the intention itself, and the audience's recognition of it—for the audience to comply with it. And this of course means good reason *from the audience's own rational point of view*. If this were not so, that is, if a Gricean intention did not declare the reasonableness of the intended response from the audience's own rational point of view, then the framer of such an intention could have no reasonable expectation of fulfilling it—could have no reasonable expectation that the audience would comply with it.

This appeal to the audience's own rational point of view is of course an appeal to the audience's commitment to achieving overall rational unity within that point of view. Yet it is a complicated sort of appeal, because no attempt is made to show exactly *why* the response intended will serve that commitment—why, that is, the audience should judge that it is best, all things considered, to make the response. This puts the audience in the position of having to *trust* the speaker. That is, the audience must take it on faith—one might say that the audience must take the speaker's "word" for it—that the response intended really is worth doing, that it really is best, all things considered from its own rational point of view. Typically, an audience arrives at this conclusion by reasoning that the speaker is reliable in two ways: first, the speaker would not intend the response unless it *believed* that the response would serve the audience's own commitment to rational unity, and second, the speaker would not believe this unless it were *true*. Now, finally, we can see the complicated nature of the appeal that a speaker makes to the audience's commitment to overall rational unity. The speaker must represent itself to the audience as reliable in both of these ways. Only in that case would the speaker have given the audience adequate reason to believe that the intended response will serve its own commitment to overall rational unity.

There is, of course, no guarantee that the speaker is reliable in either of these ways. And it is the absence of a guarantee for the first sort of reliability that affords the possibility of sincerity and insincerity. A sincere Gricean intention intends a response that the speaker actually does believe to be in conformity to an audience's own commitment to overall rational unity, whereas an *in*sincere Gricean intention intends a response that the speaker believes does not conform to this commitment.

The form of insincerity that is most often discussed is the sort of insincere assertion that constitutes a lie. Lying is generally understood to involve an intention to deceive an audience into believing something that is false by the speaker's lights. But on the present account, that is not really what makes a lie insincere. What makes it insincere is this: the speaker believes that the belief which it intends the audience to form is not warranted by the audience's own lights. Often, there is no significant difference between these two intentions.

That is because to a very large extent, speakers and audiences have a shared conception of the truth, and shared standards of evidence.[8] Although lying is the case of insincerity that is most often discussed, it is not the only case. There can be insincere orders as well as insincere assertions. Just as insincere assertions intend beliefs that the speaker believes are not reasonable from the audience's rational point of view, likewise, insincere orders intend actions that the speaker believes are not reasonable from the audience's rational point of view. (Childish pranks often take the form of an insincere order: "Go ahead and taste this, you'll really like it," offering up some delicious looking concoction that is intended to disgust the victim.)

Now that we have in hand an account of why Gricean communication affords the possibility of insincerity, let us consider why this dimension of communication is absent from long-term intentions even though they share the same complex structure. First, a quick review of the ingredients that make for the possibility of insincerity: (1) Gricean communication is a form of rational influence in which a speaker appeals to an audience's commitment to overall rational unity within its own rational point of view; (2) the speaker does not show why the response it intends would actually serve this commitment of the audience's, but merely declares that it would; (3) in declaring this, the speaker puts the audience in the position of having to trust the speaker in this matter—that is, to take it on faith that it would indeed be best, all things considered from the audience's own rational point of view, to respond as the speaker intends.

Somewhat surprisingly, *all* of these ingredients are also present in long-term intentions, even though it seems implausible to suppose that there could be such a thing as an insincere long-term intention. With respect to (1): We have seen that long-term intentions do not directly determine or cause one's future actions. Their efficacy depends rather on one's future willingness to act on them. And this presupposes that they will later be recognized as *reasons* on

---

[8] Yet this epistemic accord between speaker and audience is rarely thoroughgoing. And because this is so, I can—at least on this account of insincerity—be insincere even though I speak what is the truth by my lights. I may, for example, know that I rely on standards of evidence (such as gut feelings) that you reject. In such a circumstance, I might intend that you believe something which I know you would not find it reasonable to believe. By the lights of this account, this would constitute insincerity on my part even though what I said was an accurate expression of my own belief. Robert Adams has protested that I would be *disingenuous* in such a circumstance, but not insincere. Although his choice of words does conform better to standard English usage, that does not affect the main point here. The point is that Grice's analysis of meaning illuminates a broad class of deceptive communications to which both insincerity and disingenuousness belong—the class of communicative acts that simultaneously both invoke and abuse an audience's trust, due to the way in which they both appeal to and yet disregard the audience's own commitment to overall rational unity.

N.B.: This class of deceptive communications does not coincide with the class of acts that involve covert rational influence in the sense elucidated in the last chapter. For rational influence can be covert in that sense—that is, it can fail to disclose the real ends for the sake of which it is undertaken—without involving the complex reflexive structure of Gricean communication intentions.

which to act—that is, it presupposes that long-term intentions aim to exert a rational mode of influence. Insofar as this is so, they must aim to appeal to one's own (future) commitment to overall rational unity.[9] With respect to (2): A long-term intention does not show why the future action that it intends actually serves this commitment to overall rational unity. That is, such an intention does not reproduce for one's future self the deliberation that gave rise to it; it merely reports the outcome of that deliberation—that is, it merely conveys an all-things-considered judgment that one arrived at earlier. With respect to (3): The point of a long-term intention is to put one's later self in the position of being able to act on the basis of an earlier deliberation without having to deliberate again. And that is precisely to put one's future self in the position of trusting one's earlier self; one intends that one's future self will take it on faith that the outcome of one's earlier deliberation does indeed serve one's commitment to overall rational unity.

Why, then, does it seem so implausible that long-term intentions could be insincere in the way that Gricean communication intentions can? Here is one crucial difference between the two. Although the point of a long-term intention is to spare oneself a rehearsal one's own past deliberations, one *can* rehearse them if one wishes. Thus, one does not put oneself in the position of *having* to take it on faith that what one intended is indeed best, all things considered. One can always reconsider. In contrast, an audience may well be ignorant of the deliberations that led a speaker to form certain communication intentions. The audience may also be ignorant of the independent reasons that would count for or against the particular response which the speaker intends it to make. Indeed, the success of an insincere speech act generally depends on both sorts of ignorance. If the audience already had a settled opinion about the unreasonableness of the response that the speaker intended it to make, it would not very likely be taken in by the speaker's insincere attempt to evoke that response. And the same would be true if the audience had knowledge of the speaker's deliberations. The audience would then know that the speaker believed that the response which it intended the audience to make was unreasonable by the audience's own lights. And typically, an audience would share this belief of the speaker's. Thus the feasibility of insincere communication generally depends on significant epistemic disparities between speakers and audiences. And because there generally are no such epistemic disparities within a single person, there generally is no occasion for insincerity in a person's long-term intentions.

There is another important difference between the two cases as well. In general, an individual person would have no *motive* for being insincere toward its own self. For, setting aside the problematic case of deliberately irrational acts, there is, in general, nothing that a person would want its own self to do that it did not also judge to be best from its own rational point of

---

[9] So far, the temporal aspects of the commitment to overall rational unity have not been addressed at all. See the next section, and also section 2 of the next chapter, and the discussion of self-concern in section 2 of the last chapter as well, for a discussion of them.

view.[10] Whereas one person can have good reason, from its own rational point of view, to want another person to do something, and yet at the same time judge that action would not be best from that other person's rational point of view. Indeed, that is precisely the condition in which a person has reason to be insincere.

It has now been shown that insincerity is generally both unfeasible, and also unmotivated, in the case of long-term intentions. But it should not be thought that insincerity is always feasible or always motivated in the context of interpersonal communication. There is no reason why the epistemic disparities that make insincerity feasible should always obtain between speakers and audiences, and there is no reason why the aims and interests of speakers and audiences should always diverge in such a way as to make insincerity a reasonable option for speakers. In fact, when persons engage in joint activities, they have good reason to reduce the epistemic disparities among them, by *sharing* relevant information. And they cannot fail to have at least some common aims and interests. Thus in the context of a joint activity, insincerity may be neither feasible nor motivated, in just the way that it is neither feasible nor motivated within an individual person. Why, then, is insincerity generally *possible* between persons and not within a single person? Simply because an individual person's commitment to overall rational unity *precludes* it, and distinct persons do not share this commitment together—for on the present account that would necessarily make them the same rather than distinct.

So once again, the objection against the possibility of group persons has failed. Even if the agency of such a group person resembles the sort of joint agency that many persons can exercise together, and furthermore, even if the respect in which the group person's agency resembles joint agency is such that it depends on overt communicative acts between human beings, that does not suffice to undermine the status of the group person as an individual. Given the analogy between communication intentions and long-term intentions, there is no reason to regard the former as distinctively interpersonal phenomena unless they are accompanied by the possibility of insincerity. But insincerity would *not* be possible among the human constituents of a group person. By definition, such human beings would be bound by a commitment to achieving overall rational unity within the group. And such unity would make insincerity among them both unfeasible and unmotivated, in precisely the same way that it is unfeasible and unmotivated within the individual human-size persons we know.

That leaves just one last difference to consider between long-term intentions and communication intentions. This difference concerns a practical dimension that seems to be present in long-term intentions and that seems to be absent from Gricean communication intentions, which is that the framers of the former seem to undertake a commitment to doing something in the future

---

[10] This claim will need to be qualified when the temporal aspects of rationality are addressed later, in the next section and in section 2 of the next chapter.

while the framers of the latter seem not to undertake a commitment to their audiences' doing anything. Insofar as this difference holds, the objection against the possibility of group persons might be pressed as follows. Just as an individual person who engages in a long-term activity must harmonize its actions over time, so also the human constituents of a group person must harmonize their actions together. In the former case, the vehicle of such harmony would be long-term intentions that are formed at one time and acted upon at another, while in the latter case, the vehicle of such harmony would be communication intentions that are formed by some human constituents and acted upon by others. But there would be one crucial difference. Only the former intentions, but not the latter, would involve undertakings of commitments on the part of persons to do something, for in the latter case, one human constituent would not, in forming a Gricean communication intention, undertake a commitment to another human constituent's doing something. And the objection argues that this puts into doubt whether a group person could, in forming its intentions, undertake a commitment to doing something in the same sense that any genuinely individual person can.

This objection makes an assumption to which it is not really entitled, which is that the intentions of a group person must be analyzed as a combination of intentions on the part of its human constituents.[11] But let us grant for the sake of argument that the assumption might be true. It will be illuminating to consider what would follow from it. Yet again, it will emerge that the analogies between intra- and interpersonal relations are more striking than the claimed disanalogies.

In order to address this objection, we must consider very carefully what the commitment that a person undertakes in the course of framing a long-term intention could possibly consist in. It is very hard to provide a plausible account of it. Once we do, we shall see that such commitments have a definite counterpart in communication.

We often employ the language of commitment in order to convey a sense in which we regard ourselves as *bound* by our commitments. Yet we ought not to suppose that we are bound by them in any straightforward causal sense. That would be to suppose that the long-term intentions that we form in the present, and the commitments we undertake in forming those intentions, causally determine our future actions. And to suppose this would be to deny our future agency—that is, the sense in which it will be up to our later selves to *act* on those intentions and to follow through on our commitments. There

---

[11] Once the normative analysis of personal identity is accepted, this assumption must go by the board. As section 3 of the next chapter will make clear, even if persons depend for their existence on the exercise of rational capacities that belong by nature to human beings, the deliverances of those human capacities are *persons* who may not be identical with any human being (this is so even in the case of roughly human-size persons); and in that case, the intentional episodes that constitute the lives and rational points of view of the persons who thereby come to be would not, strictly speaking, ever belong to the human beings that make them—that is, the intentional episodes themselves and the personal lives in which they figure—possible.

is another sense of being bound by our commitments that does not wrongly deny our future agency. This is the sort of commitment that we undertake when we make promises and enter into contracts. But the sense in which we are bound to do the things that we have promised and contracted to has to do with the existence of sanctions. (These sanctions need not be the formal sanctions of a government; they can also be the informal sanctions of custom.) But of course, the sense in which one's long-term commitments are binding does not depend on the backing of a sanction.

If the framers of long-term intentions are not causally bound to do what they intend, and if they are not bound by sanctions, in what sense do they undertake commitments? The only remaining kind of commitment that seems to be available is the one that has already been appealed to many times in these pages, and that is a *normative* commitment—that is, a *rational* commitment to the *reasonableness* of certain attitudes and acts. Thus when persons frame long-term intentions, they undertake a commitment to the reasonableness of what they intend. Of course, this needs to be understood in a temporal way: it is a commitment to the reasonableness of acting on those intentions in the future. But speakers can also undertake commitments in an analogous sense. Only in their case, this needs to be understood in an interpersonal way rather than a temporal way: it is a commitment to the reasonableness, from the audience's rational point of view, of the actions that they intend their audiences to perform. Obviously, this is not something that insincere speakers do. They merely *represent* themselves as having this commitment. But when speakers are sincere, they actually *undertake* this commitment, as well as represent themselves as having it.

This last analogy between long-term intentions and Gricean communication intentions may seem less convincing than the others that have been drawn in this section. Intuitively, it seems that the commitments which individual persons undertake in the course of forming long-term intentions are acts by which they resolve to do something in the future; they are acts of *will*. And so it seems somehow wrong, or at least inadequate, to construe such commitments as mere *normative* commitments to the *reasonableness* of what is intended. Moreover, the fact that such normative commitments can be undertaken in an analogous way by speakers seems to confirm the wrongness and inadequacy of this construal, for it seems that a speaker does not, and indeed cannot, will its audience to do something—at least not in the same sense that an individual person wills its own actions. Yet we have seen that when acts of will are long-term intentions, they cannot be construed in causal terms, as involving the direct causal determination in the present of one's future actions, without wrongly denying one's future agency. And to acknowledge the independence of one's future actions from one's present intentions is to acknowledge that one's relation to one's own actions can be very much like one's relation to another person's actions. The point is not that one's long-term intentions are never efficacious. But when they are, it is because in the future, one *recognizes* them, and then *decides* that it is *reasonable* to act upon them. And the same is true of the communication intentions that are aimed at getting *another* person to do something. They too can be efficacious. When they are, it is because their audiences recognize them, and then decide that it would be reasonable to act in response to them. The only difference is this: a long-term intention and the action that constitutes its execution belong to a single rational point of view, while a communication intention and the action that constitutes its satisfaction belong to distinct rational points of view. Thus, the former fall together under a single normative commitment to over-all rational unity, while the latter do not.

With these last remarks, we have come full circle to the very point from which the whole line of objection that has been considered in this section pro-ceeded. The argument for the possibility of group persons rests on the idea that there is a difference only of degree between the sort of shared perspective from which a group of individual human-size persons can exercise their agency jointly and the single rational point of view from which an individual group person would act. The former involves a commitment to a certain lim-ited degree of rational unity within a group of persons (whatever degree is required for the success of their joint endeavor), while the latter involves a commitment to overall rational unity within a group of human beings (the degree of unity that defines individual rationality). The objection found this argument unconvincing, on the ground that a group of human beings could never really exercise the sort of agency that truly *individual* persons (which the objection takes to be human-size persons) exercise—and this would be so even if such a group of human beings was committed to achieving overall rational unity within itself. In the course of answering this objection, we have been exploring an extraordinarily close parallel between the long-term inten-tions of individual human-size persons and the Gricean communication in-tentions that speakers direct toward audiences. The last point of the parallel called into question precisely what the objection assumes. In claiming that there is a particular way in which individual persons exercise their agency, the objection assumes that there is a particular way in which the thoughts of indi-vidual persons issue in action, which is essentially different from the way in which the thoughts of one person can influence the actions of another. But we have just seen that the way in which the long-term intentions of individual persons issue in action is not essentially different from the way in which the communication intentions of speakers lead their audiences to act. In both cases, the efficaciousness of these intentions rests on just two things: a recog-nition of them and a decision that acting on them is a reasonable thing to do. And if it be asked what makes the one sort of intention an *intra*personal affair, and the other an *inter*personal affair, the answer is readily supplied by the very criterion of personal individuality that the argument for the possibility of group persons exploits, and that the objection mistakenly claimed to be in-sufficient, namely, the commitment to overall rational unity that characterizes the single rational point of view of an individual person. Thus an intention and its subsequent execution belong to one and the same person just in case both fall under the scope of the same commitment to overall rational unity. And so to repeat the conclusion of the last section, insofar as this commitment can obtain within a group of human beings, thoughts and actions that are associated with the lives of different human beings can belong to a single group person.

3. The Normative Analysis of Personal Identity: A First Full Statement

Since a group person is composed of many human beings, its identity does not consist in animal identity. And, assuming that distinct human beings do not share a single consciousness, its identity does not consist in the sort of phenomenological unity in terms of which Locke analyzed the condition of personal identity. The identity of a group person consists rather in a sort of rational and practical unity that can be characterized only in highly abstract and structural terms. These terms are the terms of the normative analysis of personal identity that will be introduced now and defended in the rest of this book.

The particular sort of rational and practical unity that constitutes the identity of a group person has already been much described and discussed in the last two sections. Yet the emphasis has often been on how this sort of rational and practical unity need *not* be tied to an individual person. We have seen that rational unity can be realized, in degree, when many distinct persons exercise their agency together in joint activities. Furthermore, there is no essential difference between the way in which distinct persons exercise their agency together in such joint activities and the way in which an individual human-size person exercises its agency over time in the course of long-term activities—except for the fact that the latter are carried out in the light of a commitment to *overall* rational unity, while the former are carried out in the light of a commitment to some lesser degree of rational unity. The commitment to a lesser degree of rational unity is what keeps the persons who engage in joint activities distinct, despite what they share by way of common ends and action. Likewise, the commitment to overall rational unity is what binds the different human constituents of a group person together as constituents of a single person, despite what they do not share by way of a common animal body and what they do not share by way of a unified consciousness.

Given these aspects of the argument for the possibility of group persons, we must allow that the facts which ground personal identity are not all or nothing, but are rather a matter of degree—as Parfit has also claimed.[12] However, Parfit applied his claim only to the case of personal identity *over* time; what he emphasized is that a certain amount of psychological (and physical)

---

[12] Parfit, *Reasons and Persons*, chap. 11.

change over time can result in a change of identity, so that one person becomes someone else. The claim here is more radical. It is that the facts which ground personal identity *at* a time are also a matter of degree. This claim is more radical, because it challenges the idea that there is a sharp distinction between intrapersonal relations, such as the relation that obtains between a person's intentions and its own actions, and interpersonal relations, such as the relation that obtains between a speaker's communication intentions and an audience's responses. There is a sense in which Parfit challenges this too. But he does it in the reverse way. He portrays the facts of personal identity as being less metaphysically deep than we ordinarily suppose. And for this reason, he thinks that in*tra*personal relations are *looser*, and hence more like interpersonal relations, than we ordinarily suppose. In contrast, the point of the last section was to show that in*ter*personal relations are *tighter*, and hence more like intrapersonal relations, than we ordinarily suppose.[13] In any event, the normative analysis of personal identity will take the general challenge to the distinction between intra- and interpersonal relations as far as possible. As far as possible, it will characterize personal identity in terms of relations that can be *either* intrapersonal *or* interpersonal.

Philosophers who have reductionist aspirations (as Parfit does) may find this approach congenial since it holds out the promise of analyzing the condition of personal identity in wholly impersonal, in the sense of person-neutral, terms. However, as the next chapter will make fully clear, the normative analysis of personal identity may be reductionist in only a weak sense. This is because it makes use of a normative ideal of rationality—the normative ideal of overall rational unity—that has a definitional, or analytic, tie to the idea of an individual person. Of course, this tie has already been heavily exploited in the arguments of this chapter. Indeed, if there were no such tie, we would lose our main ground for insisting on the possibility of group persons—in contra-

---

[13] This point has also been urged, to some extent, by Korsgaard in "Personal Identity." However, she does so with far less radical metaphysical aims and far more controversial ethical aims. According to her, Parfit errs in the same way that the whole utilitarian tradition does, in thinking of a person's life as a collection of experiences. This underestimates the unity of a person's life, or what is here being called the "tightness" of intrapersonal relations. Korsgaard also holds that persons can exercise their agency jointly. And when they do, interpersonal relations are tight in the same way that intrapersonal relations are. With this move, she looks as if she is moving toward the metaphysical position being taken in this book. Yet she explicitly rejects this position, by insisting that human-size persons are *basic* agents, on whom the unity of agency is forced by the facts of their human, and especially by their bodily, nature. This leads her to overlook, and implicitly to reject, the possibility of multiple persons within a single human being. And this shows that her approach to the metaphysical issue of personal identity is not thoroughgoingly normative in the way that this book's approach is. (A *thoroughgoingly* normative approach sets no metaphysical priority on the human body.) But furthermore, Korsgaard also departs from the line taken in this book in another way, by insisting that an emphasis on agency should bring in train some substantive ethical commitments. She maintains in particular that an emphasis on agency should undermine Parfit's recommendations in favor of paternalism. And more generally, she sees the emphasis on agency as ushering in the Kantian moral perspective. For reasons given in chapter 3, this book embraces neither of these substantive ethical conclusions.

distinction to groups *of* persons who exercise their agency together in a highly unified fashion.

Nevertheless, the project of analyzing the condition of identity for such group persons will proceed by finding a level of description that is suitable both for individual persons, on the one hand, and the sort of agency that they can exercise in the long term, and for a plurality of persons on the other hand, and the sort of agency that they can exercise jointly. But there is a problem confronting this project, which is that we lack a suitable vocabulary that can apply both to intra- and to interpersonal relations. So here are some *terms of art*.

Let a *rational relation* be defined as a relation that obtains among intentional episodes (where these include intentional states as well as intentional actions) when they are rationally assessable together in *any* of the following senses: whether they are logically consistent; whether they stand in relations of logical entailment; whether they stand in relations of inductive support; whether they stand in any other relations of evidential support; whether they stand in any relations of justificatory support that would apply in practical matters, such as a means-end relation; whether they can be ordered within a single transitive preference ranking. This notion of a rational relation is so broad that it would probably apply to any arbitrary pair of intentional episodes, whether or not they belong to the same person (or even the same century). It is, after all, in the nature of intentional episodes that they *can* be rationally assessed together, whether or not anyone is in a position to do so. But when intentional episodes belong to a single person, they *ought* to be rationally assessed together—and *by* that very person. And sometimes they ought to be rationally assessed together even though they belong to distinct persons. This will be so when the distinct persons have certain sorts of common ends.

Let *relations of reciprocal recognition* be defined as follows: they are rational relations that obtain among intentional episodes by virtue of which persons can keep track of and coordinate their various contributions to coordinated activities. A coordinated activity, remember, has the complex structure that is common to both long-term activities and joint activities: it involves more than one component action, where each such component action is conceived as a contribution to the larger coordinated activity, and each such component action would have little or no point (for the person who performs it) unless the whole coordinated activity of which it is a part were to be carried out. It is a familiar point that any action must derive part of its motivation from some sort of demonstrative knowledge—that is, the sort of knowledge that we express with demonstrative pronouns such as *I, here, now, this* and *that*.[14] So for example, I may want to drink some water, but if I do not know that *that* stuff

---

[14] Especially useful discussions of the special cognitive role of demonstrative knowledge can be found in: John Perry, "The Problem of the Essential Indexical," in *The Problem of the Essential Indexical and Other Essays* (New York: Oxford University Press, 1993); David Lewis, "Attitudes De Dicto and De Se," in *Philosophical Papers*: and Gareth Evans, *The Varieties of Reference* (New York: Oxford University Press, 1982).

in my glass is water, I will not be appropriately moved to drink it. Likewise, I may want to collect my visa, but unless I know that the name that is *now* being called is *my* name, I will not be appropriately moved to step forward and collect it.[15] When persons engage in coordinated activities, they need a complex sort of demonstrative knowledge that enables them to keep track of how the component actions of such activities relate to the whole. And the complexity of such knowledge is due precisely to the relations of reciprocal recognition that it necessarily involves. In the case of long-term activities, a person must be able to keep track of how its current actions fit into a larger pattern of past and future actions. And keeping track of this involves a reciprocal relation between the person's memories of what it has already planned and done and its anticipations of what it will later do. For in planning and carrying out a long-term activity, a person must anticipate that it will later remember what it has planned and done; and in remembering this later, it must remember having anticipated earlier that it would remember this. Similar relations of reciprocal recognition must obtain among the different participants in a joint activity, so that they can keep track of how their various actions contribute to the joint activity. This reciprocal recognition can take various forms, depending on the nature of the joint activity and the number of persons involved. But here is the canonical form that such reciprocal recognition would take in a simple two-person case: I will do this because I expect that you will do that, and I expect that you will do that because you will know that I have done this with the expectation that you will do that. For ease of exposition, these latter relations of reciprocal recognition on which joint activities rest have been characterized as obtaining among persons rather than among intentional episodes. But of course, when persons stand in relations of reciprocal recognition, there must also be relations of reciprocal recognition among intentional episodes that belong to them (in the form of beliefs about one another's states of mind).

One last term of art will be necessary in order to describe a sufficient condition of identity for group persons. Let a *unifying project* be defined as a project that can be executed only through sustained coordinated activity, and that therefore requires a significant degree of rational unity within a set of intentional episodes. Such unifying projects would include the personal projects and fundamental commitments around which individual persons organize their lives in the short or long term, and they would also include any project that requires a substantial coordinated effort on the part of many persons.

---

[15] When the last chapter argued that agents who can engage in agency-regarding relations must have *social knowledge*, it made a concession to skeptics (and others) who place such high requirements on knowledge that they are rarely, if ever, inclined to suppose that we have any. The concession was that it might do just as well to say that such agents must have *warranted social beliefs*. Readers who have these high epistemological standards were instructed to make the relevant substitutions. At this point, such readers must again make the relevant substitutions. Wherever the text refers to demonstrative knowledge, they must take it as referring to demonstrative belief.

As they have been defined, unifying projects are neither possible nor feasible unless certain *particular* sorts of rational relations obtain within a set of intentional episodes. For unifying projects have been defined as projects that are executed through coordinated activities. And we have just seen how such activities depend upon relations of reciprocal recognition, which are of course themselves rational relations. We also saw in section 2 that coordinated activities always presuppose another sort of rational relation, namely, like-mindedness—though the label "like-mindedness" was not used there to describe this relation. A long-term activity of an individual person requires like-mindedness over time, in the form of stable beliefs and values and a sustained commitment to the long-term activity. A joint activity requires like-mindedness across persons, in the form of shared beliefs and values and a shared commitment to the joint activity. Any given coordinated activity will require that other sorts of rational relations obtain within a set of intentional episodes, besides relations of reciprocal recognition and like-mindedness. However, it is hard to say anything very *general* about what these other rational relations are, except for this: when such rational relations—that is, the rational relations that are necessary for engaging in the coordinated activities through which unifying projects are executed—obtain within a set of intentional episodes, the set will approximate, to some degree, the sort of overall rational unity that an individual person must be committed to achieving, insofar as it is committed to being rational. This degree of rational unity will of course vary, depending upon the nature of the unifying project and the degree of unity that it requires for its execution.

With all of the necessary terms of art now in place, here, finally, is a *sufficient condition for the identity of a group person* who is composed of many human beings. There is a set of intentional episodes such that:

    1. these intentional episodes stand in suitable rational relations so as to afford the possibility of carrying out coordinated activities;

    2. the set includes a commitment to particular unifying projects that require coordinated activities of the very sorts that are made possible by (1);

    3. the commitment to carrying out these unifying projects brings in train a commitment to achieving overall rational unity within the set.

In closing, here are a few clarifying remarks about this first full statement of the normative analysis of personal identity.

It is striking that the analysis makes no mention of time. In fact, it aims to provide a completely general condition for personal identity that applies both at a time and over time. This attempt at temporal generality might make it appear that the analysis is incompatible with the *present aim* theory of rationality. According to that theory, a person is rationally required to take into account in its deliberations only its *current* attitudes. And it would seem to follow that the scope of a person's all-things-considered judgments never spans the different times within a person's life. If this did follow, then no sense could be made, within the present aim theory, of a commitment to overall rational unity over time. Since that is precisely how the normative analysis proposes to analyze personal identity over time, there is a strong appearance of incompatibility between it and the present aim theory of rationality.

However, the normative analysis does not require that we give up the present aim theory of rationality. And there is good reason not to give it up. After all, all-things-considered judgments are always made *at* particular times, with a view to deciding what it would be best to think and do *then*. Indeed, it has been emphasized in this chapter that such judgments, or rather the intentions to which they give rise, cannot determine (at least not in any directly causal sense) what a person will do at any other time but the present. It would seem to go along with this metaphysical picture of the causal scope of such judgments that their normative scope—that is, what they ought to consider— should similarly be confined to the present, just as the present aim theory says it is. But this does not mean that it is never in any sense rational to take into account times other than the present. What it means rather is this: if a person ought to take past and future intentional episodes into account in an all- things-considered judgment, it must have reason to do so at the time when it is making the judgment. And this will be true whenever persons are engaged in planning and carrying out long-term activities, for in the context of such activities, a person literally cannot decide what to do in the present without taking into account what it has already thought and done in the past, and what it will think and do in the future. Thus it does not follow from the normative analysis of personal identity either that the present aim theory of rationality is false or, if the theory is true, that persons do not endure over time. Rather, it follows that persons endure over time only insofar as they have commit- ments to unifying projects, and these unifying projects give them renewed reasons, at the different moments of their lives, to strive for overall rational unity over time.

It might be charged that this condition of personal identity over time is too strong. It certainly entails, as do most psychological analyses of personal iden- tity, that persons cannot survive drastic psychological change—and that this is so even when such change is gradual rather than sudden.[16] And perhaps the normative analysis requires even greater like-mindedness over time than do other psychological analyses, for other psychological analyses do not incorpo- rate the requirement of sustained commitments to long-term projects, or the underlying psychological conditions (e.g., the rational relations of like- mindedness and reciprocal recognition) on which such projects depend.

But if this requirement for personal identity over time seems too strong, that can do no damage to the claims of this chapter—which is that the condi- tion which is laid down by the normative analysis is a *sufficient* condition of personal identity that holds in the case of group persons who comprise many human beings. Insofar as a group of human beings satisfies this condition, it

---

[16] This implication of psychological analyses of personal identity is thoroughly discussed by Parfit, *Reasons and Persons*; and by Lewis, *Philosophical Papers*.

can truly be engaged with as one person in the sense which is required by the ethical criterion of personhood—and this is so both at a time and over time.

As was promised, the normative analysis of personal identity tries, as far as possible, to describe the condition of personal identity in person-neutral terms by using the various terms of art that were introduced above. Yet in the last clause, the analysis implicitly introduces the notion of an individual person, by virtue of the conceptual tie that holds between the overall rational unity and individual rationality: the former is a normative ideal that defines the latter. That is precisely why the normative analysis qualifies as an analysis of *personal identity*. However, the sense in which the analysis exploits a concept that is tied to the idea of an individual person is not obvious. It was conceded at the start of section 2 that it might be doubted whether *every* commitment to overall rational unity must amount to the same normative commitment that an individual person has when it is committed to being rational, for it seems that an individual person's normative commitment to being rational would naturally be categorical and unconditional in a way that the commitment to overall rational unity described in the normative analysis is not—that commitment being brought in train as it is by substantive practical commitments to particular unifying projects. When this issue was raised in section 2, it was set aside on the following ground: even when an agent has a merely conditional commitment to overall rational unity, that suffices to make the agent an individual person by the lights of the ethical criterion of personhood. But clearly, the normative analysis of personal identity will be more satisfying, and more compelling, if it can be shown that the notion of overall rational unity is truly *univocal*, and that it always, necessarily, embodies a normative ideal of rationality that is tied to the concept of an individual person. This matter will be taken up in the next chapter, as we consider why the normative analysis puts forward a necessary, as well as a sufficient, condition of personal identity.

meet this requirement of rationality except by preventing the existence of multiple persons within themselves, for the existence of such multiple persons would necessarily entail significant *disunity* within the human beings who house them.

The point being made here is not that common sense must therefore deny the *possibility* of multiple persons. Although we have seen in chapter 2 that a *part* of common sense does deny this possibility (the part that supports the animalist view of persons by equating persons with human beings), the aspect of common sense being considered here does not really depend on this denial. There is no *logical* incompatibility between the claim of this chapter that multiple persons are possible and the claim of common sense that human beings are rationally required to achieve overall rational unity within themselves. Taken together, these two claims simply entail that the existence of multiple persons would constitute a failure of rationality within their human hosts because their existence would involve very significant rational *dis*unity in their human hosts. (Note that this consequence might not hold in the case of group persons, insofar as the rational unity of a group of human beings need not involve any rational disunity within its human members.) But although the possibility of multiple persons can thus be logically reconciled with our commonsense attitude toward human unity and rationality, recognizing the possibility should prompt us to reexamine this attitude—namely, that it is a failure of rationality when human beings are not rationally unified—with a more critical eye.

Section 2 will undertake a critical reexamination of this attitude, in the course of establishing that the normative analysis does indeed specify a necessary, as well as a sufficient, condition of personal identity (continuing to assume, of course, that persons are agents who satisfy the ethical criterion of personhood). Along the way, section 2 will address an issue that was raised and postponed in chapter 4, concerning whether it is appropriate to portray a person's commitment to realizing the normative ideal of overall rational unity in the way that the normative analysis does, as a *conditional* commitment that is brought in train by the person's substantive practical commitments to particular unifying projects, rather than as an unconditional commitment to being rational. Another related issue was also raised and postponed in chapter 4. It concerns whether human beings could ever lose their distinct rational points of view just by virtue of the fact that they had a shared commitment to achieving overall rational unity together, and hence constituted a group person. This issue will be briefly addressed in section 3, in the context of a general discussion of the relations between persons and the human beings of which they are composed. However, this issue will not have been fully dealt with until chapter 6 clarifies the sense in which the shared rational point of view of a group of human beings would constitute a single first person point of view, despite its human multiplicity.

The most important point that will emerge from the combined arguments of this chapter is that the condition of personal identity can be analyzed in

The Sufficient Condition Is Also Necessary

THE TASK of this chapter is threefold. Section 1 will argue for the possibility of multiple persons within a single human being. Section 2 will use that conclusion to go on to argue that the normative analysis specifies a necessary as well as a sufficient condition for the identity of persons, where "person" is to be understood, of course, in the sense defined by the ethical criterion of personhood. Section 3 will address some of the remaining metaphysical issues that will have been raised by the normative analysis, and the account of the kind 'person' that entails it.

The argument for the possibility of multiple persons employs exactly the same strategy as the argument for the possibility of group persons. It begins from the premise that having and manifesting a commitment to overall rational unity is a sufficient condition for being a person in the sense defined by the ethical criterion. And it exploits the fact that certain sorts of substantive practical commitments bring this more general commitment in train— though in this case, so as to mandate overall rational unity within just a part of a human being, rather than in a group of human beings.

It is worth noticing here a point of somewhat greater generality. And that is that the normative analysis of personal identity exploits this very same fact that is exploited by the arguments for the possibility of multiple and group persons. But it does so in an *abstract* way that does not specify the human scope of the commitment to overall rational unity (part, whole, group). Instead, it specifies a *structure* of rational relations and practical commitments that yields a commitment to overall rational unity within the structure. In consequence, the normative analysis specifies a sufficient condition for the identity of multiple persons *and* of group persons *and* of human-size persons as well.

The line of argument that establishes the sufficiency of this condition for personal identity, and along with it the possibility of multiple and group persons, does not establish its necessity. The sufficiency claim alone would do for the book's main purpose, which is to provide a new interpretation and a new defense of Locke's distinction between personal and animal identity. But as it happens, once we accept the arguments in favor of the possibility of multiple persons, we must address an issue that, when properly understood, will show that the condition that is specified by the normative analysis is also necessary. The issue concerns why, and also whether, *human beings* ought to achieve overall rational unity within themselves.

According to common sense and actual practice, human beings are *rationally required* to achieve such overall rational unity. But human beings cannot

exclusively normative terms—in other words, the normative analysis is *thoroughgoingly* normative. The starting point for the analysis is of course a normative point: there is one person wherever there is one rational point of view, and there is one rational point of view wherever a certain normative commitment is in place (the commitment to overall rational unity). But the ending point is also normative: in every case, what gives rise to the normative commitment that characterizes the individual person is a certain abstract structure of rational relations. Thus the point is that in order to analyze the condition of personal identity, no mention need ever be made of any further *non*normative metaphysical condition such as the human body or the unity of consciousness. Such further metaphysical conditions are irrelevant to the analytical task because they place no restrictions at all on how the normative commitment to overall rational unity—and hence the boundaries of an individual person's rational point of view—can fall with respect to them. This point is of a piece with the point about the possibilities of group and multiple persons. And it is important to appreciate how they go together. The introduction to part I noted that other philosophers have sometimes affirmed one possibility—of group or multiple persons—without the other. In doing so, they ceded some important metaphysical role to the individual human being. Either they saw the individual human being as something that imposes a necessary unity within itself, thereby ruling out the possibility of multiple persons, or they saw it as constituting a necessary condition for individual thought and action, thereby ruling out the possibility of group persons. We can affirm both possibilities together only by denying that the individual human being places any such metaphysical constraints on the constitution of an individual person's rational point of view, or on the exercise of a person's agency from that point of view. And that is precisely denied by the normative analysis, insofar as it is thoroughgoingly normative.

1. A RATIONAL RECONSTRUCTION OF MULTIPLE PERSONALITY DISORDER

The argument for the possibility of multiple persons will take an actual phenomenon as its point of departure, namely, multiple personality disorder.

The previous chapter established that any agent who has a rational point of view, and who is committed to achieving overall rational unity within it, and who can engage in rational influence, is an agent who can engage in agency-regarding relations—and hence qualifies as a person by the lights of the ethical criterion of personhood. Prima facie, there would seem to be good evidence that human beings with multiple personality disorder might be the site of more than one individual person in this sense. Such human beings manifest distinct alter personalities who seem to function quite independently of one another. And because this is so, it is possible to rationally engage them at least *as if* they were distinct persons with distinct rational points of view.

However, it would be unwise to argue for the possibility of such multiple persons within a single human being by arguing for their actuality in cases of multiple personality disorder. For one thing, the very existence of the disorder continues to be challenged by some psychiatrists.[1] And for another, most theoretical approaches to the phenomenon take for granted the very thing that this book is calling into question, which is that a human being necessarily has just one real self. This should not be surprising. The phenomenon has for the most part been investigated by an establishment that is committed to a clinical conception of it, as a disorder that must be cured by integrating a human being's alter personalities into one unified self. And the most powerful way to justify this clinical conception is to posit a single self that underlies the various alter personalities, for that makes it possible to portray the integrative cure as a restoration of that self to its proper state of unity. Insofar as the clinical view of multiple personality disorder does justify its commitment to integrative cure in this way, it precludes the empirical conclusion that the ethical criterion of personhood invites, which is that the alter personalities of human beings who have the disorder are, at least in some cases, individual persons. Since this book will not try to refute the clinical view, it will not press this empirical conclusion. It will rest instead, as it did in the case of group persons, with a thesis about what is possible.

All the same, the argument for this possibility will take for granted some features of multiple personality disorder that are not at all in dispute. In doing so, it will rely on the popular account of the phenomenon that is provided in the biography of Sybil.[2] These features are also described in the other main popular and philosophical accounts of the phenomenon.[3]

The first feature is the most striking feature that human beings with the disorder manifest, and it has already been introduced: the alter personalities of such human beings function independently of one another to an extraordinary degree, so much so that they can be rationally engaged at least as if they were distinct persons with their own distinct rational points of view. As a result, it is not really possible to rationally engage the whole human being who hosts the personalities. (This is the obverse of the claim in the last chapter, that it is impossible to rationally engage the separate human constituents of a group person.) This fact is sometimes obscured in the popular accounts by a tendency to select one personality as constituting the human being's 'real' self, and hence as not being an *alter* personality. In general, this selection seems to be made on the following two grounds: the personality is dominant

---

[1] See, for example, Harold Merskey, "The Manufacture of Personalities: The Production of Multiple Personality Disorder," *British Journal of Psychiatry* 157 (1992): 327–40.

[2] Flora Rheta Schreiber, *Sybil* (New York: Warner Books, 1973).

[3] See especially Morton Prince, *The Dissociation of a Personality* (London: Longmans, Green, 1905; reprint (New York: Johnson Reprint Corporation, 1968); and C. H. Thigpen and H. M. Cleckly, *The Three Faces of Eve* (New York: Popular Library, 1957). For extended philosophical discussions of the disorder, see Ian Hacking, *Rewriting the Soul: Multiple Personality and the Sciences of Memory* (Princeton: Princeton University Press, 1995); and Braude, *First Person Plural*.

(i.e., it takes up more of the time and resources of the human host than the other, merely 'alter' personalities do), and it is also displays a commitment to living in a 'normal' fashion (usually, this commitment leads the dominant personality or self to seek therapy, while the other, merely 'alter', personalities oppose therapy). The name "Sybil" is used in her biography to denote precisely such a personality, namely, the personality who turned to Dr. Wilbur for psychoanalytic treatment. But the name is also used to describe the whole *human being* whom Dr. Wilbur regarded as the subject of her analysis, and who would eventually be "cured" through the integration of her various personalities. Despite this dual role, the name "Sybil" is assumed by her biographer to be univocal, precisely because the human being called Sybil is assumed to have one real self, who is the personality called Sybil. By the lights of this book, both assumptions are questionable. But even if they are granted for the sake of argument, it should not be inferred that the recounted therapy sessions between Dr. Wilbur and Sybil were encounters in which Dr. Wilbur managed to rationally engage a whole human being. It is true that the utterances and actions of the interlocutor whom she addressed as Sybil did seem to reflect a single, unified rational point of view. But that point of view did not include *all* of the thoughts and intentional episodes that belonged to the whole human being through which this Sybil spoke and acted. In fact, this point of view did not even include all of the thoughts and intentional episodes belonging to that human being *at a given time*. At all times, Sybil's utterances and actions reflected only a *portion* of that human being's intentional life. The rest of that life was divided between the other alter personalities, each of whom Dr. Wilbur was able to rationally engage separately. And so long as all of these various personalities existed, Dr. Wilbur could not rationally engage the total human being called Sybil. If she tried, the response would always be authored by one personality or another. (The goal of the therapy is well described as the goal of getting to the point where this was no longer so, and it was finally possible to engage the total human being as one person.)

The second feature of multiple personality disorder that bears on the present argument, for the possibility of multiple persons within a single human being, is that alter personalities can be 'co-conscious'. When this happens, some alters have phenomenological access to the thoughts of other alters—which is to say, they have phenomenological access to thoughts that they do not regard as their own. Very often, there is an asymmetrical relation between the personality who is regarded as the first and dominant one and the alter personalities who appear later; for the latter often have direct phenomenological access to the thoughts of the former (though not always to the thoughts of one another), while the former remains ignorant of the others' existence. Thus in Sybil's case, she reported that there had always been something peculiar about time, because there were large blank spaces of it that were empty of experiences and memories. These were times when her alter personalities were 'out'. In contrast, for many of the alters, the time when Sybil was in control were not blank spaces, because they had direct phenomenological access to Sybil's intentional life—that is, to her thoughts and actions. Yet once her therapy had progressed to a certain stage, Sybil did gain phenomenological access to some of their thoughts through memory. Her biographer provides a poignant description of her first direct phenomenological encounter, through memory, with two of her alter personalities, Mary and Sybil Ann. This is not presented as an instance where one *personality* is aware of another's thoughts, since the assumption of the biography is that Sybil is a human being rather than a personality. But nevertheless, the description gives a sense of what it would be like to have direct conscious access to thoughts and actions that one does not regard as one's own, as co-conscious alter personalities do:

> As Sybil Ann she had returned to the apartment and had been suddenly obsessed with the desire to go off on a trip. Somehow this trip had not eventuated, but while planning to go, she had looked at a purse on the dresser with Sybil Ann's eyes, thinking that she would take the purse with her and return it as soon she got settled somewhere. Observing that the name on the identification card was Sybil I. Dorsett, Sybil in the person of Sybil Ann thought: that must be the owner. The memory of being Sybil Ann was so distinct that it included Sybil Ann's confusion as to who Sybil was. (358–59)

When alter personalities are co-conscious, a similar phenomenon occurs in their *present* experience. They can be directly aware of another alter's current experiences, and this awareness can be so distinct that it includes a sense of the other's view (or ignorance) of them.

What, then, do these two features of multiple personality disorder suggest about the possibility of multiple persons within a single human being? The fact that it is possible to rationally engage alter personalities *as if* they were distinct persons suggests that each alter has its own distinct rational point of view within which it is committed to achieving overall rational unity. If this were really so, then by the lights of the ethical criterion of personhood, alters would be multiple persons within a single human being. Obviously, the identity of such multiple persons could not be given by the biological condition of animal identity since they would cohabit the same human being. Likewise, though perhaps less obviously, their identity could not be given by the phenomenological condition in terms of which Locke analyzed personal identity since some of them would be co-conscious. Thus as in the case of group persons, recognizing the possibility of multiple persons would both support Locke's distinction between personal and animal identity and yet *also* require a new interpretation of it—by tying personal identity to the identity of a rational point of view, and at the same time divorcing it from the identity of a phenomenological point of view, as well as from the identity of an animal.

However, it is one thing to say that the phenomenon of multiple personality disorder *suggests* the possibility of multiple persons within a single human being; it is quite another thing to *establish* that such multiple persons really are possible. In order to establish this, it will be helpful to move away from an empirical description of Sybil and to consider some of the conceptual issues that cases like hers raise. What we need to consider is this: in what conditions *would* there be distinct, but co-conscious, rational points of view within a single human being?

Minimally, the following two conditions would have to hold: (1) each multiple person within the same human being would have to regard some, but not all, of the intentional episodes that figure in the life of that human being as constituting its distinct rational point of view, and (2) each person would have to be committed to achieving overall rational unity just within the set of intentional episodes that constitute its own rational point of view. Clearly, these two conditions cannot hold unless there is a *principle* by which each multiple person could distinguish the intentional episodes that constitute its rational point of view from the intentional episodes that constitute the rational points of view of the other persons within the same human being. For obvious reasons, this principle cannot appeal either to bodily or to phenomenological criteria. So the question is, what other sorts of criteria might be available to such persons? The answer is, the very same criteria that apply in the case of group persons.

The last chapter argued that certain sorts of coordinated activities might require for their execution overall rational unity within a group of human beings. When this is so, the activities constitute the sorts of unifying projects that are mentioned in the last clause of the normative analysis of personal identity. And the function of such a unifying project is to provide a perspective from which the group can deliberate and act together—that is, as one person with one rational point of view. But there is an important point about such unifying projects that the last chapter did not emphasize: they actually provide the principle by which intentional episodes are distinguished as belonging to a particular group person's rational point of view, for it is in the nature of such a project to dictate how the efforts of a group of human beings must be coordinated so as to carry it out. And in dictating this, the unifying project will also dictate which human beings belong to the group. Now in general, intentional episodes belong to a group person's rational point of view just in case they figure in the lives of the human constituents of that group person. And so, insofar as a unifying project dictates the human composition of a group person, it will eo ipso determine which intentional episodes belong to the group person's rational point of view.[4]

The last chapter also brought out that unifying projects belong to a larger class of coordinated activities that includes both joint activities that are carried

---

[4] This is actually an oversimplification that will have to be corrected in section 3. On closer scrutiny, it will emerge that there is no reason to suppose that a group person's rational point of view must include *all* of the intentional episodes that belong to each of the human beings of which it is composed, rather than just a portion of them. In that case, a group person would not consist in a group of human beings; it would consist rather in parts of groups of human beings. But even with this qualification, the present point still holds, that the boundaries of a particular group person's rational point of view would be determined by reference to the practical requirements of particular unifying projects.

out by many persons together and long-term activities that are carried out by single persons over time. All such coordinated activities share a common structure: their execution involves more than one component action; these component actions are conceived as contributions to the larger activity of which they are a part; and there would be no (or little) point in carrying out these component actions unless the larger activities of which they are a part could be completed. By virtue of their common structure, all coordinated activities require for their successful execution some degree of rational unity within a set of intentional episodes. And what distinguishes unifying projects is simply that they require *overall* rational unity within such a set, thereby ensuring that the set constitutes one rational point of view. This suggests that the rational points of view of multiple persons within the same human being could be distinguished by the very same principle that applies to the case of group persons. The only difference would be one of scale: rather than there being a shared practical commitment within a group of human beings to one large-scale unifying project, there would be separate practical commitments within a single human being to many different, smaller-scale unifying projects.

To think of multiple persons in this way, as having rational points of view that are generated and circumscribed by substantive practical commitments to coordinated activities, is to think of them as things for whom the normative analysis provides a sufficient condition of identity. According to that analysis, an individual person exists when there is a set of intentional episodes such that: (1) these intentional episodes stand in suitable rational relations so as to afford the possibility of carrying out sustained coordinated activities; (2) the set includes a commitment to particular unifying projects whose execution involves the very sorts of sustained coordinated activities made possible by (1); and (3) the commitment to carrying out these unifying projects brings in train a commitment to achieving overall rational unity within the set. The thought, then, is that the identities of multiple persons and these persons' rational points of view are determined by particular unifying projects that take up less than the resources of a whole human life.

This line of thought may seem unpromising. After all, there is nothing to bar one individual person from having separate practical commitments to carrying out many different sustained coordinated activities. And in point of fact, it is quite typical for the individual human-size persons who actually exist to have commitments to many distinct long-term activities, each of which requires a sustained coordinated effort over time. So it is not immediately clear how or why commitments to such sustained coordinated activities—what the normative analysis calls "unifying projects"—would provide a principle by which to distinguish the separate rational points of view of distinct persons.

Once again, the case of group personhood provides a useful insight. We have seen that not all large-scale coordinated activities are such that they would require *overall* rational unity within a group of human beings. When they do not, they do not constitute the sorts of unifying projects that give rise to group persons. But group persons are possible nevertheless, at least insofar as it is possible that *some* coordinated activities would require overall rational unity within a group of human beings, and groups of human beings could in principle have practical commitments to such activities. Similarly, there is no need to suppose—and indeed it would be wrong to suppose—that separate practical commitments to different coordinated activities within a single human being always generate multiple persons within that human being. But nevertheless, some of them might. This would happen if these different coordinated activities did not require overall rational unity within the whole human being and yet did require it within some part of that human being. And of course, this would not be some bodily part, such as a hand or a foot, but rather some portion of the intentional episodes and activities that figure in the life of the human being.

It will be easiest to explain how commitments to certain sorts of coordinated activities might generate multiple persons within a single human being by way of contrast with a case where they do not. Let us take for granted that I am an individual person with a commitment to achieving overall rational unity within a particular human life. But as it happens, I am also committed to pursuing the following different activities: philosophical work; a teaching career; the study of music. Now insofar as I pursue these different activities in the light of my commitment to overall rational unity, the following must be true: (1) whenever I pursue one of them, I judge that it is best, all things considered, for me to do so then, and (2) the scope of the "all" in such all-things-considered judgments ranges over my commitments to all of the different activities. This ensures that I never pursue these coordinated activities in complete independence of one another. Rather, I always bear in mind how pursuing one would affect my ability to pursue the others. And I also rank the activities in importance so that I can judge which it would be best to pursue on occasions when there are opportunities to pursue several and I must choose one.

Now imagine that coordinated activities very similar to mine were pursued within the life of a single human being—except that unlike mine, these activities were *not* pursued in the light of a commitment to overall rational unity within that human life. Rather, the activities were pursued completely independently of one another—that is, without regard for how the pursuit of each might affect the pursuit of the others, and without any effort to rank them in importance, and without any effort to arrive at all-things-considered judgments that take them all into account. This description perhaps sounds like a description of irrationality, or at any rate of a chaotic psychological economy. But it could equally well be a description of a case where several distinct persons exercise their agency in complete independence of one another. We would have no difficulty, for example, in applying the description to three human-size persons, one of whom was a philosopher, one a teacher, and one a musician. Each such person might well pursue its central activity—what the normative analysis would call its "unifying project"—without any interest in or commitment to pursuing the activities that the others pursue. Furthermore, each might pursue its unifying project without any regard for how that might affect the ability of the others to pursue theirs—and indeed, without attaching any importance at all to their activities. We might fault these human-size persons for single-mindedness. And we might fault them for a failure of regard for others. But we should not try to convict them of irrationality, for each of these human-size persons would pursue its unifying project by arriving at and acting upon all-things-considered judgments. And in principle, the same could hold for multiple persons within a single human being.

So let us now consider this possibility in greater detail. The thought is that there might be, within a single human being, a philosopher, a teacher, and a musician. Each cares only to pursue its own unifying project, and none regards its unifying project as requiring the resources of the whole human life. (We can imagine, for example, that each wants just three or four hours a day—the philosopher to read and write, the teacher to prepare and give lectures, the musician to study, listen, and practice.) As a result, each of these persons wants to pursue its unifying project by devoting a portion of a human life to it. But now suppose that each has phenomenological access to all of the intentional activity that goes on within that human life. This would bring in the feature of co-consciousness. In such a case, each would have phenomenological access to intentional activity that it regarded as extraneous to the pursuit of its unifying project. So, to take a very limited example, the philosopher might have phenomenological access to a desire to sit for hours practicing the piano. But there would be no reason for the philosopher to regard that desire as a basis for deliberation and action—that is, there would be no reason for the philosopher to regard the desire as belonging to its rational point of view. Despite the fact that the philosopher was conscious of this desire, and despite the fact that the desire figured in the life of the human being whose resources the philosopher wished to use, the desire would not impinge on the philosopher's pursuit of its unifying project; because that project does not require the resources of the whole human life in question, the philosopher is free simply to disregard that desire—even while it, as it well might, lets the desire be acted upon. On the other hand, the philosopher's unifying project would require overall rational unity within a specific part of the intentional life that goes on in that human being. This part would include views about which intellectual endeavors are most worthy of pursuit, which philosophical problems ought to be tackled, which figures in the history of philosophy should be taken seriously, which philosophical journals are worth reading. It would also include plans for particular philosophical articles and books that the philosopher might be engaged in writing, as well as memories and anticipations of past and future contributions to those works. These are the intentional episodes that are relevant to the philosopher's unifying project. That is, it is these episodes that the philosopher ought to take as a basis for deliberation and action; it is these that constitute its distinctive rational point of view.

It may well come to someone's mind to object that this imaginary philosopher could not really constitute a person who was entirely distinct from the teacher and the musician who by hypothesis cohabit the same human being. The objection might run as follows: the philosopher cannot reasonably disregard the desires that animate the teacher's and the musician's unifying projects, for all of these different projects might naturally lead these purportedly separate persons into conflicts. And this is so even if these persons do not wish—and by hypothesis they do not wish—to monopolize the human being whose resources they share; they might still come into conflict about who is to do what when. And obviously, they cannot resolve such conflicts without taking one another's desires into account in their deliberations. However, far from proving the objection, this only serves to show that *multiple* persons can have reason to enter into certain sorts of *cooperative* arrangements in order to share a common resource—as can any *other* individual persons who need to share resources. Such arrangements always require persons to achieve a degree of rational unity together. But in general, such unity falls very far short of the sort of overall rational unity that ought, ideally, to be achieved within the rational point of view of an individual person. In the case at hand, the philosopher, teacher, and musician may arrive at a time-sharing arrangement that settles who is to do what when without arriving at all-things-considered judgments about what they should together think and do, for apart from this need to settle conflicts about time sharing, each can be indifferent to the thoughts and actions of the others. These acts of cooperation can be seen, then, as precisely that—acts of *cooperation* by *three distinct persons*.

To repeat, these multiple persons would satisfy the condition of personal identity that is specified by the normative analysis of personal identity. Each would consist in a set of intentional episodes that stands in suitable rational relations so as to afford the pursuit of sustained coordinated activities, and each would be committed to pursuing particular unifying projects whose execution involves such coordinated activities, and these unifying projects would mandate overall rational unity within the set—which is to say, itself. Because each multiple person would thus have a commitment to achieving overall rational unity within itself, each could be rationally engaged as an individual person in its own right. Each would therefore satisfy the ethical criterion of personhood.

It is of course an empirical question whether and to what extent the alter personalities of human beings with multiple personality disorder satisfy the ethical criterion of personhood. The popular descriptions suggest that some do and others do not. In Sybil's biography, her alter personalities are generally depicted as representing different *aspects* or *sides* of the total Sybil that she had not managed to integrate into one unified self—generally because they represented aspects of herself that she wished to repress and deny. This depiction seems especially appropriate with respect to the alters who displayed childish personalities. They did seem to function as mere *personalities* through whom Sybil *herself* could manifest regressive behavior. But many of Sybil's alters were not juvenile in either thought or manner. Very often, they had definite and distinct practical commitments that reflected a high degree of reflection, both about their own situation and about Sybil's (they did distinguish these two things). And in general, they were committed to carrying out separate projects that were not shared by the other alters and that indeed the other alters had reason to oppose. As a result, the alters did not reason from the unified rational point of view of the total human being Sybil; they reasoned almost exclusively from the perspective of their separate practical commitments. Given the arguments of this book, this means that they reasoned from their own distinct rational points of view, as distinct persons.

Whether or not this conclusion is accepted in Sybil's case, several points deserve mention. First, the facts just described above, which invite the conclusion that some of Sybil's alter personalities satisfied the ethical criterion of personhood, are the very facts by virtue of which it was possible for Sybil's analyst to engage her alters at least *as if* they were distinct persons. Second, Sybil's alters had enough of a sense of self and separateness and individual practical commitment that they actually *opposed* the clinical goal of integration—that is, the goal of overall rational unity within the human being Sybil. (This opposition was often voiced as a concern about the prospect of their death.) Finally, there is a question about the *rationality* of this opposition. To the extent that distinct practical commitments leading to distinct rational points of view within a single human being are *sustainable* and *effectively pursuable* (as in the more artificial case described above, of the philosopher, the teacher, and the musician who cohabit the same human being), it is not clear why it is necessarily *irrational* to oppose the goal of overall rational unity within the human being.

This last point might seem to suggest that the arguments of this section are aimed at undermining the clinical goal of integration for human beings with multiple personality disorder. That is not so. The point being made here has far less straightforward implications for that goal. Let us suppose that some alter personalities did qualify as distinct persons. By hypothesis, they would have their own rational points of view from which to assess the merits of integration, and they would be able to see that integration would, for them, be tantamount to death. Yet all the same, they could in principle have reason to view integration as a worthy goal. This would be so in the following condition: they judge that there are things worth doing which would require integration (say, a certain sort of "normal" life with a marriage and a career), and they judge that these things are *more* worth doing than the separate projects that they can pursue on their own, as distinct persons who act individually rather than together as one. In this condition, the alters would have *internal* reasons to integrate into one human-size person (just as several human-size persons can have internal reasons to integrate into one group person). So if, in this condition, the alters opposed integration, they would be irrational by their own lights. By drawing attention to this internal justification for integration, this section does not rule out that there might be other, *external* justifications as well—that is, justifications that would not be recognized by the alters. In that case, clinicians might still regard themselves as justified in pursuing the goal of integrating alter personalities, even though they could not convict the alter personalities of irrationality for opposing the goal. This, of course, is a familiar sort of paternalism, which may sometimes be justified, and which one finds in many other areas of value and action over and above the one we are discussing.

So to repeat: The aim of this rational reconstruction of multiple personality disorder has not been to undermine the clinical goal of integrating alter personalities. The aim has been rather to bring out that alter personalities approximate, and may even meet, the condition of being multiple persons within a single human being; and to the extent that they do approximate this condition, it is not necessarily irrational for *them* to oppose the clinical goal.

2. JUSTIFYING THE COMMITMENT TO OVERALL RATIONAL UNITY

This section will argue that the normative analysis specifies a necessary as well as a sufficient condition of identity for things that satisfy the ethical criterion of personhood. (However, it should be borne in mind that the book's thesis about the possibility of multiple and group persons does not depend on the success of this argument. That they satisfy a condition that is sufficient for personal identity is enough to secure their status as individual persons in their own rights.) Along the way, the argument of this section will also provide an answer to a very general question that chapter 4 raised, concerning whether ideals of rationality impose categorical as opposed to merely hypothetical demands. The answer is that they do not, and indeed they cannot.

The argument begins where the last section left off. We have seen that it would, in general, be rational for multiple persons within a single human being to oppose being integrated into one human-size person, because they would have substantive practical commitments to unifying projects that would have to be either foregone or altered for the sake of integration. These same practical commitments ensure that multiple persons would satisfy the normative analysis of personal identity. Here is a *restatement* of that analysis: there is a set of intentional episodes such that: (1) these intentional episodes stand in suitable rational relations so as to afford the possibility of carrying out coordinated activities; (2) the set includes a commitment to particular unifying projects that require coordinated activities of the very sorts that are made possible by (1); (3) the commitment to carrying out these unifying projects brings in train a commitment to achieving overall rational unity within the set. The important point is that the substantive practical commitments that multiple persons would have to unifying projects would bring in train a further commitment to achieving overall rational unity, and the latter commitment is characteristic of the individual point of view of an individual person. That, of course, is the general *reason* why the condition specified by the normative analysis is a *sufficient* condition for personal identity, namely, that it includes a substantive practical commitment to unifying projects that bring in train a commitment to achieving overall rational unity. It will emerge that the condition is *necessary* for the very *same reason*.

Let us first consider a very swift argument for this conclusion, and then reconsider the argument more carefully in the light of various queries and objections. As we reconsider the argument, we will have occasion to critically examine our attitudes concerning whether and when human beings ought to achieve overall rational unity within themselves, and hence whether we ought to regard fragmentation into multiple persons as a failure of rationality on the part of human beings.

The swift argument is as follows: the ethical criterion of personhood entails that it is a necessary condition on personal identity that a person have a commitment to achieving overall rational unity within itself; insofar as a person does have this commitment, the person must regard itself as having some *reason* to achieve overall rational unity; it is impossible to derive an *ought* from an *is*; so a person must have some other evaluative commitments that supply it with a reason to achieve overall rational unity, and therewith give rise to its commitment to achieving such unity; these other evaluative commitments would supply a reason to achieve such unity only insofar as they were commitments to carrying out unifying projects (this is a matter of definition); it is, therefore, a necessary condition on personal identity that persons have substantive commitments to unifying projects, just as the normative analysis specifies.

It must be admitted that this conclusion does not square well with our attitudes toward human rationality and unity, especially as those attitudes are manifested in connection with multiple personality disorder. We tend to presume that human beings who have the disorder ought to achieve overall rational unity within themselves. Yet it cannot be presumed that these human beings actually have substantive practical commitments to unifying projects that would require them to do so. And so the question arises, is there some other reason why human beings ought to achieve overall rational unity within themselves, *besides* substantive practical commitments to unifying projects? And if such a reason could be found, would it show that having substantive commitments to unifying projects is not, after all, a necessary condition on personal identity?

Perhaps there is a more naturalistic account of what grounds the commitment to overall rational unity—an account that, unlike the argument above, manages to bridge the gap between *ought* and *is*, and so does not need to posit unifying projects in order to find a reason to achieve overall rational unity. Here is such an account: human beings by nature have certain rational capacities; the natural function of these rational capacities is to deliver rational unity; therefore, human beings ought to achieve overall rational unity within themselves, and for no other reason than that it is in their nature to do so.

The conclusion of this naturalistic account is a non sequitur. All that really follows from it is that human beings *can* achieve overall rational unity within themselves. Now, perhaps there are some circumstances in which *ought* follows from *can*. But it cannot follow in this case. We have seen that human beings also *can* employ their rational capacities so as to achieve rational unity within groups and parts of human beings. That puts human beings in the position of having to choose from *among* these alternative practical possibilities. And of course, they need reasons for this choice. What reasons might there be, besides commitments to unifying projects that require a specific *level* of unity, within a part, or a whole, or a group? It might be suggested that rational unity is good *for its own sake*. But this provides no immediate help, since all of the options would deliver some rational unity. It might also be suggested that *more* rational unity is *better*. But if so, that would not entail a commitment to overall rational unity within human beings; rather, it would entail a commitment to integrating into one single group person who comprised all human beings. Finally, it might be suggested that the *best* level of rational unity is the human level. With this suggestion, we find the semblance of a reason why human beings ought to achieve overall rational unity within themselves. But it does not show that there is some reason, besides substantive commitments to unifying projects, for achieving overall rational unity, since human beings who had this reason would have such a commitment to such a unifying project, namely, the project of leading a *rationally unified human life*.

These reflections about the connection—or rather the lack of one—between human nature and the commitment to overall rational unity are generalizable. They serve to bring out what would be wrong with *any* attempt to analyze the condition of personal identity without incorporating substantive practical commitments to unifying projects. If the analysis is to give the condition of identity for things that satisfy the ethical criterion, then it must ensure that individual persons have a commitment to achieving overall rational unity within themselves. Now, in order that there be such a commitment, there must of course be rational capacities through whose exercise rational unity can be achieved. But the commitment to overall rational unity must also have *boundaries*, boundaries that determine the scope of the "all" in all-things-considered judgments. So let us ask whether and how any metaphysically given boundaries might serve in this capacity—such as the boundaries that demarcate human beings, or human brains, or single consciousnesses, or functional systems, or material bodies. It would be wrong to suppose that the mere existence of such boundaries provides a reason to achieve overall rational unity within them. And if they do not provide such a reason, they cannot constitute the condition of personal identity. It is *logically* possible, of course, that the things that are demarcated by certain metaphysically given boundaries just *do* have a commitment to achieving overall rational unity within them. But in that case, those things would have substantive commitments to unifying projects, for example, the projects of achieving a rationally unified human life, or a rationally unified brain, or a rationally unified consciousness, or a rationally unified functional system, or a rationally unified material body. So we would not really have been given an *alternative* to the normative analysis of personal identity, which portrays the commitment to overall rational unity as grounded precisely in commitments to such unifying projects.

In the light of these more general reflections, the swift argument for the necessity of the condition put forward by the normative analysis of personal identity should seem more powerful. That argument insisted that persons need a *justification* for their commitment to overall rational unity, and since an *ought* cannot be derived from an *is*, persons must have other substantive commitments to unifying projects in order to justify it. And that is why the normative analysis specifies a necessary, as well as a sufficient, condition of personal identity. Those who think that the *is-ought* divide can be bridged may not have been impressed by that argument. So we considered whether human nature might be the *is* that can deliver this particular *ought*. We saw that all that human nature can supply are the rational capacities by which rational unity is achieved. But those capacities do not by themselves dictate what *level* of rational unity human beings *ought* to achieve. That is, they fail to determine the *scope* of anyone's commitment to overall rational unity. We have also seen that no other metaphysically given boundaries will necessarily determine that scope either. Of course, their existence may be *taken* as a reason to achieve a certain level of rational unity. But that would be to *undertake* a particular unifying project, which is precisely what the normative analysis requires for personal identity.

Let us now turn to the question of whether the normative ideals of rationality impose categorical as opposed to merely hypothetical demands. If they did, that would cast doubt on a central part of the rationale for the normative analysis of personal identity, namely, the claim of the analysis to exploiting a conceptual or definitional tie between the idea of individual rationality and the idea of overall rational unity. If it turns out that what truly defines individual rationality is a categorical imperative to achieve overall rational unity, then the analysis could not claim to capture it, because the analysis portrays a person's normative commitment to achieving such unity as merely conditional—conditional upon having further substantive commitments to unifying projects that require such unity.

However, the argument of this section has exposed a fundamental incoherence in the idea of a categorical imperative to achieve overall rational unity. This incoherence stems from the fact that persons are capable of achieving not only different degrees, but also different *levels*, of rational unity. It follows that any imperative to achieve overall rational unity would be essentially incomplete, and indeed its very intelligibility would be compromised if the imperative failed to specify the *boundaries* within which such unity ought to be achieved. And this raises the question, what sets these boundaries? Or to put it another way, what determines the *scope* of the normative requirement to achieve overall rational unity? This section has shown that nothing *can* set these boundaries and determine this scope except a substantive commitment to a unifying project. That, then, is what any intelligible imperative to achieve overall rational unity—intelligible in the sense that it is not essentially incomplete and underdescribed—must specify. But of course, in specifying this, the imperative would be specifying a *condition* on which its demands are conditional. Thus there can be no such thing as an unconditional or categorical imperative to achieve overall rational unity.

Here is another way of putting the same conclusion: the merely conditional commitment to achieve overall rational unity that figures in the normative analysis of personal identity is the *only* sort of commitment to rational unity that there can be, so it is no objection against the analysis that it fails to provide for the idea that persons are subject to an unconditional requirement of rationality to achieve such unity. Admittedly, this conclusion goes against some fairly deep-seated presumptions about the nature of rationality and the necessity of its demands. But here are some further consequences of the overall argument that serve to bring out that the normative analysis does manage to capture at least some *part* of these presumptions. Although the requirement to achieve overall rational unity within one's rational point of view is never categorical but always hypothetical, it does not follow that persons can ever fail to be committed to achieving such unity. On the contrary, it is *necessarily* the case that persons have this normative commitment—at least if they are persons in the sense defined by the ethical criterion of personhood; the criterion entails that persons must have the commitment, and so it also entails that persons must fulfill whatever condition the commitment is conditional *on*. That is precisely what the normative analysis captures, thereby delivering both a necessary and a sufficient condition of personal identity.

3. Some Remaining Metaphysical Issues

The last chapter and this one have shown that this book does deliver, as promised, a new defense and a new interpretation of Locke's distinction between personal identity, via a new, normative analysis of personal identity. This section will consider some further metaphysical issues that the arguments for the normative analysis raise. In doing so, it will continue to extend the account of the kind 'person' that follows from the ethical criterion of personhood.

The normative analysis says that an individual person exists just in case there is a set of intentional episodes standing in suitable rational relations, and the set includes practical commitments to unifying projects that bring in train a commitment to overall rational unity within the set. There is a broad sense of "psychological," which contrasts with such terms as "material" and "biological" and "physiological," under which this analysis qualifies as a purely psychological analysis of personal identity, for it mentions no material, biological, or physiological conditions. But there is also a narrower sense of "psychological" that construes all psychological relations as strictly intrapersonal relations, and that generally assumes that such intrapersonal relations must obtain within a single animal, or within a single consciousness, or both. Of course, the normative analysis does not qualify as a psychological analysis in this narrower sense, since it deliberately employs the term "rational relations" in such a way as to cover both intra- and interpersonal relations, and since it also conceives rational relations as relations that can hold between distinct organisms and consciousnesses. All the same, the normative analysis cannot be said to make use of any terms that are clearly *non*psychological. And from a metaphysical point of view, it faces some of the same issues that are faced by all purely psychological analyses of personal identity.

In recent philosophical discussions, the main question about psychological analyses of personal identity concerns whether they can accommodate all of the relevant logical and metaphysical aspects of the identity relation, especially its transitivity, its one-one character, and its necessity. But as chapter 2 has already made clear, neo-Lockeans have shown that there are many ways to handle these issues within a purely psychological analysis of personal identity. Since this book offers no new arguments with respect to these issues, it will leave them to one side. Instead, it will, with just one exception, focus on metaphysical issues that are *uniquely* raised by the normative analysis of personal identity, and the account of the kind 'person' from which it derives. The first issue concerns the relation between persons and human beings. The next concerns what kind of possibility is being affirmed, and on what grounds, when it is affirmed that multiple and group persons are possible. The third issue concerns the sense in which the normative analysis of personal identity is a reductionist analysis. This is an issue that arises for all purely psychological analyses of personal identity, and for other analyses as well. But the reductionist character of the normative analysis has an implication that is not shared, or at least not claimed, by any other analysis of personal identity, which is that the boundaries between persons are vague, not only over time (which many reductionists have affirmed), but even at a time.

Personal and Human Nature

The positive arguments for the possibility of group and multiple persons make a number of claims about human nature. These claims include: human beings have a *potential* for distinctively personal activities and relations; this potential cannot be realized without *generating* rational points of view from which persons deliberate and act; human beings are not *born* with such rational points of view—that is, they are not born persons in the sense defined by the ethical criterion of personhood; human beings do not, strictly speaking, *become* persons either, if that implies that the persons who come to be must be identical with human beings; human beings are, rather, the *site* of personal lives.[5]

There might seem to be a regressive paradox here. Persons are distinguished by having certain rational and practical capacities. And it might seem that human beings could not have a potential for distinctively personal activities and relations unless they already possessed the distinctive capacities of persons as part of their native endowment. It might also seem that this potential could not be realized except by exercising these distinctively personal capacities. But these are capacities that can be exercised only by a person, and only from that person's particular rational point of view. So it might therefore seem that human beings would already have to *be* persons in order to *generate* persons.

This appearance of paradox harks back to the second of the two issues that chapter 4 raised and postponed (the first was addressed in the last section; it concerned whether it makes sense to portray a person's commitment to achieving overall rational unity as a merely contingent and conditional commitment): if a group of human beings did join their rational and practical forces so as to integrate into a single group person, would they not inevitably retain their own distinct rational points of view? The presumption that human beings would and indeed must retain distinct rational points of view goes hand in hand with the presumption that now animates the charge of paradox, namely, that human beings must start out with their own distinct rational points of view, which they also never lose, no matter how much rational unity they achieve with other human beings.

The idea that human beings are not born with rational points of view, but rather have a potential to generate rational points of view that were not there before, does not really present a paradox so much as a puzzle. It is very similar to other puzzles that are raised by questions of genesis, especially in the sphere of reason and knowledge. For example, it is hard to understand how we can acquire a new concept on the basis of experience, because it seems that that would involve distinguishing instances of the concept, and it seems that that is something we could not do except by applying the concept—which

[5] Does this mean that two things can occupy the same place at the same time? Yes. See Wiggins, *Sameness and Substance*, for a vigorous defense of this idea that proceeds from essentialist assumptions. These assumptions entail, against Gibbard, that a statue and a piece of clay might be composed of exactly the same matter, and exist at exactly the same place and time, and yet be distinct—because they differ in their modal properties. (See Allan Gibbard, "Contingent Identity," *Journal of Philosophical Logic* 4 [1975]: 187–222.) However, the claim being made here does not really depend on this essentialist argument, for in general, there will always be differences between persons and human beings *besides* modal differences—in particular, spatio-temporal differences. This is so even in the case of human-size persons, since their lives never begin at human birth and sometimes end before human death.

But of course, it would only be if the life of a particular person coincided *exactly* with the life of a human being that the question would arise whether they were identical or distinct. See Michael Della Rocca, "Essentialists and Essentialism," *Journal of Philosophy* 93 (1996): 186–202 for a critique of the claim that essentialism would require them, or Gibbard's statue and piece of clay, to be distinct.

suggests that we must already possess an empirical concept in order to acquire it. This puzzle about concept acquisition might lead some philosophers to conclude (rashly) that all concepts must be innate. But if we are willing to allow that, somehow, we can acquire new concepts from experience that we did not have before, then we ought also to allow for a similar phenomenon in the practical sphere. Somehow, human beings do realize their potential for distinctively personal activities and relations, and in doing so, they generate rational points of view *that were not there before*. This point is worth making as a general point that applies not only to group persons comprised of human beings, to whom it *obviously* must apply, but even to human-size persons to whom its application may not be quite so obvious. Human beings are not born with temporally extended rational points of view, which take the past and the future into account. This is rather a human *development*. The arguments that have been presented here merely add that the result of this sort of human development need not be a one-one correspondence between human beings and rational points of view, not even at a time.

Of course, even if there were no such one-to-one correspondence—that is, even if there actually were group persons and multiple persons—it surely seems empirically accurate to say of our planet, right now at any rate, that no rational points of view are ever realized in anything but human matter. For group persons and multiple persons, even were they to exist on our planet right now, would, from what we actually know right now on our planet, be composed of human material. That, at any rate, is all that has been argued for here, namely, that there is potential for personhood in *human* beings, whether it flowers in human-size persons or in group persons or in multiple persons. This does not rule out that other animals could have the same potential for distinctively personal activities and relations that human beings have. And perhaps even machines could have this potential. It would always be easy to tell if this potential for personhood were actualized in anything besides a human being. As chapter 3 made clear, the ethical criterion imposes strong epistemic requirements on personhood: persons are essentially the sorts of things that are knowable by other persons, for otherwise, they could not engage in agency-regarding relations with other persons and would not satisfy the ethical criterion of personhood.

Whether it really is possible that some persons are realized in machines, say, depends on whether the functionalist theory of mind is correct, according to which the same mental events, states, and relations can be multiply realized in very different sorts of material conditions—both organic and nonorganic. This brings us to our next metaphysical issue.

What Kind of Possibility Is Being Affirmed?

Just as this book is agnostic about Locke's claim that the unity of consciousness has no organic basis in animal identity, so also it is agnostic about the functionalist thesis of multiple realizability (the reasons why will be given below). Given so much agnosticism, the following question must be addressed: How can the book *affirm* the possibility of multiple and group persons with so much confidence when it does not affirm but *remains agnostic* about the possibility that Locke envisaged in his thought experiment about the prince and the cobbler, which is that a single consciousness might be transferred from one body to another? In neither case has it been claimed that we have any *actual* cases in hand to prove them. (Remember, although the argument for the possibility of multiple persons within a single human being does appeal to the actual phenomenon of multiple personality disorder, it does not claim that alter personalities actually *are* such multiple persons.) So why then the differential response to Locke's possibility on the one hand and the possibility of group and multiple persons on the other? What makes the two cases of what is imagined to be possible so different, that one possibility should be described in agnostic terms and the other in affirmative terms?

Locke seemed to think that his thought experiment about the prince and the cobbler entitled him to affirm that a single consciousness could be transferred from one body to another. But all that the experiment really shows is that he could *conceive* this possibility. And that does not suffice to show that it is a *real* possibility, in the sense of being consistent with the laws of nature. After all, we can also conceive the possibility that we are not bound by gravity to the earth's surface. But we cannot take this conception to be of a real possibility, since it is inconsistent with our scientific understanding. The difficulty for Locke is that his conception might similarly be undermined by advances in our cognitive scientific understanding. Whether it will be so undermined depends upon whether we can provide an adequate *explanation* of the unity of consciousness without appealing to the condition of animal identity. The gravest shortcoming of Locke's own discussion of personal identity is that he failed to acknowledge the need for such an explanation—or even the possibility of one. As chapter 1 explained, he regarded the unity of consciousness as a brute fact that has no ground or explanation in any biological (or indeed any other metaphysical) condition. That is precisely why he thought that the same consciousness could be transferred from one human body to another.

Unlike Locke's, this account of personhood and personal identity has not tried to avoid the explanatory task that confronts it. On the contrary. It is precisely by taking on that explanatory task that the account earns its right to affirm that the possibilities which it envisages, of multiple and group persons, are real possibilities. What, then, is the explanatory task? To explain why persons are committed to achieving overall rational unity within themselves.

It will soon emerge that this explanation has already been presented, but without being labeled as such, for it is really contained in the normative analysis of personal identity. It will also emerge that the explanation can be accepted, along with its implication about the possibility of multiple and group persons, *without* waiting for any future advances in cognitive science. That is why this book is entitled, in a way that Locke was not, to its possibility claim.

However, before proceeding to the explanatory task that will vindicate the book's affirming of a possibility claim, it is worth digressing, to consider a philosophical perspective from which it *appears* to be no better off than Locke's (or, alternatively, that Locke is no worse off in his possibility claim than this book is in its possibility claim). From this perspective, it appears that *his* claim can also be vindicated without waiting for advances in our cognitive scientific understanding. If it can be shown that this is *merely* an appearance, then one would have made clear why Locke s position demands agnosticism.

The perspective in question is the perspective of functionalism, where functionalism is not taken to be an empirical theory about the nature of the mental, but is taken rather to be an analytical doctrine about the concept of the mental. According to this version of functionalist doctrine, it is in principle possible to analytically reduce *all* mental concepts to functional terms. Such a functionalist reduction of the mental would indeed vindicate Locke, for it is a defining feature of functions that they can be multiply realized in very different material conditions. It follows that a single functional process could be successively realized in a series of different material conditions (think again of the sort of calculation described in chapter 1, that begins in the head, then proceeds to pen and paper, and expands to include a calculator, and is finally completed by a sophisticated computer). And so, insofar as the phenomenological unity of consciousness can be reduced to functional terms, it seems that it too could be successively realized in a series of different material conditions—including different human bodies, just as Locke envisaged.[6]

There are several points that need to be registered in response to this functionalist vindication of Locke.

First, the availability of a functionalist account of the possibility that he affirmed in his thought experiment does not mean that *he himself* was entitled to affirm it. Functionalism offers a particular *explanation* of the unity of consciousness, in the light of which we can make sense of the possibility that the individual consciousnesses of the prince and the cobbler could be switched. In contrast, Locke denied that there is, or even could be, any such explanation.[7]

Second, even if Locke were to avail himself of the functionalist explanation of the unity of consciousness, that would not mean that the normative analysis was any worse off than his. Just as functionalism would entitle Locke to affirm

---

[6] See Daniel Dennett's "Where am I?" in *Brainstorms*, (Cambridge, Mass.: Bradford Books, 1978) for a highly entertaining account of this possibility as it would be provided for if functionalism is true.

[7] There is, however, a family resemblance between Locke's understanding of what a single consciousness is and the functionalist understanding of it. He seemed to think of it mainly in *relational* terms—that is, as a relation that a person has in the present to its own present and past thoughts. And the effect of his arguments about personal identity was really to abstract this relation away from all material conditions, much as the functionalist aims to do for each and every mental kind. But of course, Locke was not embarked on that functionalist project. And in fact, his empiricist epistemology does not square well with that project. He took for granted that our experiences have an *irreducibly qualitative* aspect that cannot be explained in any other terms. And that is precisely what functionalism denies.

the possibility that he envisaged, so also it would entitle us to affirm the possibility that the normative analysis leads us to envisage, of multiple and group persons. After all, the point of functionalism's multiple realizability thesis is not just that the same mental functions can be realized in different sorts of *stuff*, organic and nonorganic alike; the thesis also implies that there are no restrictions of *scale*. This means that the same mental functions can be writ large or small, precisely as in the cases of group and multiple persons. (However, this is usually thought to be an *objection* to functionalism, since it has the counterintuitive consequence that there could be a single mind that was as large as the whole universe.)[8]

But third, this book chooses not to rest its case for multiple and group persons on the truth of functionalist doctrine. This is not because it regards the doctrine as subject to philosophical refutation on the usual sorts of grounds that philosophers offer, such as that the phenomenological and normative aspects of the mental defy functionalist reduction.[9] It is rather because there is room for skepticism about whether the doctrine really is a purely *analytical* doctrine that can be confirmed or infirmed only by philosophical argument, and hence has no *empirical import* by virtue of which it can be confirmed or infirmed by scientific findings in psychology and the surrounding disciplines of cognitive science. Insofar as functionalism is a theory with empirical import, then given our current state of knowledge about the nature of the mental, we ought to be agnostic about its truth—and in that case, we ought also to remain agnostic about the possibility that Locke raised in his thought experiment, just as chapter 1 urged.

One of the attractions of functionalism is that it would allow us to retain a quasi-Cartesian intuition about the irreducibility of our mental concepts to material terms within a materialist metaphysics,[10] for although it is true that no mental functions can actually exist except by being materially realized, the multiple realizability thesis ensures that there can be no reduction of such functions to material terms. There is certainly an analytical connection between the concept of a function and the thesis about multiple realizability. But of course, functionalism is an analytical doctrine about the *mind* only

[8] For a discussion of this and other difficulties facing functionalism see Ned Block, "Troubles with Functionalism," in *Perception and Cognition*, ed. W. Savage, Minnesota Studies in the Philosophy of Science, vol. 9 (Minneapolis: University of Minnesota Press, 1978).

[9] The literature claiming and discussing that the phenomenological element in mentality cannot be captured is enormous and well known. For a valuable discussion of the issues, even if it is by those who eventually think a modified and supplemented functionalism can accommodate the phenomenological element, see Sydney Shoemaker, "The Inverted Spectrum," *Journal of Philosophy* 79 (1982): 357–81; and Ned Block, "Are Absent Qualia Impossible?" *Philosophical Review* 89 (1980): 257–74. For the claim that functionalism cannot capture the normative element in mentality see Saul Kripke, *Wittgenstein on Rules and Private Language* (Oxford: Basil Blackwell, 1982), pp. 35–37; and John McDowell, "Functionalism and Anomolous Monism," in *Truth and Interpretation: Perspectives on the Philosophy of Donald Davidson*, ed. Ernest Lepore (Oxford: Basil Blackwell, 1986).

[10] See Jerry Fodor, *Psychological Explanation* (New York: Random House, 1968).

insofar as there is also an analytical connection between our mental concepts and the concept of a function. If there were such an analytical connection, then functionalist doctrine would indeed be insulated from all empirical refutation. We would be in a position to reject, a priori, any scientific claim that tried to restrict the multiple realizability thesis, such as a claim to the effect that certain mental phenomena, for example, pain or a feeling of elation or the unity of consciousness, are realizable *only* in specific organic conditions. And to be in that position would be to know, a priori, that there can be no illuminating *explanation* of mental phenomena except along functionalist lines. There could, of course, be accounts of how certain mental phenomena *happen* to be realized in the neurophysiology of certain animals. But such accounts could never shed any light on the *nature* of those mental phenomena, for their realizing conditions would necessarily be extrinsic to their multiply realizable nature. However, although we know this to be true, a priori, of *functions*, it is hard to be sanguine that we also know this to be true, a priori, of all *mental* phenomena. Those who are sanguine about this are likely to take the persisting interest that the mind-body problem holds in philosophy as a sign that they are right. Indeed, one good way to state the problem is in terms of an explanatory gap. In these terms, the problem is that we do not see any prospect of explaining mental phenomena by anything so conceptually and metaphysically distant from the phenomena as matter. And again, one of the attractions of functionalism is that it situates the mental in a material world, without in any way lessening the conceptual and metaphysical distance between them.

Now, if functionalism is an *analytical* doctrine, rather than an empirical theory, then it must be the case that this conceptual distance between the mental and the material could *never* be lessened by any advances in our scientific understanding. But there is an obstacle standing in the way of accepting this conclusion, which is that our concept of the *material* is not a very definite or stable concept. And the question we must ask ourselves is whether we really know now that this concept can never undergo a transformation, in the light of developments in the physical and biological sciences, that would close the explanatory gap that there now is between it and our mental concepts. Chomsky has pointed out that our concept of the material has already undergone enough of a transformation that it no longer gives rise to the metaphysical problem that Descartes faced, concerning the relation between mind and body.[11] For Descartes's conception of bodily interaction required direct contact, and his metaphysical problem was that this conception does not afford an understanding of how mind-body interaction is possible. But since Newton posited action at a distance, and since the stock of physical concepts has grown to include molecules and quarks, it is no longer clear precisely what stable features in our conception of body should absolutely rule out a systematic account of its relation to mind (or vice versa)—even one that affords more

[11] Chomsky, *Language and Problems of Knowledge.*

explanatory insight into the material basis of the mental than functionalist doctrine affords or allows to be possible.

These reflections do not, of course, amount to a philosophical refutation of functionalism. But they do call into question whether functionalism really is a purely analytical doctrine with no empirical import. They reveal that our concepts of materiality are open-ended empirical concepts, and as such they are subject to revision in the light of theoretical advances. It may be that such advances will never lead us to doubt the truth of functionalism and its thesis that the material conditions in which mental phenomena are realized are extrinsic to them (owing to their purely functional nature). But it does not appear to be an a priori truth that there could never be such theoretical advances, that is, advances that suggest a deeper connection between certain mental phenomena and certain realizing material conditions.[12] Insofar as this is not an a priori truth, then given the current state of our knowledge, we ought to be agnostic about the truth of functionalism. And that means that we ought also to remain agnostic about the possibility that Locke affirmed in his thought experiment, as chapter 1 urged.

So to return to our original question. Why is it that this book is entitled to affirm the possibility of multiple and group persons, while Locke (and neo-Lockeans who rely on functionalism) must wait for confirmation from cognitive science—at least if they are affirming more than a bare conceptual possibility? Because it provides an account of personhood and personal identity that *does* adequately address the particular explanatory issue that it raises. This

---

[12] It might help to give an example to illustrate how a theoretical advance could reveal a deeper explanatory connection between mind and matter than functionalism allows. Unfortunately, given the current state of our understanding, it is difficult to give a convincing example. What we need to imagine, is this: developments in cognitive science generate a clear explanatory need that we cannot fulfill without finding such a connection. William James thought that his psychology generated precisely such a need. He was committed to the idea that the notion of *habit* ought to be given a primary place in any adequate psychological theory. And this led him to subscribe to an extraordinary physiological principle: in any organism that is sophisticated enough to acquire and sustain habits, growth must take place *in the direction of* recently acquired habits. This principle has many potential applications and implications. For instance, it can explain why, when we are young, exercise routines into which we have recently trained ourselves are easier a few days hence: the muscular growth that has occurred in the intervening time has been in the direction of the recently acquired habit, that is, it has been of the sort required for the repeated performance of the exercise routine. More generally, the principle can explain why the young learn more easily than the old: they are still growing. But most importantly, the principle helps to explain why habits are sustainable in an organism at all, young or old, for it says that even the sort of growth involved in cell replacement and general body maintenance will be in the direction of, and hence will preserve, our acquired habits. It makes no difference here whether James's physiological principle is true, or even whether it is consistent with current neurophysiological theory. The interest of the principle lies in two things: first, it is a *physiological* principle that James introduced, and thought he needed, in order to account for the possibility of certain *psychological* facts, namely, the acquirability and sustainability of habits in growing organisms. And second, the principle itself would require theoretical backing from, and possibly theoretical change within, biological science more generally. See William James, *The Principles of Psychology* (New York: Dover Press, 1950), chap. 4.

issue is not what explains the unity of a person's consciousness, but what explains a person's commitment to overall rational unity.

It might seem that there is no room for explanation here, since the ethical criterion of personhood *defines* persons in such a way that nothing will count as a person unless it has a commitment to overall rational unity. Yet this stipulative definition does leave room for an explanation. We can still ask, what is it *about* individual persons *by virtue of which* they have this commitment? Or, to formulate the question in a way that connects the explanatory issue with the issue of personal identity: what is it about the condition of a person's identity that ensures that a person will be committed to achieving overall rational unity within that condition?

The normative analysis of personal identity provides a clear answer to this explanatory question: the condition of personal identity includes substantive practical commitments to unifying projects, and it is *by virtue of* having such practical commitments that a person also has a commitment to overall rational unity. And section 2 has shown that there is no other condition besides such a commitment to a unifying project that *could* give rise to the commitment to overall rational unity. That is why the normative analysis provides a necessary condition of personal identity.

However, the normative analysis entails the possibility of multiple and group persons only if the condition that it specifies is sufficient as well as necessary for personal identity. And if it were not sufficient, then it could also be charged that the explanation that it provides of a person's commitment to overall rational unity is not really complete. To see what such explanatory completeness would consist in, compare the functionalist explanation of the unity of consciousness. Its completeness would be ensured by the multiple realizability thesis, for that thesis would obviate all appeal to any *further* ground of such unity beyond functionally defined facts. But can we similarly conclude that there is no further ground of a person's commitment to overall rational unity beyond the particular structure of rational relations and practical commitments that the normative analysis specifies as the condition of personal identity? It might seem that this *cannot* be concluded, precisely because the argument for the normative analysis begins from an agnostic stance with respect to functionalism. Thus, the normative analysis is intended to be consistent with the possibility that mental phenomena might *not* be multiply realizable. And indeed, it is intended to be consistent with the possibility that the specific intentional phenomena in terms of which it analyzes personal identity might be realizable only in human beings. Bringing this point together with the discussion a little earlier about the relation between human and personal nature, one can say: the normative analysis allows that the potential for distinctively personal activities and relations might belong only to human beings. But if human matter might be required for the existence of persons, and if the normative analysis makes no mention of human matter, how can the normative analysis claim to provide a complete explanation of what grounds the commitment to overall rational unity? Because the explanandum is a *com-*

mitment, which calls for a *normative* explanation that serves to *justify* it. That is why human matter per se has no explanatory role to play.[13] And the same would be true of any other material condition that might accompany personal identity if functionalism were true, and intentional episodes could be multiply realized in any sort of material condition. No such material condition could ever justify, and hence would not explain, a person's commitment to overall rational unity.

These reflections on functionalism bring out one important reason why the explanation that the normative analysis provides of a person's commitment to overall rational unity need not wait for confirmation from cognitive science. The explanation is completely *neutral* with respect to larger issues concerning the constitution and the causal basis of mind. But there is another, more obvious reason why the explanation need not wait for scientific confirmation: it is a *normative explanation* that supplies a justificatory, rather than a causal, ground of what it explains. Accordingly, the possibility that it entails is not a strictly theoretical possibility that would require scientific backing. It is rather a *practical* possibility. And all the backing it requires is the insight that we persons have into the structure of our own rationality and agency, for in general, we are able to think and act, except perhaps on some highly restricted and arcane matters, without a deeper scientific understanding of the constitution and causal ground of our own intentional activity. And without such scientific understanding, we are also in a position to see that certain possibilities represent genuine practical possibilities for us. The claim of this book is that the possibilities of multiple and group persons are among them.

How can we be sure that these are real possibilities for us?

First, we must answer the more general question: how do we *ever* know that something is a real practical possibility for us, especially if it is something that we have never yet done or even tried to do? There are three conditions that we would have to fulfill. One absolutely necessary condition is that we should find the possibility in question conceivable. We cannot *intentionally* do what we cannot conceive. (It should be noted that conceivability is, in many cases, more than a necessary condition; it is sometimes also an enabling condition. For example, the fact that we can conceive a constitutional government is a large part of what makes it really possible and, indeed, actual.) However, the mere fact that we can conceive a practical possibility does not yet show us that it is a real possibility for us. So second, we need to know *how* we would go about trying to realize the possibility in question. More specifically, we need to know that we have the relevant abilities, and we need to know how we could appropriately exercise these abilities in an effort to realize the possibility. And finally, it must be the case that none of our general knowledge (where that includes both common sense and science) points to

---

[13] As the last section explained, a person could have a substantive practical commitment, *in the light of which* it was committed to achieving overall rational unity within a certain portion of human matter. But it would be the substantive commitment, and not the human matter itself, that justified the latter commitment to unity.

any in principle obstacle to our success in realizing the possibility, if we were to try to realize it.

Here are some simple cases to illustrate the relevance and sufficiency of these conditions for knowing that something is a real practical possibility for us.

It is a real practical possibility for me to walk twenty miles in a day. I can certainly conceive this possibility. And I certainly know that I have the relevant ability, which is the ability to walk. Moreover, it is obvious how I would have to exercise this ability in order to try to walk twenty miles in a day. And finally, none of my general knowledge points to any in principle obstacle to my succeeding. I know that any human-size person who is in my overall state of health and fitness can walk at a certain pace (say, between two and five miles per hour), and sustain that pace for long enough to complete twenty miles in a day.

Now compare the possibility of my jumping one hundred feet into the air. This is not a real practical possibility for me. Of course I can conceive it, and I know what ability I would have to exercise and in what ways in order to realize it. But I also know that there is an in principle obstacle to my realizing it: I lack the requisite strength to jump so high, and moreover, I could never acquire such strength.

The case of jumping contrasts with another case that is beyond my present ability but that is nevertheless a real possibility for me, namely, the possibility that I could run ten miles without stopping. Although I cannot do this in my current physical condition, I know what sort of physical training would enable me to realize it, and I know that this training is within my general capacities. On the other hand, I cannot imagine being *moved* to undertake such training. And I feel nothing but aversion when I think of the prospect of running so many miles. My aversion is so great, in fact, that I shall probably never do it. Yet I do have the requisite ability to do it, and there is no in principle obstacle to my succeeding if I tried. So it is a real possibility for me.

This last point, about the difference between motives and abilities, will be crucial when we turn to the cases of group and multiple personhood. There is a temptation to view these as cases of something that is *psychologically impossible* for us. But we shall see that this view has more to do with whether we can be *moved* to pursue them, than with our *ability* to do so. Consider the Chinese ritual in which a daughter tries to save her dying mother's life by cutting off a piece of her living flesh and putting it into a soup for her mother to eat.[14] It would, in one sense, be psychologically impossible for me to perform either end of this ritual, for no incentive would ever move me to perform it. Yet I do have the relevant abilities to perform it, and I could exercise them in the requisite ways if I wanted to. So, despite being a psychological impossibility for me in one sense, it is a real practical possibility for me all the same. The same is true of the possibilities of group and multiple personhood; these can be real practical possibilities for us even if they should prove to be

---

[14] This scene is enacted in the film *The Joy Luck Club*, directed by W. Wang.

psychologically impossible because we find them highly, and even horribly, undesirable.

Let us consider more closely, then, why these are real possibilities for us. We can certainly conceive them. All we need conceive is that groups of human beings, and parts of human beings, could have the commitment to achieving the sort of overall rational unity that characterizes the individual rational point of view of an individual person. We certainly know what abilities we would need to exercise in order to realize these possibilities. In order to realize them, we would have to devise and embrace unifying projects that would require the relevant level of rational unity—either at the level of a group of human beings or at the level of a part of human being. And in order to do this, we would need to exercise the very rational and practical abilities that we already exercise in our own lives, when we embrace and pursue our personal projects and achieve the level of rational unity they require. The only issue that remains, then, is whether there is an in principle obstacle against our succeeding if we were to try to exercise these abilities in order to realize the possibilities of group and multiple persons. Since the obstacles might be different in the two cases, let us consider them separately.

It might be alleged that it is not really feasible for a group of human beings to achieve any very significant degree of rational unity. It is undeniable that such a group might well face enormous obstacles in trying to arrive at and execute all-things-considered judgments. For example, the human members of the group might need to confer and communicate more often than there is time for, or they might face computational problems of daunting size and complexity when they try to rank their preferences together or try to assess their practical opportunities. However, even if these obstacles proved to be insurmountable, that would not preclude the possibility of group persons. In order to qualify as an individual person, a group of persons need not actually achieve overall rational unity within itself. It would need only to be *committed* to achieving such unity. And falling short of that commitment is perfectly consistent with having it. Indeed, it is par for the course. Overall rational unity is, after all, a normative ideal of which every finite person is bound to fall short—and that includes all actual human-size persons as well as any group or multiple persons who might come to be. This brings to light an important caveat: we must not exaggerate the actual facts about actual human-size persons in the course of arguing against the possibility of group persons. And it would be an exaggeration to suppose that any actual person ever has come very close to realizing the ideal of overall rational unity. In fact, we fall so far short that some philosophers have suggested that we jettison the idea of an all-things-considered judgment from our philosophical psychology and theories of action.[15] Their thought is the obvious one, that we cannot, in fact, ever

---

[15] Daniel Dennett has suggested this in *Elbow Room: The Varieties of Free Will Worth Wanting* (Cambridge: MIT Press, 1984), though he has subsequently conceded that the unfeasibility of all-things-considered judgments does not preclude our commitment to the rational ideal of arriving at and acting upon them. See his "Reply to Slate and Rovane," *Philosophical Topics* 22 (1994): 558–62.

consider *all* things. And that is another way of saying that perfect overall rational unity is *not* a real practical possibility for us; we cannot ever succeed in realizing it. Yet we can embrace overall rational unity as a normative ideal. In order to do so, this is all that is required: that we conceive the ideal; that we can measure our own distance from it; that we can understand criticisms of us that draw attention to the ways in which we fall short of it; that we know how to and are able to take steps in order to approximate it better in the light of such criticisms. There is no reason to think that the practical limitations on groups of human beings are so severe that all this is not just as feasible for them as it is for us human-size persons. And it ought not to be overlooked that such groups might show great ingenuity in overcoming the special difficulties they face, which are not shared by human-size persons. For example, they could overcome their special communicative and computational difficulties simply by appointing an executive authority whose charge would be to make their all-things-considered judgments and to guide the coordination of their practical efforts accordingly.

The obstacles that might be alleged against our fragmenting into multiple persons would naturally be very different from those alleged against our integrating into group persons. Multiple persons would actually face *lesser*, and not greater, communicative and computational challenges than we human-size persons face. What else, then, might pose an obstacle to our ever succeeding in realizing this possibility? The answer is nothing. All we would need to do is embrace several different unifying projects that would give us reasons for achieving rational unity along different lines than we presently do—not within all of the intentional episodes that we presently regard as our own, but within different subsets of them (much as was described in section 1 of this chapter). Surely this is something that we have the ability to do. What it mainly entails is doing *less* of what we *already* do when we try to achieve overall rational unity within ourselves—for example, resolving fewer contradictions, making less of an effort to rank various preferences (in the sense of not trying to rank them all together), arriving at all-things-considered judgments that take less into account. Of course, when we try to imagine actually wanting to pursue this possibility, we might feel at a loss. How could we, who have a commitment to achieving overall rational unity within ourselves, set about trying to lose that commitment, and to want less rational unity than we already have? Although it is worth considering how this poignant motivational question might be answered, it is first important to remember that multiple personhood can be a real practical possibility even if it should prove to be psychologically impossible for us, in the limited sense that we do not want to realize it (just as in the case above, of the Chinese ritual). The point is that there is no in-principle obstacle to our realizing it if we *did* want to—which is what makes it a real possibility for us.

In any case, we should not underestimate the extent to which we might actually come to want to realize the possibility of multiple personhood. Imagine, for example, that you had a very strong urge to pursue a personal project that is generally forbidden, or at least very strongly disapproved of, in your particular social milieu. Thus on the one hand, you see that your personal project cannot be justified, given your social ties; yet on the other hand, you are unwilling to give up either the project or the social ties. Now, if your project cannot coherently be pursued within the context of your social ties, then the best thing for you to do would be to give up on your commitment to overall rational unity, and to opt instead for a "double" life—a fragmented human life in which two distinct persons figured; for the only other prospect you would face would be one of constant pain and frustration as you struggled to reconcile two practical commitments that are, ultimately, unreconcilable. And if you were able to see that this is so, then you might well regard the prospect of fragmentation into multiple persons with relief, and maybe even with enthusiasm.

However, it is not the intention here to show that there actually is good reason for us to pursue either of the practical possibilities that have been raised, of multiple or group personhood. It may be that these possibilities will never be realized in fact, because there is nothing *worth doing* that would require us to realize them. But this does not mean that they are not really possible. It remains true that we have the requisite rational and practical abilities by which we *could* realize them in principle, if only we had a reason for doing so.

The larger point here can be summarized as follows. Even if Locke were to have considered the explanatory question about what allows for the possibility he envisaged (something he never did because he thought it unexplainable), the *sort* of explanation that is needed for his sort of possibility is the sort that forces one in our present stage of knowledge to be agnostic about his possibility. But the case is different with the possibility claim being made in this book. The possibility in question is a practical possibility for persons. And we persons are in a position to determine that this possibility is a real possibility for us without our having to wait for the deliverances of science. We know what our rational and practical abilities are (indeed, we could not be persons in the sense defined by the ethical criterion of personhood unless that were so); and we know how we could exercise our abilities in order to realize the possibilities in question; and we recognize no obstacle to our doing so except a lack of motive. So apart from the issue of ability, the only other issue on which the possibilities being affirmed here depend is a normative one, concerning what would constitute a good *reason* for us to pursue these possibilities. Both of these issues are directly engaged by the normative analysis of personal identity. It describes the condition of personal identity in such a way that everything on which the normative commitment to overall rational unity depends is in place—*both* the rational and practical abilities whose exercise yields such unity (in degree) *and* the substantive practical commitments to unifying projects that *justify* the commitment. In consequence, the analysis fully explains how it is that the normative commitment to overall rational unity arises. And that is why it can support counterfactual claims about how the commitment *could* arise in groups and also in parts of human beings—thereby giving rise to group and multiple persons who are not identical with any animal.

The point of the contrast with Locke is not to show that he was wrong to distinguish a phenomenological point of view from the bodily point of view of a particular animal. It is merely to bring out that we do not presently *know* that these two things can come apart. Whereas, we *do* know that a rational point of view can come apart from both of these other kinds of point of view. Because this is so, and because we have good reason to equate the condition of personal identity with the condition in which there is a single rational point of view, we can conclude with Locke that there is *a* distinction between personal identity and animal identity, even while remaining agnostic about his own interpretation and defense of that distinction.

Is the Normative Analysis Reductionist?

Probably all psychological analyses of personal identity, including the normative analysis, are in some sense reductionist. However, the normative analysis is not reductionist in its aspirations. And its interest certainly does not lie in its reductionist character, insofar as it has that character. Its interest lies rather in the following facts: it follows from the ethical criterion of personhood; it implies the possibility of group and multiple persons; it therefore supports a version of Locke's distinction, thereby resolving the central philosophical dispute about personal identity. But since the issue of reductionism has been so central to recent work in personal identity, it ought to be considered whether and in what sense the normative analysis is reductionist. At the very least, this will serve a clarifying purpose. It will also set the stage for a further metaphysical issue that is uniquely raised by the normative analysis, concerning the possibility of overlapping persons.

The normative analysis certainly satisfies Parfit's main criterion for being a reductionist analysis, which is that it portray personal identity as consisting in "nothing but" certain sorts of events standing in certain sorts of relations, and that it posit no "further fact" such as a Cartesian ego (or any other sort of substantial essence).[16] The normative analysis mentions nothing but certain sorts of intentional episodes standing in certain sorts of rational relations. (Intentional episodes are events in the broad sense that Parfit has in mind, which includes not only actions and occurrent thoughts, but also standing psychological attitudes, states, and dispositions).

However, Parfit describes this sort of reduction as "weak reduction." He contrasts it with something he calls "strong reduction." It is a much harder question whether the normative analysis would qualify as strongly reductionist by Parfit's criteria. In order to so qualify, it would have to describe persons in wholly *impersonal* terms. The analysis does go a long way toward providing such a description. It makes no *direct* mention of persons. And as far as possi-

---

[16] See Parfit, *Reasons and Persons*, chaps. 10–13.

ble, it employs terms that can apply neutrally to intra- and interpersonal phenomena. Indeed, chapter 4 explicitly *defined* the terms "rational relation," "relation of reciprocal recognition," "coordinated activity," and even "unifying project" in such a way that they can apply indifferently to phenomena involving several persons or just one. We have seen that despite its deliberately person-neutral terminology, the normative analysis can nevertheless lay claim to having captured the condition of personal identity, because the condition that it specifies includes a commitment to achieving overall rational unity, and such unity defines what it is for an individual person to be fully or ideally rational.

An opponent of reductionism might protest that there are two quite different ways in which the normative analysis fails to analyze personal identity in *purely* impersonal terms. First, it illicitly smuggles the concept of an individual person into its analysans. Second, the relata in terms of which it analyzes personal identity always owe their identity to the particular person to whom they belong. So let us consider the extent to which these charges are true—but always bearing in mind that it does not matter if they are true, since the normative analysis would retain its interest even if it did not succeed in analyzing personal identity in purely impersonal terms.

The first charge fastens on the analytical connection just noted above, between the concept of overall rational unity and the concept of individual rationality. The thought behind the charge is that by incorporating the first of these concepts, the normative analysis really smuggles in the second. However, the mere existence of an analytical connection between these two concepts does not by itself show that the normative analysis implicitly makes use of the concept of an individual person. It might be that overall rational unity can *define* individual rationality without being in any way conceptually *dependent* on the notion of an individual person. Indeed, this thought is encouraged by the fact that rational unity is achievable in degree by groups of persons as well as by individual persons. Yet it must also be admitted that there is much to discourage this thought. We seem to have no *other* conception of rational unity than as an *ideal* that *individual* persons ought to achieve in their deliberations and actions by arriving at and acting upon all-things-considered judgments—or in other words, by achieving *overall* rational unity within themselves. And insofar as groups of persons do achieve degrees of rational unity, it seems that we have no way of understanding what this is except as an approximation of the ideal that holds for individuals.

Suppose that this is so. Then the concept of overall rational unity is not a strictly impersonal concept. And because the normative analysis makes use of the concept, it fails to be strongly reductionist. The analysis might also be charged with a certain kind of circularity. But just as it does not matter to the larger purposes of this project whether the normative analysis is reductionist, it also does not matter whether it is in this way circular. Even if the normative analysis does travel in a circle between the concept of an individual person and the concept of overall rational unity, it is a nontrivial and illuminating circle.

For en route from the one concept to the other, it traces a series of analytical connections between the following concepts: rational relation, like-mindedness, reciprocal recognition, coordinated activity, unifying project. But of course, this series of analytical connections does not serve to show that the normative analysis is, after all, strongly reductionist.

The second respect in which the normative analysis might fail to be strongly reductionist concerns a metaphysical, rather than a conceptual dependence, of the analysans on the analysandum. It might be charged that the intentional episodes in terms of which the normative analysis analyzes personal identity depend for their identity on the individual person in whose lives they figure. And in consequence, the analysis would have failed, in another way, to provide for a purely impersonal characterization of personal identity.

This claim of metaphysical dependence is often associated with Strawson's criticism of the *no-ownership* doctrine of the self, according to which mental particulars owe their identity not only to a particular *self*, but to a particular *body*.[17] The sort of body that Strawson had in mind was an animal body. Since the normative analysis does not take animals to be persons, there is a sense in which its status as a strongly reductionist analysis—that is, an analysis of persons in *impersonal* terms—is not threatened by Strawson's thesis. But of course, that would be to miss the intended meaning of his thesis, which is that mental particulars owe their identity to the *persons* to whom they belong. When we join this reading of the thesis with the normative analysis of personal identity, we get the following result: a given intentional episode owes its identity to the particular structured set of intentional episodes that constitutes the identity of the person to whom it belongs. Even if this is true, it is not clear that it poses any threat to or limitation on the reductionist character of the normative analysis. Although it preserves the metaphysical dependence that Strawson affirmed, of mental particulars on personal identity, it also entails a reciprocal dependence that Strawson did not affirm, of personal identity on mental particulars. This metaphysical interdependence of persons and intentional episodes complicates the issue of reductionism. Given the first direction of dependence, it would seem that the normative analysis does fail to characterize persons in purely impersonal terms. But given the opposite direction of dependence, it would seem that the analysis does not employ any irreducibly personal terms either.

However, it has not yet been established that the normative analysis either entails or presupposes the direction of metaphysical dependence on which Strawson insisted. The process by which persons (in the sense defined by the ethical criterion of personhood) acquire social knowledge of one another suggests a reason for thinking that it does.

Contrary to the natural Strawsonian assumption, persons cannot be identified by any *straightforwardly* bodily criterion. That would be inconsistent

---

[17] Sir Peter Strawson, *Individuals* (London: University Press, 1959), chap. 3.

with the admission of the possibility of multiple and group persons, who do not stand in a one-one relation to human bodies or to any other sort of independently identifiable bodies—independent, that is, of the process of identifying the structure of rational relations and practical commitments that, according to the normative analysis, constitute a person. What, then, is the process by which this structure is identified? It is a process of determining that certain events admit of intentional explanation, and hence qualify as actions that implement all-things-considered judgments. And the process of determining this involves identifying the other intentional episodes that constitute the rational point of view from which such all-things-considered judgments proceed. Thus it is a holistic process in the following sense: the ascription of each individual intentional episode to a person is provisional, depending upon whether it can be situated in relation to other intentional episodes, so that taken together, these episodes can be seen as constituting the sort of unified rational structure that characterizes the rational point of view of an individual person.

The holistic nature of the process becomes very clear when we imagine the following sorts of cases: we assume that we are confronted with a human-size person, but then discover that we are really interacting with a multiple or a group person. So for example, we might initially interpret the utterance "I intend to complete a college degree" on the human being Sybil's lips as expressing an attitude that would explain the actions of a roughly human-size person. But then we discover that it is really the utterance of an alter personality. What does this discovery consist in? That it makes no sense to interpret the utterance as implementing an all-things-considered judgment whose scope includes all of the thoughts associated with the human being Sybil. There is too much in that human being's behavior that is inconsistent with the intention of going to college (or even declaring the intention), and more generally, there is too little rational unity overall in that human being to interpret any of its behavior as actions that proceed from a single human-size rational point of view. But it does make sense to interpret the utterance as implementing an all-things-considered judgment whose scope includes a *subset* of the thoughts associated with the human being Sybil. That subset does exhibit the requisite rational structure so as to constitute a single rational point of view, the point of view of one of Sybil's alter personalities. The same holistic process is at work in the case of group persons. Thus we might initially think that a human being sitting behind a desk at corporate headquarters is a roughly human-size person, only to find ourselves confronted with utterances and actions that make sense only as the outcome of a larger corporate point of view. (This example should not be taken as an affirmation that all, or even any, existing corporations actually qualify as group persons—it merely takes advantage of a resemblance between the former and the latter; similarly, the remarks above about Sybil should not be taken as an affirmation that alter personalities generally qualify as multiple persons.)

The holism that is at work here is not dissimilar to the *structure* (not substance) of the sort of holism that Wittgenstein, Quine, and Davidson claim is at work in the interpretation of speech.[18] We lose our right to suppose that we have interpreted speech correctly if our interpretations entail too many false beliefs. Likewise, we lose our right to suppose that we have interpreted intentional behavior correctly if our interpretations entail too little rational unity, for then we cannot see it as the behavior of a single person who is committed to realizing the ideal of rational unity.

If we take this holism seriously, then we ought not to suppose that intentional episodes can exist except in the life of a person, for they cannot exist without occupying a position in the sort of rational structure that constitutes a person. But does this give force to the Strawsonian thesis, that intentional episodes literally owe their *identity* to their subject? It does, if it gives us reason to affirm the following counterfactual: the same intentional episode could not exist in any possible world except as an episode in the life of the particular person in whose life it actually figures in this world. Now, it is far from clear that the sort of holism just discussed above actually entails the truth of this counterfactual. But there is a more *radical* holism that would entail it. This radical holism was advocated by William James in *The Principles of Psychology*, where he declared that each individual thought reflects the *whole* of what has gone before it in the same mind, so that it is impossible for one person to think the same thought twice.[19] It does seem to follow from this sort of holism that an intentional episode is *essentially* an episode in the life of a particular person and could not exist in any possible world except as an episode in that life—and moreover, as an episode in that life lived exactly as it is lived in the actual world. If this is true, then perhaps the normative analysis is vulnerable to the second charge, that it fails to reduce persons to impersonal terms because intentional episodes owe their identities to the persons in whose lives they figure.

However, there is no need to refute *either* of these charges which conclude that the normative analysis is not strongly reductionist in Parfit's sense, of reducing persons to *purely* impersonal terms. It does no harm to the project if the normative analysis implicitly appeals to the concept of a person by bringing in the concept of overall rational unity, or if the notion of an intentional episode is not a purely impersonal notion. To repeat, the aim has not been to arrive at any reductionist conclusions, strong or weak. The aim has simply been to resolve the philosophical dispute about personal identity on the basis of a substantive account of what kind of thing a person is.

But just for the record, the account *has* delivered a weakly reductionist conclusion. An individual person consists in *nothing but* the structure of ra-

---

[18] See Ludwig Wittgenstein, *Philosophical Investigations* (New York: Macmillan, 1953), sec. 207; Willard van Orman Quine, *Word and Object* (Cambridge: MIT Press, 1960), chap. 2; Donald Davidson, *Inquiries into Truth and Interpretation* (New York: Oxford University Press, 1984), essays 9–12.

[19] James, *Principles of Psychology*, chap. 9.

tional relations and practical commitments that the normative analysis of personal identity specifies. And this weakly reductionist conclusion has been instrumental in resolving the dispute about personal identity, for it entails that the condition of personal identity is not the condition of animal identity.

Overlapping Persons

According to Parfit, weak reductionism entails that the facts that constitute personal identity—namely, that certain sorts of events stand in certain sorts of relations—are not "all or nothing," but can obtain in degree.[20] Within standard psychological accounts of personal identity, here is what this thesis about degree is generally taken to mean: personal identity is constituted by certain facts that obtain when mental events are bound by such relations as memory, anticipation, similarity, and so forth; and because more or fewer of these relations can hold over time, and for longer and shorter periods of time, these identity-constituting facts are a matter of degree. In everyday terms, the point is that persons undergo psychological change over time, and there is an issue about how *much* psychological change a person can undergo (e.g., how much memory loss or how much change in evaluative outlook) without ceasing to be altogether and giving way to a new person. And insofar as such psychological change is a matter of degree, there may be no nonarbitrary way to specify this boundary between two persons, which marks the death of one and the birth of another.

In general, discussions of this issue about personal identity over time take for granted that no similar issue arises for personal identity at a time. The assumption seems to be that the latter issue is easily settled, perhaps by appeal to whether events coexist within a single animal body or a single consciousness. Given such an appeal, the facts that ground personal identity at a time might be all or nothing even though the facts that ground personal identity over time are not. But the normative analysis of personal identity makes no such appeal to bodily identity or phenomenological unity. Instead, it portrays personal identity at a time in exactly the same way that it portrays personal identity over time—as grounded in certain sorts of rational relations that hold among certain sorts of intentional episodes, namely, the sorts of relations and episodes that make deliberation and coordinated activities possible. These relations can hold in varying degrees at a time as well as over time. And it would seem to follow that the boundaries between one person and another can be just as hard to pin down at a time as over time.

However, this vagueness of boundaries between persons at a time is, in an important way, unlike the vagueness of boundaries between persons over time. Within most psychological analyses of personal identity, the latter vagueness is associated with a *spectrum* of gradual psychological change, and

[20] Other reductionists agree. See, for example, Lewis, "Survival and Identity," in *Philosophical Papers*; reprinted in Amelie Rorty, ed., *The Identities of Persons* (Berkeley: University Press, 1979).

the problem is that there is no nonarbitrary basis on which to *mark* the temporal boundaries between persons on this spectrum. But the normative analysis does not imply that there is a similar spectrum at a time, so that one person gradually shades off into another simultaneously existing person. What it implies is rather that it may be hard to settle whether a particular intentional episode belongs to one person rather than to another. And the possibility that it raises is that a single such episode might actually figure in the life of more than one person.[21]

It is not entirely clear that this possibility of overlapping persons is actually *entailed* by the normative analysis of personal identity. For perhaps one could with consistency embrace the analysis and yet—perhaps on some independent metaphysical ground—deny that persons could overlap in this way. But at the very least, the analysis does invite us to examine the possibility.

Initially, it seems highly counterintuitive to suppose that persons could overlap, in the sense of having intentional episodes in common. And there are probably many reasons why this seems counterintuitive, some of which are worthier of consideration than others. The main reason why is that we do not normally have the possibilities of multiple and group persons in view when we consider the issue of personal identity. And that leaves us free to suppose that the facts that constitute personal identity at a time *are* all or nothing in the way that neo-Lockeans seem to take for granted (such as the facts of bodily identity and phenomenological unity, which arguably *are* all or nothing). But if we keep the possibilities of multiple and group persons in view, it is not hard to see that the boundaries between persons might be vague, and in such a way that they could be said to overlap.

Suppose, for example, that at the beginning of Sybil's analysis, her alter personalities qualified as completely distinct multiple persons within the same human being. It is not hard to imagine that after the analytical process had begun, there might be moments when the boundaries between these alters became vague. How might such vagueness give rise to overlap? Some intentional episodes associated with the human being might figure in the rational point of view of more than one alter, with the result that several alters might take the *same* belief or desires as a basis for action. This is not, of course, a point about psychological attitude-*types*—as when we say that you and I both have the same desire, say, the desire to go to China, for the *particular episodes* in our lives that constitute these desires on our parts would be quite distinct. What is being suggested here is that this may not always be so. A single intentional episode might animate the thoughts and actions of two distinct persons. Thus imagine that a single episode of desiring to please the analyst might figure in the lives of two distinct alters. This desire would naturally manifest itself quite differently in each alter because of the way in which

---

[21] As chapter 2 noted, Lewis's solution to the problem about branching entails the same thesis, that distinct persons may have intentional episodes in common. But on his understanding, when persons thus overlap at a particular time, they share *all* of their intentional episodes at that time. In contrast, the suggestion being made here is that persons can have just a few episodes in common at a time, and thus *partially* overlap at a time.

it interlocked and interacted with other episodes in their lives. It might lead one alter to engage in less destructive behavior while leading the other to be less timid.

If the case just considered seems unconvincing, consider a case of group personhood. For simplicity's sake, the discussion of group persons in chapter 4 portrayed them as being composed of *whole* human beings. Although that portrayal fit in well with the particular example that was used there, of a certain sort of marital arrangement in which two human beings literally function as one person, there is no reason why a group person should not be composed of just *parts* of human beings. So suppose that the Philosophy Department of Yale University became a department that showed the requisite rational unity, and thereby satisfied the condition of being a group person. (Remember, this would require that rational relations of like-mindedness obtain within the department, and that the department embrace commitments to unifying projects that brought in train a commitment to overall rational unity.) That group person would be composed of many human beings. But the scope of its commitment to overall rational unity would not very likely include *all* of the intentional episodes associated with each of those human beings—even at given moment in time, for many of those intentional episodes would be irrelevant to the deliberations and actions of the Yale Philosophy Department. This is really just another application of the point that was made in section 1 with respect to a philosopher and a musician who are multiple persons within the same human being. The philosopher is free to ignore in its deliberations certain intentional episodes within that human being, such as the musician's desire to practice the piano, because they are irrelevant to its philosophical projects. Likewise, the Yale Philosophy Department can ignore in its deliberations many of the intentional episodes in the lives of the human beings of which it is composed. Imagine, then, that thirteen *persons* are composed of twelve *human beings*. Twelve of the persons are roughly human-size persons (that is, each of them is composed of the greater portion of a single human being), while the thirteenth is the Yale Philosophy Department, who is composed of parts of all twelve human beings. What stands in the way of supposing that the boundaries between the twelve human-size persons and the Yale Philosophy Department might be vague in the sense under discussion, of giving rise to overlap? Suppose, for example, that one of the human-size persons believes that Yale University should do more to improve the lives of the citizens of New Haven, and this belief leads the person to do such things as write letters to that effect to various administrators as well as to the *Yale Daily*. There is no reason why this *very same belief* should not also enter into the deliberations of the Yale Philosophy Department—for instance, when it deliberates about how to dispose of its excess property, such as double copies of books and unused office equipment.

There are two different sorts of protest that might be raised against this portrayal of a group person. First, it might be protested that it is indeed the very same belief that animates the human-size person's actions and the Yale Philosophy Department's actions, and the reason why is that there can be no such a thing as a group person who is distinct from its human members. Second, it might be protested that insofar as there is such a thing as a group person who is distinct from its human members, then all of the particular intentional episodes that figure in its life must belong to it and to no other person. The second protest is a general protest against the possibility of overlap, whether the persons involved be group persons or multiple persons or human-size persons. And only it really addresses the issue at hand. The first protest simply misses the point of the last chapter's argument for the possibility of group persons. But just in case anyone has missed that point, here is a quick response to their protest here.

The example about the Yale Philosophy Department brought out that the same intentional episode would generate a very different outcome when it figured in the separate deliberations of the human-size person and of the philosophy department—one would write letters while the other would dispose of its excess property. These outcomes would be different partly because the two persons in question would face very different practical possibilities. Quite literally, there are things that a human-size person can do but that a philosophy department cannot, and vice versa. Now consider the deliberative perspectives from which these different sets of practical possibilities would be entertained. If a philosophy department can do very different sorts of things than a human-size person can, so also its deliberations about which of these things to do will take into account a very different set of attitudes, for unless it is a department that has only one human member, it will take into account attitudes that are associated with more than one human life. Thus, although the same belief might figure in its deliberations and in the deliberations of a human-size person, that belief will carry a different weight or normative force in the two cases. In each case, the belief will enter into a quite different rational structure, which is constituted by quite different attitudes. That is precisely why the same belief, namely, that Yale University ought to do more to improve the lives of the citizens of New Haven, can generate different outcomes in the two cases—letter writing and the disposal of excess property. Now, the first protest, against group persons, cannot deny the possibility of such different outcomes. Nor can it deny that these different outcomes would be generated by different background conditions—that is, that the letter writing would arise from the private deliberations of a human-size person while the disposal of excess property would be prompted by the discussion and resolution of a philosophy department. But these different background conditions are the different rational structures that were just mentioned above. So the protest would have to be that these rational structures do not suffice to constitute the distinct rational points of view of distinct persons. But insofar as they are bound by a commitment to overall rational unity, and hence deliver actions that implement all-things-considered judgments that reflect them, this protest is simply out of place.

The more pertinent second protest grants everything that has been claimed in connection with the example about the Yale Philosophy Department *except this*: that the very same intentional *episode*, of believing that Yale University should do more to improve the citizens of New Haven, could figure both in the life of that department and in the life of a human-size person. In support of this protest, it might reasonably be pointed out that nothing absolutely forces us to make this claim. We are always free to count the same belief twice over, so that there are distinct episodes of believing in which the two persons have a belief of the same type (they believe the same proposition). However, if the protest is really to stick, it is not enough to point out that nothing forces a count of one, whereby the two distinct persons emerge as having a single episode of believing in common. It would have to be established that something *does* force a count of two, so that they do not have the belief in common.

Certain views of personal identity might have forced this on us, such as the animalist and Cartesian views. This would have been so insofar as animals and Cartesian egos cannot, by their very nature, have overlapping mental lives. But no reductionist view of the person could ever enforce such deep metaphysical divisions between persons as these views do. And certainly, the normative analysis of personal identity does not.

But perhaps we are looking at the wrong end of things. Rather than consider what facts about *persons* might have precluded their having intentional episodes in common, perhaps we ought to consider what facts about *intentional episodes* might preclude this. Yet it is not clear what features of them would preclude it.

Suppose, for example, that all such episodes must have a phenomenological character, by virtue of which they are apprehendable in consciousness.[22] Should this feature of phenomenology preclude the possibility of overlapping persons? No. For one thing, the notion of overlapping consciousnesses is perfectly intelligible. And for another, the normative analysis provides a way of conceiving overlapping persons without overlapping consciousnesses. The normative analysis implies that phenomenological unity is neither necessary nor sufficient for personal identity, and so it implies that a single intentional episode could belong to distinct persons even if it did not belong to distinct consciousnesses.

Let us consider next the feature of holism, whether the sort of radical holism that was briefly discussed above might preclude the possibility of overlapping persons. According to this radical doctrine, the content of each intentional episode in a person's life is determined by its relations to everything else that has gone before in that person's life. So it is impossible that *the very same episode* could figure in the lives of two persons, unless they were perfect psychological duplicates of each other. But of course the thesis about the possibility of overlapping persons was not intended to be restricted in this

---

[22] Cognitive scientific research makes this claim highly dubitable. See Daniel Dennett, *Consciousness Explained* (Boston: Little, Brown and Co., 1991) for a description of some mental phenomena that seem to lack a phenomenological character. But see Nagel, *View from Nowhere*, for a qualified endorsement of the claim—namely, that it is essential to any mental phenomenon that it at least be *capable* of manifesting itself in consciousness.

way. The whole point of it was rather to suggest that the very same intentional episode could figure in two quite different psychological economies. And it must be conceded that a very radical holism would undermine that point. Yet to concede this is not to concede very much, for such a radical holism would also entail that two distinct persons (who were not perfect psychological duplicates of each other) could never have intentional episodes with the same contents, nor could one person ever have distinct intentional episodes with the same content. So it would appear that the thesis that persons could share intentional episodes in common is no worse off than the thesis that they can believe the same propositions or think the same thought twice.

This book will not try to refute the doctrine of radical holism. And in that sense, it will not try to prove the possibility of overlapping persons. It merely wants to urge that the possibility should be taken seriously, along with the possibilities of multiple and group persons. Why should it be important to do so? Because taken together, these possibilities call into question the *metaphysical givenness*, and *separateness*, of the individual person. Within the framework of value theory, there have been many attempts to call the separateness of persons into question—by arguing in Kantian fashion that persons are in the position of having to reason universally for all persons, or by arguing as Sidgwick did for a parity between prudence and altruism, or by arguing for the broadly Hegelian conclusion that ethical issues arise for persons only insofar as they belong in a constitutive way to a particular community. But virtually all such value-based challenges to our separateness have something in common, which is the assumption that there are basic *metaphysical* boundaries between us persons that we manage to transcend by virtue of our rational and social nature. And this seems to be so even on the Hegelian view, according to which we are socially constituted beings. For it does not follow from that view that one and the same episode of thinking something can figure in the lives of distinct persons. Yet that may be the ultimate metaphysical consequence of the ethical criterion of personhood. Of course, the ethical criterion also challenges our separateness by emphasizing our ability to engage in agency-regarding relations, which involves *projecting* ourselves into the rational points of view of others and viewing evaluative issues from personal perspectives other than our own. But this ability *might* have been just another way in which our rational and social nature allows us to transcend the metaphysical boundaries between us—boundaries that are given and that never change. The really interesting possibility that the ethical criterion raises is that these boundaries do not need transcending, because we already live on both sides of them, and moreover, we can always redraw them.

This brings to an end the discussion of a range of metaphysical issues that emerge out of the normative analysis of personal identity that the book offers. There is one very large and significant metaphysical issue that remains to be discussed, which has to do with what makes a rational point of view a *first person* point of view, and that is the theme of the next and last chapter.

The First Person

ALTHOUGH the normative analysis of personal identity ushers in a new interpretation of Locke's distinction between personal and animal identity, it does
preserve his idea that the identity of a person is bound up with the identity of
a point of view—only it is a rational, as opposed to a phenomenological (or
animal), point of view. The procedure by which the normative analysis was
arrived at guaranteed that it would preserve this idea, for the ethical criterion
of personhood stipulates that persons are agents who can engage in agency-
regarding relations, and we have seen that each such agent must have its own
distinct rational point of view.

But if a rational point of view is to be a *person's* point of view, it must be a
first person point of view. There is of course an intuitive sense in which it must
be a first person point of view. It is the point of view from which a person
deliberates, and the goal of deliberation is to arrive at (and implement) all-
things-considered judgments whose very topic is first personal, namely, what
it would be best for *me* to do, all things considered. But all the same, there is
a question about whether the characterization of a rational point of view that
is implicit in this book s normative analysis of personal identity can provide
for an adequate rendering of various aspects of the first person, given how
remote its entire approach and rhetoric are from an overall Cartesian picture
and given its conceptual separability from the phenomenological point of
view. The first section of this chapter will deal directly with the challenge of
providing such a rendering. The second section will deal with the same subject of the first person but not directly with this challenge, for the challenge
will have been met in the first; rather, it will deal with some implications for
the ethical notions of accountability and of self-concern, to the extent that
these notions also seem to involve first personal relations.

Perhaps the hardest challenge is to show that the characterization provided
here can do justice to the privileged status of first person knowledge as being
immune from the sorts of error to which other sorts of knowledge are generally subject. This privileged status of first person knowledge is commonly
explained by appeal to a kind of Cartesian immediacy—that is, by appeal to
the idea that a person has direct phenomenological access to its own thoughts
and also to itself as the thinker of those thoughts. However, if a rational point
of view in the sense put forth in this book qualifies as a first person point of
view, then having such direct phenomenological access to an item cannot be
either necessary or sufficient for having a first person *relation* to it—that is, the
relation of *ownership* that a person has to its own intentional episodes; for it

has been established that such direct phenomenological access is not necessary within the rational point of view of a group person (whose human members may not be phenomenologically unified), and it is not sufficient within the rational point of view of a multiple person (who may be co-conscious with other multiple persons within the same human being). It follows that Cartesian immediacy cannot be either necessary or sufficient for first person *knowledge* either. And this consequence leaves us with the challenge of accounting for the privileged status of such knowledge without recourse to any Cartesian epistemological assumptions, and instead accounting for it within the framework of this particular account of the kind 'person', which derives from the ethical criterion of personhood and which entails the possibility of group and multiple persons.

It might be thought that there is a further, much broader obstacle that stands in the way of accommodating the first personal aspect of a person's point of view within this account of the person. Quite apart from the privileged status of first person knowledge, there seems to be a deep metaphysical difference between a person's relation to its own self and its relation to other persons. But this account of the person, as we have explicitly seen in chapter 4, seems to threaten the very *distinction* between intra- and interpersonal relations. It brings out that some distinctively intrapersonal relations have perfect counterparts in interpersonal relations. It also contends that where there are differences between intra- and interpersonal relations, these differences are often merely differences of degree. And finally, it suggests that two distinct persons could share, and hence both have a first person relation to, the very same thought. All of these scramblings that the account engenders in the distinction between intra- and interpersonal relations might seem to call into question whether there is anything which is truly distinctive about the first person relation that a person bears only to its own self and its own thoughts. However, this further obstacle is not really an obstacle at all, because it is quite wrong to think this is being called into question here. All that is being called into question is the Cartesian understanding of the first person, which places an exclusive emphasis on epistemological considerations. In contrast, this account will lay emphasis on certain *normative* considerations that can equally well account for the distinctive features of the first person—but without erecting a barrier, of either an epistemological or a metaphysical nature, between persons.

At the beginning, the book announced that even though it would begin its argument with what it called an "ethical criterion" of personhood, the analytic work in the account of personal identity was to be done by a normative analysis, where the term "normative" was intended in a very broad sense that has to do with rationality in general, and not with ethical considerations in particular. Thus the term "ethical" in the ethical criterion was not intended to mark any analytic work being done by ethical considerations in the normative analysis of personal identity, but only to mark certain implications for how a certain ethical prejudice involving hypocrisy could be generated by a failure to properly apply the criterion of personhood in terms of agency-regarding relations. So, to repeat, the normative analysis of personal identity makes no use or mention of any ethical concepts; its normativity resides solely in the fact that it characterizes the condition of personal identity as the condition in which there is a single *rational* point of view, which is governed by a commitment to achieving overall rational unity within it. Similarly, when this chapter will appeal to normative considerations in its rendering of the first person, it will focus on the normative relation that a person bears to its own self and its own intentional episodes by virtue of being the subject of such a rational point of view.

However, in addition to this normative relation, there are certain specifically *ethical* relations that also qualify as first personal, namely, accountability and prudential self-concern. These are ethical relations that a person can bear only to its own self and its own intentional episodes. Chapter 3 noted that these self-oriented ethical relations have figured centrally in other arguments for Locke's distinction. Locke's own argument fastened on accountability for one's own actions, and many neo-Lockeans have fastened on prudential concern for one's own well-being. Unlike the special features of the first person discussed in section 1, these ethical first person relations do not pose a challenge to the account of this book, because there is nothing in the book that repudiates any particular account that may be given of them in the way that the Cartesian account of the special features of the first person is repudiated by this book's normative account of them. All the same, something must be said to address the implications of this account of the first person for these self-oriented ethical relations. Section 2 will therefore explore the extent to which these latter ethical relations are, and are not, provided for by the normative first person relation that a person, in the sense defined by the ethical criterion, bears to itself and its intentional episodes.

1. The Distinctive Features of the First Person

If the rational point of view of a person, in the sense defined by the ethical criterion of personhood, is a first person point of view, then there must be a way to render the meaning of the first person singular pronoun so as to capture the sense in which this is so. That is, it must be possible to render the meaning of this pronoun in such a way as to make it intelligible that multiple and group persons as well as human-size persons could think and express first person thoughts. Once this has been accomplished, then it can be considered how well this rendering accommodates the distinctive features of the first person, especially the features that seem to invite Cartesian epistemological assumptions concerning the special status and source of first person knowledge.

A Revisionist Rendering of "I"

No form of thought can count as first personal unless it is reflexive; it must involve a conception of *oneself* as the subject as well as the object of the thought in question. This reflexivity of first person thoughts is expressed with the first person singular pronoun, by which a person reflexively *refers* to itself. And such reflexive self-reference seems to constitute the very meaning of the pronoun.

These remarks about reflexivity leave many questions about the meaning of the first person singular pronoun unanswered. For example, the normative analysis of personal identity says that a person is a set of intentional episodes that stand in suitable rational relations. That raises the question whether the meaning of the first person singular pronoun ought to be rendered so as to reflect the analysis. In addition, there is a question about how the reflexive character of an *act* of first person reference ought to be rendered within the terms of the analysis.

If the meaning of the first person singular pronoun is to be rendered so as to reflect the normative analysis of personal identity, then it must be understood as *referring* to a set of rationally related intentional episodes. Moreover, the pronoun may also be understood as incorporating the description "set of rationally related intentional episodes" as part of its *sense*. But of course, its sense must also include the *reflexive* aspect of first person reference. Now, any *act* of first person reference will occur in the context of a particular thought. And given the normative analysis, the most natural way to render the reflexive character of such an act is in terms of the token-reflexivity of the particular intentional episode in which the act of reference occurs. Thus when the meaning of the first person singular pronoun is rendered so as to reflect both the normative analysis of personal identity and the reflexive character of first personal thought, the pronoun's whole meaning is: the set of rationally related intentional episodes of which *this* (the present episode) is a member.

One virtue of this rendering of the first person singular pronoun is that it shows how multiple and group persons can think and speak in the first person. More specifically, it shows how a first person utterance can fall from the lips of a human being and yet refer to something besides that human being. It refers to the set of rationally related intentional episodes to which that utterance belongs. That set might be one among many multiple persons who cohabit the same human being, or the set might be a group person who is composed of many human beings (or rather, suitable parts of them).

This rendering of the meaning of the first person singular pronoun will not, of course, be faithful to the meaning of the English term "I" or its counterparts in other natural languages. The use of those terms is informed by commonsense beliefs about persons, many of which stand opposed to Locke's distinction between personal and animal identity, and hence opposed to the normative analysis of personal identity. It must certainly be admitted that users of "I" need not explicitly think of themselves in accordance with the normative analysis when they think and speak in the first person. That is, when they think in the first person, they need not have it in mind that they are a set of rationally related intentional episodes. They might think of themselves in accordance with the animalist analysis instead. Or their uses of "I" might not be informed by a commitment to any particular analysis of personal identity at all.

But in the context of the present project, the point of rendering the meaning of the first person singular pronoun is not to capture the precise meaning of the English term "I." It is rather to show what first person modes of reference and thought come to once the ethical criterion of personhood and its implications are accepted. Since the ethical criterion is itself a revisionary proposal, it is only to be expected that it should bring in train a revisionist rendering of the meaning of the first person singular pronoun.

The ethical criterion actually requires two different sorts of revision with respect to our understanding of the first person.

First, as has just been acknowledged, it renders the meaning of the first person singular pronoun in a way that accords with the normative analysis of personal identity, rather than with common usage (clearly, most uses of the pronoun do not reflect either a commitment to or even a conception of the normative analysis).

But more philosophically important, the second revision has to do with abandoning our Cartesian intuitions about the nature and basis of first person knowledge—in particular, about what accounts for its privileged status. The most striking bits of evidence for the privileged status of first person knowledge are: (1) the referential guarantees that seem to attend uses of the first person singular pronoun and (2) the special authority that persons are accorded when they report their own states of mind. It is generally assumed that these aspects of the first person cannot be explained without invoking Cartesian epistemological assumptions, which posit direct phenomenological access to the items known. However, for the obvious reasons that were recounted in the opening remarks of this chapter, such a Cartesian explanation could not apply in the cases of group and multiple persons. This account proposes to explain the special status of first person knowledge without recourse to a Cartesian epistemology. In fact, it will not make any assumptions at all about *how* persons may come to know themselves and their own minds.

A revisionist account of anything can be accepted only if it preserves enough of what it proposes to revise so as to avoid the charge of having changed the subject altogether. So although the revisionist rendering of the first person singular pronoun need not accord in all ways with the common meaning of the English term "I" (or its counterparts in other natural languages), it must nevertheless incorporate some central aspects of that common meaning. And if the resulting account of the first person is *neutral* on some of the epistemological issues that normally play a central role in such accounts, that neutrality must be justified. The proposed account of this book is marked by such epistemic neutrality, and so this justification will be a large part of this section's concern. That is, it will be shown that the central and important features of the first person can be accommodated without bringing in the usual Cartesian epistemological assumptions.

The most central and important feature of first person reference and thought is its reflexive character. When a person thinks of itself in a first person mode, it recognizes that it is both the subject and the object of its thought. That is, it recognizes its identity with the object of its thought. This way of thinking of oneself cannot be reduced to any nonreflexive terms. I have at my disposal many nonreflexive ways of referring to myself—by my proper name, my nicknames, and various individuating descriptions of myself. But because these are nonreflexive ways of thinking of myself, none of them can replace my uses of "I" without loss of meaning. This irreducibility is shown by the fact that my first person thoughts play a distinctive motivational role that is not shared by my nonreflexive thoughts about myself.[1] For example, I may wish that the person who is playing out of tune would stop, and it may be that the person I am thinking of is myself, but I will fail to stop playing unless I know in a first person way that it is *I* who is playing out of tune.

On the revisionist rendering, the first person pronoun means "the set of rationally related intentional episodes of which *this* one is a member." It thus incorporates the reflexive character of the first person in terms of the reflexive term "this," which refers to the thought in which it occurs. As a piece of phenomenology, this rendering of the first person singular pronoun is unconvincing. When I learn that *I* am the one who is playing out of tune, I do not seem to think anything so complicated as "the set of intentional episodes of which *this* thought is a member is playing out of tune." And this is not because I do not accept the normative analysis of personal identity on which the rendering of "I" is based. As a matter of fact, I do accept it. But even more importantly, it would not make for much greater phenomenological plausibility to leave out that particular analysis of personal identity and to substitute the roughly equivalent, but noncommittal, rendering of "I" as "the thinker of this thought." Except when I am thinking about the nature of first person thought, I do not seem ever to think thoughts like "the thinker of this thought is playing out of tune."

However, although it may be a bad piece of phenomenology, as a piece of philosophical psychology the revisionist rendering of "I" is actually illuminating. The special motivational role of "I" is shared by other demonstratives, in particular, by "now" and "here." By "motivational role" is meant just the role they essentially play in the production of actions, such as stopping playing in the example above or, as in the next two examples, meeting a seminar and asking for a ticket. I may intend to meet my seminar at the regular appointed

<hr />

[1] On the irreducibility of the reflexive pronouns, see Hector Castaneda, "He: A Study in the Logic of Self-Consciousness," *Ratio* 8 (1966): 130–57; and Roderick Chisholm, *The First Person* (Minneapolis: University of Minnesota Press, 1981). On their special motivational role see John Perry, "The Problem of the Essential Indexical," in *The Problem of the Essential Indexical*; and David Lewis, "Attitudes De Dicto and De Se," in *Philosophical Papers*.

time, but if when the time comes I do not know that the seminar meets *now*, I will fail to act on my intention. And I may need to ask for my airline ticket at the first class check-in counter, but if when I get there I do not know that the first class counter is *here*, I will not ask for my ticket. In all cases, the special motivational roles of these demonstratives are associated with their irreducibly reflexive character. Just as the reflexive character of "I" can be rendered in terms of the token-reflexivity of the thought or utterance in which it occurs, likewise for "now" and "here." For the moment, it does not matter that "I" is being rendered in accordance with any particular analysis of personal identity such as this book's normative analysis. That is, it will do just as well to focus on the fact that the aim is to render "I" roughly as "the thinker of this thought"—the special twist, by way of any particular analysis, on what a thinker is can safely be ignored. In other words, for the moment, it is enough to think about rendering "I" by the circumlocutory "the thinker of this thought," and there is no need to render it by the circumlocutory "the set of rationally related intentional episodes of which *this* (the present one) is a member." The point at the moment is this: just as "I" can be rendered as "the thinker of *this* thought," "now" can be rendered as "the time of *this* thought" and "here" can be rendered as "the location of the thinker of *this* thought at the time of this thought." These renderings of "now" and "here" have no greater phenomenological plausibility than does the rendering of "I" on which they are based. But it cannot be denied that to trace the motivational roles of all of these demonstratives to a common source would be a significant theoretical gain. And that is precisely what is accomplished by the circumlocutory renderings of them just proposed. The motivational roles of "I," "now," and "here" can all be understood by appeal to a single reflexive aspect that they have in common, namely, the token-reflexivity of the thoughts and utterances in which they occur, which is expressed by the phrase "*this* thought."

This theoretical gain notwithstanding, it might be protested that none of these renderings is faithful enough to ordinary commonsense psychology to be any more convincing as a bit of philosophical psychology than as a bit of phenomenology. This may seem to be especially true of the revisionist rendering of "I." Most users of the first person singular pronoun have never even encountered the normative analysis of personal identity as a set of rationally related intentional episodes. It therefore seems impossible that their understanding of the meaning of that pronoun should reflect that analysis.

At the same time, nothing can satisfy the ethical criterion of personhood unless it satisfies the terms of normative analysis. And satisfying the terms of normative analysis is not something that a person can do without *knowing* it—not in the sense of knowing that it satisfies this particular analysis of personal identity, but in the sense of knowing the *facts about itself* by virtue of which it satisfies the analysis. The analysis requires that a person be committed to unifying projects that bring in train a commitment to overall rational unity, and it also requires that a person's thoughts, actions, and other intentional episodes stand in the sorts of rational relations that would enable it to plan and pursue those unifying projects. And a person simply cannot have such commitments, or satisfy the background psychological conditions that would enable it to fulfill those commitments, without knowing it. The term "knowing it," and the idea generally of knowing that one has these commitments, and so forth, which is being insisted on is not, of course, intended to suggest that an agent has it always on the surface of its mind and awareness as it thinks or utters first person thoughts; it is intended rather in the ordinary sense of assenting readily if asked whether it has these commitments, and so forth.

Thus anyone who satisfies the ethical criterion of personhood and the normative analysis of personal identity has fairly elaborate knowledge about the rational relations that obtain among the various intentional episodes of its life. And in point of fact, most actual users of the first person pronoun do satisfy the ethical criterion, and hence do have such knowledge. Moreover, their uses of the pronoun are often informed by this knowledge. For example, whenever I remember a past event of my life, I implicitly know that there is a rational relation (in this case memory, which is a special case of what the normative analysis calls "relations of reciprocal recognition") that obtains between my present intentional episode and some past intentional episode; similarly when I anticipate future intentional episodes and intend future actions. In fact, it is an explicit part of the content of these sorts of intentional episodes that they stand in specific rational relations—of remembering, anticipating, or intending—to other intentional episodes. And this generally goes hand in hand with a specifically first person content: I remember what *I* did; I anticipate and/or intend what *I* will do. Because all of these uses of "I" are so highly informed by knowledge of the various rational relations that obtain among intentional episodes, it is not so outlandish to propose that a reference to such relations be built into the very meaning of the first person singular pronoun.

One of the primary motives behind this proposal is that it helps to complete the argument for the possibility of group and multiple persons by showing how it is that they are capable of first person reference and thought. It seems clear that in their cases, first person thinking will involve an explicit conception of how rational relations constitute their existence over time. That is what will guarantee that their first person thoughts refer to the right things— themselves. Given the discussion so far, there are two grounds for supposing that thoughts on the part of group and multiple persons which involve the content "the set of rationally related intentional episodes of which *this* one is a member" are first person thoughts: they involve the sort of reflexive content that characterizes first person reference, and this reflexivity brings in train the special motivational role that characterizes first person thoughts. Although this way of rendering the first person is not entirely faithful to ordinary usage nor to the phenomenology of all that can be counted as first person thinking, the fact that it does preserve these two central features of the first person speaks in its favor.

All the same, it is one thing to say that uses of the first person are informed by knowledge of rational relations, and it is quite another to say that it is part of the meaning of the first person pronoun that it allude to such relations. Since the motive for saying the latter is expressly semantically revisionist, it is worth exploring its consequences more carefully. One of its consequences seems to be this. Not only is it the case that an act of first person reference may include, as part of its meaning, a description of the sort of thing to which it refers, namely, a set of rationally related intentional episodes; also, an act of first person reference might rest on and be *mediated by* such a description. This does not mean that the proposed rendering of the first person singular pronoun precludes the possibility that first person thinking might involve a feat of direct self-reference. It simply allows that first person reference can also be indirect. That is, it allows that referring to myself in the first person might involve my having to figure out which series of rationally related intentional episodes I am. Although it seems improbable that I should ever actually be in the position of having to figure this out, it is not improbable that a group or multiple person should be in that position. The trouble is, that is part of what underlies the commonsense intuition that these agents would not really be persons. Their inner lives would not have the properties that invite a Cartesian epistemology of mind, because such figuring out is entirely alien to that epistemology of mind.

This of course leads directly to the second respect in which this account of the first person is revisionist—namely, its deliberate neutrality on the epistemological issues that are generally regarded as basic to a proper understanding of the first person.

Referential Guarantees and First Person Authority

In the light of the discussion above of what first person thinking would come to in the case of group and multiple persons, one motive for epistemological neutrality should be apparent. It is to allow that such group and multiple persons would be capable of genuinely first person thought even if their knowledge of themselves and their thoughts did not conform to the Cartesian picture, according to which self-knowledge involves direct phenomenological access to the items known. But another, and ultimately more important, motive for epistemological neutrality is that it helps to bring out some of the limitations of the Cartesian picture even with respect to the sort of first person knowledge that actually existing human-size persons possess.

There are two phenomena associated with the first person that seem to support the Cartesian picture. They are the referential guarantees that attend uses of the first person singular pronoun and the first person authority that attaches to reports of one's own states of mind. Both of these sources of apparent epistemic privilege need to be examined in greater detail. Then it must be considered what sort of first person privilege the proposed revisionist rendering of the first person singular pronoun can and cannot accommodate. It will emerge that the best way to understand the nature and significance of first person knowledge is to demote epistemological considerations from their customary central position, and to substitute in their place normative considerations. In other words, the most important aspect of a first person relation is not a person's special way of knowing itself and its thoughts, but rather the normative relation that a person bears to its own thoughts.[2]

The first referential guarantee associated with uses of the first person singular pronoun is the guarantee of existence affirmed by Descartes's *cogito* argument. In each use of the pronoun, whether in speech or in thought, it seems that there must be a referent. Descartes was impressed by the idea that this could be known by the user—who is the referent—even if the user knew nothing else but that it was thinking a thought in the first person mode. But he went even further than to affirm the guaranteed existence of the referent of the first person pronoun; he also affirmed that every act of thought—even those without an expressly first person content—implicitly gives its thinker first person knowledge of its (the thinker's) own existence. This stronger claim was famously denied by Lichtenberg. Given the normative analysis of personal identity, it might be suggested that even the weaker Cartesian claim could in principle be denied; for it seems that there could in principle be a thought with a first person content that was not situated in a larger set of intentional episodes, and by the lights of the normative analysis, that would be a first person thought without a thinker. (An example of this might be an attempt at first person thinking from the imagined point of view of a group person that does not really exist.)

Within the framework of the normative analysis, the only thing that might stand in the way of this possibility, of a first person thought without a thinker, is holism about the mental. On a holistic picture, what makes a thought the particular thought it is—with its particular content and psychological role—is its relations to other thoughts in the same system of thoughts, that is, in the same mind or, as the normative analysis would have it, in the same set of rationally related intentional episodes. Perhaps this implies that there cannot, after all, be an isolated thought that is not situated in a thinker. Insofar as that is true, the suggestion above is false—there cannot be a first person thought whose referent fails to exist.

This holistic version of the *cogito* argument provides an interesting interpretation of Kant's Transcendental Deduction. He claims that it must be pos-

[2] See Akeel Bilgrami's *Self-Knowledge, Holism and Intentionality* (Cambridge: Harvard University Press, forthcoming) for an argument to the effect that the problem of explaining first person authority is wrongly posed as a problem in epistemology. Thus he goes even farther than the epistemological neutrality aimed for here. He claims that one ought *never* to ask, except in treating the exceptional sort of case, *how* self-knowledge is achieved. In his view, a proper and complete understanding of this special character of self-knowledge lies *wholly* within the domain of questions of responsibility and value.

sible to attach the "I think" to each of my thoughts. And he argues that this is not possible unless all of my thoughts stand in relations to one another in such a way that they together realize the sort of rational unity that is conferred by the categories of the faculty of understanding. The resemblance between this Kantian idea and the normative analysis of personal identity, in terms of a rational structure that gives rise to a commitment to overall rational unity, is undeniable. One important difference, however, is that Kant stresses that this unity is a merely formal unity. This comes out most clearly in the first paralogism, whose aim is to show that the Cartesian view that the pronoun "I" refers to a substantial soul is mistaken. This formal emphasis notwithstanding, it has been convincingly argued that Kant's "I think" can be given a metaphysical interpretation, one that accords well with normative analysis of personal identity.[3] On this interpretation, any actual use of "I" must refer to a particular system of thoughts, where what makes it a *system* of thoughts is the fact that the thoughts stand in the very relations of formal unity that Kant emphasized as belonging to the meaning of the "I think." Thus nothing counts as a self or person unless it exhibits this formal or rational unity, as per the normative analysis. But at the same time, it requires a particular, existing self to realize this formal unity, and this self is the referent of "I." If this interpretation of the Transcendental Deduction is accepted, then it can be read as a refutation of Humean skepticism about the self. And if something roughly like the Kantian argument, so interpreted, is accepted, then it would seem that there cannot be a first person thought whose referent fails to exist. And something roughly like the Kantian argument seems to be licensed by the holistic conception of mind.

If the holistic conception of mind should be rejected, then it must be allowed that there can be isolated thoughts. It would seem to follow that there can be isolated first person thoughts. And in that case, the normative analysis of personal identity, along with its revisionist rendering of the first person pronoun, would fail to guarantee the existence of a referent for all uses of that pronoun. This hardly seems to be a ground for rejecting either the analysis or the rendering. If there can be isolated thoughts, then there can be thoughts that do not belong to persons. And if such isolated thoughts can have a first person content, then there can be uses of the first person pronoun that fail to refer. It may be that neither of these is a genuine possibility. But even if these are possibilities, the following would minimally still be true: whenever a *person* uses the first person singular pronoun or has a first person thought (an "I-thought," as it is called), the "I" is guaranteed to have a referent. This is of course a trivial truth. But there is absolutely no reason why an account of the first person need do any more, in order to be acceptable, than the minimal thing of preserving this trivial truth. That is, an account of the first person need not license the inference

[3] See Patricia Kitcher, *Kant's Transcendental Psychology* (New York: Oxford University Press, 1990).

from the existence of a thought to the existence of a thinker; it need not support the first step on Descartes's path from hyperbolical doubt to certain knowledge.

The second referential guarantee that has been claimed for uses of the first person singular pronoun is that they are immune to "referential error through misidentification."[4] Other referring terms are clearly subject to such error: a speaker (or thinker) can use a referring term, and then identify the wrong thing as its referent. For example, I may gaze at the New York skyline and say, "The IBM Building is beautiful in the twilight," while the building on which I fasten my gaze, and which I take to be the IBM Building, is actually the Seagram Building. It is not clear how such cases are best construed. On the most natural construal, the words "the IBM Building" refer to the IBM Building, while my act of reference in using those words is a reference to the Seagram Building.[5] But it might do just as well to say that both I and my words refer to the IBM Building, and that I mistake the Seagram Building for the referent. This second way of describing the case fails to capture an important sense in which I seem to be talking and thinking of the Seagram Building. But what it does capture is the way in which I take myself to be thinking and talking about the very thing to which my words refer. In any case, the important point is that I may make a mistake in identifying the referent of the words "the IBM Building." To claim that uses of the first person singular pronoun are immune to such referential error through misidentification is to say that I cannot mistake anything which is not myself for the referent of my uses of "I," which of course refer to myself.

This claim of immunity can be challenged. Suppose that upon entering a store I look up at a video monitor, and on the basis of what I see I think to myself that I have terrible posture, but then, as I walk on I realize to my relief that it was not me but the person ahead of me whom I had just seen slouching across the screen. Here is a case in which I have mistaken someone who is not myself for myself, and in which I can be taken to refer to that other person with my use of "I." There is of course a temptation to deny that I can be taken to refer to anyone else with my use of "I," and to deny this is to try to save "I's" immunity to referential error through misidentification. This can be done by insisting that I must really have had *myself* in mind all along, and that I simply mistook a certain video image for an image of myself. But that is rather like saying that when I looked up at the New York skyline I really had the IBM Building in mind all along, and that I simply mistook the Seagram Building for it. In both cases, this sort of construal leaves something out—namely, that there is something I have in mind which is not the referent of the words I am

---

[4] The phrase is Shoemaker's. See his "Self-Knowledge and Self-Awareness," *Journal of Philosophy* 65 (1968): 555–67.

[5] This would be close to what Donnellan calls a "referential use" of a definite description—except of course that this is a case of a proper name. See his "Reference and Definite Descriptions," *Philosophical Review* 75 (1966): 281–304.

using. Just as I did in some sense think of the Seagram Building when I said of whatever I was talking about that it looks beautiful in the twilight, I also did in some sense think of the person whose image was on video display when I said of whomever I was talking about that she has terrible posture. And that is enough to show that uses of the first person singular pronoun are not immune to referential error through misidentification—a person can make a mistake in identifying the referent of its uses of that pronoun.

Nevertheless, it might still be claimed that uses of the first person are *virtually* immune to referential error through misidentification, and that any account of the first person ought to explain this. One bit of evidence for this claim can be drawn from considerations having to do with the interpretation of speech. Even if I have no clue about which building really is the IBM Building, my use of the words "the IBM Building" can still be interpreted as referring to it anyway. Indeed, that may be the best way to make sense of my utterances containing those words. In all such utterances I may intend to be talking about whatever is generally referred to by those words. Such an interpretation would of course leave me enormous scope for referential error through misidentification. I could constantly use the words "the IBM Building" while looking at other buildings, and in such a way that what I said was true of the other buildings but not of the IBM Building, and I could still mean to refer to the IBM Building. However, the case is different with "I." If I should constantly use the term "I" in such a way that on each occasion what I said was true of something else but not myself, that would call into question whether I could possibly mean to refer to myself with "I." In other words, it would call into question whether in my mouth "I" really was the first person singular pronoun. Thus interpretation does seem to proceed on the assumption that uses of "I" are virtually immune to referential error through misidentification.

Although this is not yet an explanation of *why* uses of "I" are not prone to errors of misidentification, the explanation does not lie far off. In the context of communication, speakers are—and must be—accorded a great deal of knowledge of the external world. Moreover, they must themselves be counted as parts of that external world, and they must be counted as knowing this, and their uses of "I" must be consistent with such knowledge about themselves. Indeed, this is absolutely required if they are to be capable of communication at all. For example, a speaker must have the sort of self-knowledge that coincides with the knowledge that its audience has of it—and that it knows its audience has of it. Otherwise, it would not be possible for the speaker even to address its audience. This of course goes a good distance in explaining why an audience can assume that a speaker's uses of "I" are not prone to referential error through misidentification. The self-identifying knowledge in relation to an audience that is presupposed by any communicative effort is substantive knowledge on the part of a speaker of which thing in the world it is. And that knowledge is sufficient to give a speaker a firm referential grip on itself. (Once again it should be noted, in proviso, that the word *knowledge* here is intended not to convey that it is in the forefront of one's mind and awareness every time someone communicates.)

Not only does communication presuppose that persons have such substantive self-identifying knowledge; action in general presupposes this, for action requires that a person identify itself in relation to the things in the world that bear on its actions—for example, if a person is cleaning a house, it must identify itself in relation to various rugs and chairs and tables and mops and faucets. If a person did not have self-identifying knowledge that was adequate to meet its practical needs, with the result that it could not successfully carry out its practical endeavors, that would call into question whether it was an agent at all. This explains why a person's referential grip on itself is firmer and truer than its referential grip on other things—in other words, why first person singular reference is by and large immune to the sort of error through misidentification that is common in other kinds of reference. There is no other single object in the world, besides itself, of which a person must have identifying knowledge in order to be a thing that can communicate and act. That is, a person's *general* ability to speak and to act would never be compromised by the fact that it systematically misidentified any other *particular* thing, say, by always confusing the dean of the law school with someone else, or by never managing to pick out the North Star in the night sky; but this general ability would be compromised if a person could not correctly situate itself among many of the objects in the world around it—if it could not locate itself in social as well as physical space and time, so as to makes its practical way through them. (This is even true of group and multiple persons, even though the issue of their location is somewhat more complicated than it is in the case of human-size persons.)

This explanation of virtual immunity to referential error—by appeal to the presuppositions of communciation and action—accords very well with the normative analysis of personal identity and the revisionist rendering of the first person singular pronoun that goes along with it. The governing assumption about persons underlying these proposals is that persons satisfy the ethical criterion of personhood. That ethical assumption absolutely entails the further metaphysical assumption that persons are reflective rational agents who have a capacity for social knowledge and social interaction, including communication. So if it is true that agency and communication presuppose that persons have reliable self-identifying knowledge, that suffices to explain why it should be true of persons that their first person thoughts are relatively immune to referential error through misidentification.

If this explanation is not satisfying, the source of dissatisfaction must derive from its deliberately un-Cartesian orientation. What it fails to capture is the Cartesian idea that one's referential grip on oneself in first person thought is absolutely independent of any knowledge of oneself as a thing in the external world—indeed, it is supposed to be independent of any knowledge of anything in the external world. It is important to see that a commitment to this idea does not entail a commitment to the related Cartesian idea that a thinker is an immaterial thing. It might be supposed that brains in vats, and certain deranged persons can think first person thoughts without any knowledge of the external world, even though they are items in it. And furthermore, the proposed rendering of the first person singular pronoun does not absolutely preclude the possibility of first person thought in these conditions. On this rendering, the pronoun refers to a set of rationally related intentional episodes via a token-reflexive thought that belongs to the set. If such a set has a conception of what such a set is, and also has token-reflexive thoughts that accomplish reference to the particular set that it in fact is, then it thinks about itself in the first person—even if it should fail to have knowledge of the external world.

However, even though the proposed rendering can thus in principle allow for this Cartesian possibility, its rationale clearly goes against it. The point of the rendering is to capture what first person thinking and reference come to for persons in the sense defined by the ethical criterion of personhood, and a set of intentional episodes that lacked all knowledge of the external world could not satisfy the criterion, because it would not have the requisite knowledge by virtue of which it could engage in agency-regarding relations. So by the lights of the account of the kind 'person' being developed in this book, it would not really be a person. It would at best be a potential person. Recall also from the discussion in chapter 3 where agency-regarding relations were first introduced into the account of the kind 'person', it was frankly admitted that if skepticism about the external world were true, that would disable thought from being the thoughts of persons. And this raises the question whether the Cartesian idea is even relevant to an assessment of the revisionist rendering of the first person, which is meant to capture what persons who are not in the predicament of Cartesian ignorance do when they use the first person pronoun or think an "I-thought."

The answer to this question turns on the answers to two further questions: whether it is essential to first person thought that such thought be possible in a state of metaphysical doubt, and whether, if this is essential, this is also compatible with the proposed rendering of the first person singular pronoun. The second question has just been answered in the affirmative. But it might be suggested that that answer was wrong because it reflects a misunderstanding of what the first question, about first person thinking in a state of metaphysical doubt really means. When Descartes affirmed that first person knowledge of one's own existence is possible in the absence of knowledge of the external world, he also supposed that it is possible without any other knowledge besides knowledge of one's current thought. Thus in his view a subject of a first person thought need not have any knowledge or conception of a larger set of intentional episodes to which its current thought belongs. So it would appear that he did conceive first person thinking in a way that is incompatible with the proposed rendering of the first person pronoun as "the set of rationally related intentional episodes of which *this* one is a member." His idea seems to be rather that a first person thought reaches out to its subject just by virtue of its reflexive content, with no support from any identifying beliefs about oneself, including the conception of oneself as a set of related thoughts. If that were so, then the elaborate explanation provided above of the virtual immunity of the first person pronoun from referential error through misidentification would be completely unnecessary. Indeed it would have ignored the very aspect of the first person that, in the Cartesian view, constitutes its epistemological significance and privilege, namely, that the referential connection in first person thought is so immediate that there is no opportunity for misidentification.

The pull of this idea in discussions of the first person is strong. Even philosophers who are prone to think that Cartesian doubt is unintelligible like to suppose that first person thought requires no other knowledge whatsoever. It has been suggested, for example, that someone could think a first person thought while in a combined state of sensory deprivation and amnesia.[6] In these epistemically impoverished conditions a thinker of a first person thought might well be without any particular conception or knowledge of the referent.[7] And so it might well be a case where, if a feat of self-reference were managed, it would indeed be just by virtue of its reflexive content. But one wants to ask *what* it is that would have been referred to in such a case. After all, the other demonstratives share the very same reflexive character of the first person pronoun, and they do not refer to a person. "Now" refers to times, "here" refers to places, and "this" in its reflexive use refers to the thought or utterance in which it occurs. So if a use of the first person pronoun by a sensorily deprived amnesiac is to refer to the right thing, it would seem that it should incorporate as part of its meaning some minimal conception of the sort of thing to which that pronoun refers, namely, "a subject of thought." And to concede this is tantamount to conceding that the proposed revisionist rendering of the pronoun is on the right track. According to that rendering, the first person singular pronoun is roughly equivalent to "the thinker of this thought." All it adds is that the thinker is a person, and that a person is a set of rationally related intentional episodes. Since it has been shown that the example of the sensorily deprived amnesiac does not have the effect of making the circumlocutory rendering of "I" as the "thinker of this thought" to be fundamentally wrong, the question arises whether the example shows that there is something fundamentally wrong with this even more circumlocutory addition.

[6] G. E. M. Anscombe considers this possibility in "The First Person," in *Mind and Language*, ed. S. Guttenplan (New York: Oxford University Press, 1975).

[7] Anscombe, ibid., follows Wittgenstein (cf. *The Blue and Brown Books* [Oxford: Basil Blackwell, 1958]) in supposing that if first person thought really is possible without any substantive self-identifying knowledge, and if, moreover, it is absolutely immune to referential error through misidentification, then the first person singular pronoun does not refer at all. But there are overwhelming reasons to reject that supposition. The first person pronoun can occupy every grammatical position that a referring term can occupy, and there seem to be valid inferences from "I am tired" (spoken by Liz) to "Liz is tired" and "Someone is tired."

The interest of the example of such an amnesiac is supposed to lie in the fact that it illustrates how an act of first person reference might hit its mark in the absence of self-identifying knowledge, and indeed of all knowledge. To suppose that it can illustrate this is to suppose that it is an example in which there is an abiding person who thinks an isolated first person thought that does not stand in a set of rationally related thoughts. It was granted above for the sake of argument—in connection with the first purported referential guarantee attending the first person, the guarantee of existence—that it might be possible that an isolated first person thought could occur that was not situated in a larger set of related thoughts. However, it was also argued that in such a case the Cartesian inference from the existence of a thought to the existence of a thinker might not be valid. Now, the same possibility of an isolated first person thought has resurfaced in connection with the second referential guarantee attending the first person, the immunity to referential error through misidentification. In this case, it was granted for the sake of argument that there is an abiding person to whom the first person pronoun refers, a person who suffers from sensory deprivation and amnesia. But to grant this may not be compatible with the normative analysis of personal identity. So before trying to assess what the example about the sensorily deprived amnesiac might show about first person reference, it must first be determined what object, in such a case, could serve as the referent.

Suppose that a human-size person goes into a combined state of sensory deprivation and amnesia, and there is a complete rupture of all the sorts of rational relations that, according to the normative analysis, would constitute its personal identity over time. It would certainly go against a part of common sense to say that such a rupture would constitute the death of one person or that it might, depending on what developed by way of rational relations over time after the rupture, usher in the birth of another. But given the many arguments of this book, it should be clear that there are good grounds on which to say this. And to say this is to deny that there is a single person who precedes, then suffers, and finally recovers from the condition of sensory deprivation combined with amnesia. Now, reconsider the isolated first person thought that is supposed to occur in this condition. It is no longer clear *who* would be thinking that thought. If the thought should occur at the time of the rupture, it would belong neither to the person who preceded it nor to the person who might succeed it—it would belong to no one. For this reason, no act of first person reference would have been accomplished in the thought. But furthermore, even granting that there would at least have been an attempt at first person reference, it is not clear what conception of the referent would have been brought to bear so as to distinguish it as an attempt at specifically first person reference, as opposed to some other reflexive form of reference (such as "now," "here," or "this thought"). And so it is not clear what this case shows about the proposed rendering of the first person pronoun that issues from the normative analysis or about any other rendering of it.

The case would be different if the sensory deprivation and amnesia were not accompanied by such a total rupture of rational relations over time. If, for example, the amnesia was not so total that it amounted to an incapacity for thought, and if there was a critical mass of abiding beliefs and values, and if these abiding psychological attitudes made deliberation possible even during sensory deprivation, then it might make sense to suppose that there was an abiding subject who persisted through the amnesia and sensory deprivation. But such a subject could certainly think itself in accordance with the proposed rendering of the first person pronoun as a set of rationally related intentional episodes, since its first person thoughts would not be completely isolated.

Thus the case of a sensorily deprived amnesiac does not directly show that the proposed rendering of the first person pronoun is unacceptable. The point of exploring the case was to try to see whether it might shed light on the Cartesian idea that self-knowledge is possible in the absence of all other knowledge, and whether that idea shows that it is an essential feature of first person reference that it be accomplished without any identifying self-knowledge or elaborate self-conception. The case takes the Cartesian idea to an extreme by offering an example of a completely isolated first person thought that is not informed by any substantive self-knowledge or self-conception. Although Descartes certainly granted the possibility of such a thought, it may be that, even by his own lights, he should not have granted it. As he reasoned his way from dreams and demons to the thought that he is deceived, and eventually to the conclusion that he exists, and that God exists too, he needed at each stage to conceive his current thought in relation to the previous stages of his reasoning. That is, he had to conceive himself as an abiding subject of various thoughts, and he had to conceive his thoughts as not isolated, but as standing in various rational relations. All of this amounts, of course, to the very conception of himself that is required by the proposed rendering of the first person pronoun, as "the set of rationally related intentional episodes of which *this* one is a member."

If the Cartesian view of self-knowledge provides a strong reason for rejecting the proposed rendering of the first person pronoun, it has more to do with an allegiance to the coherence of skepticism than with the possibility of a completely isolated first person thought. It was the announced aim of the present approach to be epistemologically neutral. Such neutrality involves leaving all epistemological possibilities open, *including the possibility of a demonstration that skepticism is incoherent.* And the reason for this is that the question of Cartesian skepticism bears directly and importantly on the subject of the first person because most attempts at a coherent articulation of the skeptical position, like Descartes's, turn on and *require* exempting first person knowledge from skeptical doubt and elevating it to a privileged status. And the real point of insisting on epistemological neutrality was precisely to avoid this Cartesian assumption about the privileged status of self-knowledge. That is, the point was to remain neutral on the question *how* self-knowledge might be achieved, and to focus instead on what is responsible for its first personal character—what makes it *self*-knowledge. This has nothing to do with the relative independence of self-knowledge from knowledge of the external world, or knowledge of oneself in relation to things in that world. It has to do instead with its reflexive character, and with its special motivational role, and with some normative properties that will be discussed below.

If the referential guarantees that attend uses of the first person could not be explained *except* by appeal to the Cartesian view that self-knowledge is privileged and requires no knowledge of the external world, that would constitute a powerful reason for abandoning epistemological neutrality. But these referential guarantees *can* be explained in other terms, terms that explicitly connect self-knowledge with knowledge of the external world. It has already been shown how substantive knowledge of oneself as a rationally unified thing that is situated among other things in the external world can also underwrite those referential guarantees. To try to avoid all appeal to knowledge of the external world in an account of the first person would obscure why this is so. It would obscure the way in which the basic capacities of persons for action and interpersonal engagement necessarily depend on their having such substantive knowledge about themselves. The central point is that remaining epistemologically neutral does not require that knowledge of the external world be either denied or assumed. If such knowledge is denied, then the referential guarantees attending uses of the first person might best be explained along Cartesian lines. But if such knowledge is assumed, then those guarantees admit of another sort of explanation.

The main rationale for epistemological neutrality—for not insisting on the Cartesian picture of self-knowledge—has little to do with the revisionist nature of the normative analysis of personal identity, and the resulting revisionist rendering of the first person pronoun. It has to do with making the best overall sense of what first person thinking comes to for actually existing persons—that is, for things that have the distinctive ethical status of persons because they act in the world and engage with another as persons. But this is not to say that there is no revisionist aspect to this account of the first person as it has been elaborated so far. The account deliberately allows that multiple and group persons can have first person thoughts despite the fact that in their case there is probably no possibility of first person reference without substantive empirical knowledge of their identities.

Cartesian grounds are not the only grounds on which it has been suggested that first person reference does not ride on identifying self-knowledge. Another ground has to do with the theory of reference. Even if reference is always informed by descriptive individuating knowledge of the referent, it is usually the case that more than one thing could in principle satisfy a given description. And so it would seem that, in general, if a referring term is to refer uniquely, it must be in virtue of something besides an individuating description. The obvious candidate is a demonstrative relation that reaches out from the term to only one of the many things that might satisfy the descriptions associated with the term. And of course, such demonstrative relations depend on the very sort of reflexive content that characterizes the first person pronoun.[8] So, for example, suppose that I want to use the term "Empire Szechuan" to refer to a particular restaurant, but my descriptive knowledge of that restaurant comes to no more than that it is a Chinese restaurant on the upper west side of Manhattan that delivers passable food and that has the word *empire* in its name. As it happens, this description is true of more than one restaurant. But I can nevertheless refer to just one of them if I have at my disposal a suitable demonstrative tie to it, such as that it is the restaurant in which *I* am sitting *now*. Although it was clearly an advance in the theory of reference to give demonstrative reference a central place, it does not solve all problems in the theory of reference. In fact, the specific problem that demonstratives are meant to solve—namely, how singular reference can be accomplished in the absence of individuating descriptive knowledge that is adequate to distinguish the referent from all other things—cannot be counted as solved until a complete theory of demonstrative reference has been delivered.

It has already emerged in the course of discussing the Cartesian view of the first person that the reflexive component of a demonstrative term cannot secure reference to one thing rather than another unless the term also incorporates as part of its meaning an indication of the sort of thing to which it refers. That is part of what makes "I" different from "here" and "now." The suggestion made earlier in connection with the special motivational role of first person thoughts was that demonstrative terms all share the same reflexive element; they can all be rendered as making the thoughts in which they occur token-reflexive. Thus "I" is the "thinker of *this* thought," "now" is the "time of *this* thought," and "here" is "the location of the thinker of *this* thought at the time of *this* thought." These renderings leave it open—and deliberately so—that demonstrative modes of reference might depend heavily on descriptive individuating knowledge. If that is so, they might not constitute a fundamental basis of reference.

It may be, then, that the special motivational role of thoughts containing demonstratives is enough to distinguish demonstratives as demonstratives—that is, as terms with a reflexive aspect—whether or not they constitute a nondescriptive basis for reference. So for example, my ability to refer to myself in the first person might depend on the fact that my descriptive individuating knowledge of myself is adequate to distinguish me from all other things—knowledge such as that I am the daughter of DKR, author of such-and-such article on branching self-consciousness, and so forth. This is compatible with granting that my uses of "I" cannot be paraphrased by using the descriptions that would capture my self-individuating knowledge, since thoughts expressible with the latter would not play the distinctive motivational role that is played by my first person thoughts. If "I" is paraphrasable at all, it is only by other demonstrative terms that also involve reflexivity, such

---

[8] See Strawson, *Individuals*; and Evans, *Varieties of Reference*.

as "the thinker of this thought." But to reiterate, this is compatible with supposing that reference to oneself in the first person might depend on having substantive self-identifying knowledge.[9]

These remarks do not, of course, show that demonstratives do not constitute a basis for singular reference that is independent of individuating descriptive knowledge. Indeed, in the spirit of epistemological neutrality, it ought to be left just as open that they might as that they might not. But as with the case of the Cartesian view of the first person, it must be considered whether a theory of singular reference based on indexicals provides a reason for abandoning the stance of epistemological neutrality. That is, it must be considered whether an account of the indexical basis of reference would show that the first person singular pronoun *must* be rendered as referring *without* mediation by any descriptive content such as "the set of rationally related intentional episodes of which *this* one is a member," and whether this being so would provide a reason for supposing that the pronoun simply cannot be rendered as it has been rendered here, as having such a descriptive content.

Gareth Evans offers an account of demonstrative reference that does seem to cast doubt on such a rendering of the first person pronoun. According to him, first person and other demonstrative thoughts not only play a distinctive motivational role; they also play a distinctive cognitive role. Their cognitive role has to do with certain ways of gaining and retaining information. Thus "here-thoughts" are associated with ways of gaining information through perception in the sense that perception provides information about how things are *here*. And first person thoughts are associated with ways of retaining information through memory in the sense that memory is a repository of information that is specifically about *my* past. In Evans's view, it makes no sense to think of memory as providing me with information about someone's past and then to infer that that person is *myself*. Rather, memory necessarily provides me with information about myself, and automatically licenses first person judgments—without any inference, and certainly without any explicit self-identifying beliefs, such as that the person of whom I have information through memory is myself. Evans calls this "identification-free" reference.

Now, if it were a necessary condition on first person reference that it be identification-free, that would call into question whether the proposed rendering of the first person pronoun was in the end acceptable, for a large part of its rationale is precisely to allow for identification-dependent first person reference. Insisting that identification-freedom is a necessary feature of first person reference would also call into question the appropriateness of the explanation offered above of the second referential guarantee associated with the first person, its virtual immunity to referential error through misiden-

[9] For a more extended discussion of how all of the distinctive features of the first person may be reconciled with the claim that first person reference is mediated by individuating knowledge and descriptions, see my "Epistemology of First Person Reference," *Journal of Philosophy* 84 (1987): 147–67.

tification. That explanation was that communication and action require reliable self-identifying knowledge, and that that suffices to explain why uses of the first person on the part of persons who satisfy the ethical criterion are in general immune to error through misidentification. But obviously, if it was in the nature of first person reference that it did not involve any identification to begin with, then there would be no scope for referential error through misidentification and no need for the explanation in terms of reliable self-identifying beliefs and knowledge.

There is no reason to deny that Evans's account of the connection between first person thought and memory might provide an accurate description of how things are with many actually existing human-size persons. And there is no reason to deny that if his general account of demonstratives is correct, then there is such a thing as identification-free reference, and it might serve as a basis for identification-dependent reference. However, there is good reason to deny that it is a necessary condition on first person reference that it be identification-free in his sense.[10] If I have a poor memory, then I may have to rely on a journal in order to know about my past actions. If, after reading in my journal, I have the first person thought that I promised a friend that I would visit her in Finland, my reference to myself is identification-dependent, for my first person thought is based on the belief that the person who wrote the journal entry made the promise, and that that person is myself. It certainly does not undermine the first person character of this thought that its reference to myself is mediated by a description like "the person described in this journal is me." The thought will play the special motivational role that is characteristically played by first person thoughts: it will dispose me to keep the promise to go to Finland (at least insofar as I have a general commitment and disposition to keep promises).

This example about the journal can be generalized in a number of important ways. Not only does it demonstrate that a first person thought can play its distinctive motivational role even if it involves an identification-dependent form of self-reference. It also introduces some specifically normative and indeed ethical dimensions of the first person. Insofar as I take the entries in my journal to record my past thoughts and actions, I must regard them as things for which I can appropriately be held accountable. And insofar as some of these past thoughts are long-term intentions—like the one couched in the promise to visit a friend in Finland—I must regard myself as in some sense committed to carrying them out. This is not to say that I cannot change my mind. But it is to say that it would be a change of *my* mind. And what makes it a change of my mind is this: the intention was formed in a context of a commitment to overall rational unity, where that commitment ensures that

---

[10] For a vigorous defense of the claim that identification-freedom is necessary for first person reference, see John McDowell, "Reductionism and the First Person," in *Reading Parfit*, ed. Jonathan Dancy (Oxford: Oxford University Press, forthcoming). For a more detailed response along the same lines presented here see my "Self-Reference: The Radicalization of Locke," *Journal of Philosophy* 90 (1993): 73–97.

both my earlier intention and my present decision about whether to carry it out are derived from a single rational point of view. That is why, unlike the intentions of others, which may not give me a reason to act, my own long-term intentions do give me reason to act. It is also why, if I decide not to carry out my intention, that requires some explanation and justification. This is so even if my knowledge of my earlier intention is based on a journal entry rather than on direct memory of it. All of this depends of course on seeing the journal as reflecting, and even embodying some of the rational relations over time in virtue of which I have a sustained rational point of view over time. But the role of the journal with respect to the maintenance of my rational point of view can go well beyond supplying me with a sort of surrogate memory. My journal can literally be the vehicle by which I achieve rational unity over time. It can be the means by which I hold on to and keep track of my unifying projects—that is, the substantive practical commitments in the light of which I have reason to strive for overall rational unity. And it can also be the place where I work out what I should think and do in light of these commitments. As a result, it can constitute a sort of blueprint for future thought and action.

To see a journal in this way, as something that might play an integral role in the maintenance of rational and practical unity over time, sheds light on the question of first person authority. Like the referential guarantees associated with the first person, the special authority that attaches to first person reports of one's thoughts is generally regarded as requiring epistemological explanation. Nevertheless, the present account will maintain its stance of epistemological neutrality. For suppose—and there is good reason to suppose—that the ethical criterion of personhood entails first person authority. That is, suppose that the agents who can engage in agency-regarding relations, and who are therefore capable of rational engagement with one another, must be accorded special authority when they report knowledge of their own states of mind. It still would not matter *how* a person's first person knowledge of its own thoughts is achieved. In particular, it would not matter whether such knowledge was based on direct phenomenological access, or whether it was inferred from evidence, such as that provided in a journal. The paramount consideration in deciding whether a form of knowledge is *self*-knowledge is whether the knower stands in appropriate *normative* relations to the item known, that is, whether it is committed to taking that item into account in its deliberations and assessing it together with the other intentional episodes that belong to its rational point of view as it strives for overall rational unity within that point of view. This normative relation to one's own thoughts certainly requires an epistemic relation as well: one cannot consider in one's deliberations intentional episodes of which one is ignorant. Yet there is no particular restriction on *how* the requisite epistemic relation to one's own intentional episodes is achieved. This is clearly shown by the example about the journal.

The point relevant to the larger theme of this book is that it is also shown by the cases of group and multiple persons. In the case of co-conscious multiple persons, one such person could have direct phenomenological access to an intentional episode without regarding that episode as its own, regarding it rather as belonging to a companion person within the same human being. Since these distinct multiple persons would have distinct rational points of view, it follows that direct phenomenological access is not sufficient for first person knowledge of an intentional episode. Nor is it necessary. A group person could achieve knowledge of its intentional episodes without such direct access, so long as it had mediated access through relevant group records and procedures. In both cases, and indeed in all cases, an object of knowledge belongs to the rational point of view of the knower, and hence is an object of first person knowledge, just in case it stands in the appropriate normative relation. It must fall within the scope of the knower's commitment to overall rational unity; it must be something that the knower ought to take into account in its all-things-considered judgments. That is why direct phenomenological access may fail to deliver first person knowledge in the case of (co-conscious) multiple persons, and it is also why mediated access through records and procedures can deliver first person knowledge in the case of group persons.

This conclusion is not based on an independent argument; it is merely a consequence of the ethical criterion of personhood and the normative analysis of personal identity. Given the way in which the identities and rational points of view of persons have been analyzed, in terms of a structure of rational relations among intentional episodes, the first person relation that obtains between persons and their own intentional episodes must likewise be analyzed in the same structural and relational terms. Thus the main indicator of a first personal relation must be that a person stand in normative as well as epistemic relation to its own thoughts and deeds.

That completes the case for how all the special features of the first person can be captured within the terms of the normative analysis of personal identity and the ethical criterion of personhood from which that analysis issues.

2. SELF-ORIENTED ETHICAL RELATIONS

The aim of this section is to see how the rationally based normative relation that a person bears to its own intentional episodes provides for two ethical first person relations: the sort of accountability that a person bears only for its own thoughts and actions and the sort of prudential self-concern that a person has only for its own well-being.

However, the aim of this section is not by any means to give a *complete* account of either accountability or self-concern. No book of readable length could possibly cover that comprehensive ground after having traversed the issues it already has. The aim is merely to uncover *one* rational basis for accountability and self-concern that persons automatically have, just by virtue of satisfying the ethical criterion of personhood. This does not rule out that there might be other bases for them as well—both nonrational and rational.

There are two reasons why it is worth uncovering this rational basis of accountability and self-concern. First, it is always useful to find a rational basis for our attitudes when it can be found. Second, finding this particular rational basis for these particular attitudes will help to complete our understanding of what it means to embrace the ethical criterion of personhood. More specifically, it will help to complete our understanding of the distinctive ethical significance that persons possess, for themselves as well as for one another.

Chapter 3 established that the ethical criterion constitutes an ethically uncontroversial but nevertheless ethically important starting point for an account of the kind 'person'.

The uncontroversiality of the criterion derives from the following facts: persons, qua agents who can engage in agency-regarding relations, face a choice concerning whether and when to engage in such relations with one another; this is an ethically significant choice because it always *matters* to persons whether others engage in agency-regarding relations with them; the ethical significance of this choice is something that persons can recognize, and indeed cannot fail to recognize, no matter what their other substantive ethical commitments might be. Despite its ethical uncontroversiality, the ethical criterion personhood is nevertheless important because it helps to define and expose a particular form of prejudice, which consists in a hypocritical denial of personhood. Here is why: the agents who can engage in agency-regarding relations can engage in certain sorts of distinctively interpersonal relations (such as reasoning with one another), in which they engage with one another *as persons*; they are guilty of a hypocritical form of prejudice when they explicitly *deny* that something is a person, and yet at the same time implicitly *acknowledge* that it is a person precisely by engaging in distinctively interpersonal relations with it.

This importance of the ethical criterion of personhood would stand even if it could not be shown that the agents who satisfy it are rationally accountable for their own actions or have reason to be prudentially concerned for their own well-being. Persons would still bear an ethical relation to one another (because they all occasion and face the same ethically significant choice) even if they did not bear these self-oriented ethical relations *to themselves*. And it would still be *important* for persons to overcome hypocritical prejudice against one another by not allowing certain kinds of differences among them—as human-size persons have historically allowed differences of race and gender—to obscure their common nature as persons who all belong to the same ethical kind. Yet it might prove difficult to overcome such prejudice in the case of group and multiple persons. And learning that there is *more* to our common personal nature, from an ethical point of view, might help to lessen the difficulty. In particular, it might help to learn that they, like us, are objects of ethical significance for themselves as well as for others because they have reason to regard their own actions as something for which they are rationally accountable, and because they have reason to regard their own well-being with a special kind of prudential concern. And it might help to learn that all of this is so just by virtue of the common nature which the ethical criterion entails that *all* persons have, as rational, reflective, and social agents who can engage in agency-regarding relations.

The uncontroversiality of the ethical criterion of personhood is not at all compromised by the fact that it entails this extra, self-oriented ethical significance of persons. But this uncontroversiality does come at the cost of not delivering everything that might be sought in an ethical theory. We have seen that the ethical criterion insists upon the ethical *significance* of regard for agency, and yet it does not accord such regard any particular position on a scale of ethically significant values. Likewise with respect to accountability and self-concern; the sense in which they are provided for by the ethical criterion does *not* determine what place they should occupy in our ethical outlook, for that is a matter of ethical contestability.

Rational Accountability

On Locke's understanding, the question whether a person is accountable for its actions is not distinct from the question whether the person deserves reward and punishment for those actions. And he saw the first person relation of ownership that a person bears to its own actions—which he construed as the relation of consciousness—as a necessary condition for such accountability:

> And therefore whatever past Actions it cannot reconcile or appropriate to that present *self* by consciousness, it can no more be concerned in, than if they had never been done: And to receive Pleasure or Pain, *i.e.* Reward or Punishment, on the account of any such Action, is all one, as to be made happy or miserable in its first being, without any demerit at all. For supposing a Man punish'd now, for what he had done in another Life, whereof he could be made to have no consciousness at all, what difference is there between that Punishment, and being created miserable? (2.27.26)

The ethical criterion also draws a connection between personal accountability and the first person relation that a person bears to its own actions. However, it does not share Locke's preoccupation with the question of punishment. Nor does it share Locke's phenomenological interpretation of the first person relation. It claims rather that a person must have first person *knowledge* of its actions. And such knowledge of one's actions need not involve direct phenomenological access to them through consciousness. What it must involve is a normative relation to them. It involves seeing one's actions as having proceeded from—in the sense of being justified by as well as caused by episodes within—one's own rational point of view.

This normative first person relation makes persons accountable in the following sense: they are appropriate objects of evaluation and criticism, and hence praise and blame, where these evaluative actions are literally *callings to account* for one's actions, in which a person is asked to give, and to defend, and to critically examine the reasons on which it has acted.

The fact that persons in the sense defined by the ethical criterion are appropriate objects of praise and blame in this critical-evaluative sense does not guarantee that they *deserve* reward and punishment. But the former is at least a necessary condition for the latter, for as Locke understood, punishment is supposed to be a *meaningful* infliction of pain, and this requires a first person relation to the action for which one is being punished. But the first person relation in question cannot stop with mere knowledge of the action for which one is being punished. Punishment cannot be meaningful unless one also grasps the critical or sanctioning *attitude* that the punishment embodies. And this attitude is not generally directed at what a person *happened* to bring about through its actions, but rather at what the person *intended*. Thus the critical scope of punishment takes in a person's *reasons* along with its *actions*. And as a result, it presupposes the sort of rational accountability that the ethical criterion provides for.

There are various considerations that might be brought to bear, over and above the fact that persons are rationally accountable in this sense, in order to justify our practices of punishment. Perhaps it can be shown that these practices serve other values that we hold to be important. Or perhaps it can be shown that punishment has certain beneficial consequences. Or perhaps we feel that nothing else besides the infliction of harm on a wrongdoer can give proper expression to our moral attitudes.[11] In keeping with its spirit of ethical uncontroversiality, the ethical criterion neither entails nor precludes any of these justifications of punishment.

However, it might be objected that these supplemental justifications would fail to consolidate a certain intuition, which is that persons *deserve* to be punished for their wrongs. In fact, these supplemental justifications probably *cannot* consolidate this intuition, since the intuition is, presumably, that persons deserve to be punished for their wrongs regardless of whether the general practice of punishment can be justified in any other way—such as that it serves our other values, or generates good consequences, or satisfies our emotional needs.

The quick response to this objection is that the intuition to which it appeals is controversial, and hence not something which this account of the person needs to preserve. But the objection merits a somewhat more consid-

---

[11] Sir Peter Strawson provides such an expressivist justification of punishment in "Freedom and Resentment," in *Freedom and Resentment and Other Essays* (London: Methuen, 1974)—though he would not appreciate the label "expressivist." Nevertheless, he situates the question of desert (along with the issues of freedom and responsibility, which are really his primary concern) in relation to what he calls our "reactive attitudes." These attitudes combine the rational-critical dimension of accountability that has been emphasized here, along with certain emotional responses to one another, such as resentment, indignation, and so forth. And his point is very much that we could not justify any of our practices surrounding blame and punishment without bringing in this emotional dimension of our moral responses.

ered response, for it may be that the intuition about desert is as much a *meta-physical* as an ethical intuition. That is, it may be that persons are thought to deserve punishment for their wrong actions because of their metaphysical relation to them as *authors* and *causal generators* of them. And so it might be objected that the present account of the person is not exempted from having to consolidate this intuition on the ground that aims at *ethical* uncontroversiality. After all, the account does aim to characterize the distinctive sort of agency that persons possess. And if there is such a thing as metaphysically grounded desert, it would, presumably, belong to distinctively personal agency.

The topic that has been raised by this objection is really the topic of autonomy or freedom. And the topic has been conspicuous by its absence throughout this book. The main difficulty with the topic is that there are simply too many diverse conceptions of autonomy and freedom. On some conceptions this account of the person clearly entails that persons are free, while on other conceptions it does not so clearly entail this. Locke's conception of freedom, as acting in accordance with one's will, is certainly provided for within this account—only it is interpreted more specifically, as acting in accordance with the dictates of one's rational point of view or one's all-things-considered judgments. The account also provides for another kind of freedom, which consists in a person's capacity for *self-change* in light of reflection, for insofar as persons have a normative commitment to achieving overall rational unity within their rational points of view and insofar as they have a capacity to act on this commitment, they must have a capacity to revise their attitudes in the light of critical self-evaluation—which is just to say, they must have a capacity for self-change.[12]

Perhaps some might be prepared to take these kinds of freedom that are presupposed by the ethical criterion of personhood to ground desert—certainly Locke thought the first sufficient by itself. But it is not obvious that everyone would, or even ought to. It seems perfectly coherent to suppose that persons can act in accordance with their wills (in the sense of acting on all-things-considered judgments) and that they can revise their attitudes (so as to satisfy their normative commitment to overall rational unity) without suppos-

---

[12] See Harry Frankfurt, "Freedom of the Will and the Concept of a Person," *Journal of Philosophy* 68 (1971): 5–20 for an account of freedom that emphasizes this capacity. He claims that actions are free when they are in accord with one's desires, and one's will is free when it is in accord with one's *higher-order* desires—for example, second-order desires to have certain first-order desires. And these higher-order desires are, of course, desires by which an agent can, in principle, *change* its lower order desires. However, it should not be thought that the account of reflective rational agency that has been developed in this book shares the same *hierarchical* structure that Frankfurt attributes to personal agency. He supposes that the direction of self-change is always from higher-order desire to lower-order change, whereas this account simply posits a general commitment to overall rational unity, in the light of which a person might have reason to revise *any* of its attitudes, no matter whether they are of the first, second, or *n*th order. Thus the direction of self-change is not from higher to lower order; it is rather from a state of less rational unity to a state of greater rational unity.

ing that it is ever justifiable to inflict harm on persons—even if they have acted wrongly.

If it should be insisted that punishment cannot be justified without consolidating the intuition about desert, and if it also should be insisted that this intuition requires specifically *metaphysical backing* in some aspect of personal agency (so that punishment cannot be justified on the normative grounds briefly mentioned above, namely, that it serves other values, generates good consequences, or fulfills expressive needs), and finally, if should be insisted that the two kinds of freedom that are provided for by the ethical criterion of personhood do not consolidate the intuition, then we have only two options. We can conclude that punishment is not justified, or we can find some metaphysical aspect of personal agency that does consolidate the intuition. This book has no novel suggestion about how the latter option might be pursued. But it does in its turn want to insist on the following points in response to the intuition that there is such a thing as desert, and that desert must have a metaphysical ground in personal agency: first, the interest of this book's account of personal agency does not lie in its ability to consolidate this intuition, but rather in its implications about the possibility of group and multiple persons; second, there is no reason to suppose that acknowledging these possibilities of group and multiple persons will make the task of consolidating the intuition about desert any harder than it otherwise would have been; and third, the intuition should not make us doubt any of the book's positive claims about the nature of personal agency.

The last point deserves to be expanded. In many ways, the keynote of this account of the kind 'person' has been that the normative dimensions of personal agency ought to be emphasized over its causal dimensions. Quite apart from the task of consolidating an intuition about desert, there might be a worry about whether the arguments for the possibility of group and multiple persons have been made easier—and indeed whether their soundness might even be compromised—by this emphasis. For it might be thought that a proper understanding of the causal production of actions in agency might show, somehow, that groups and parts of human beings are not the sorts of things that can be agents, and hence persons, in their own rights. Likewise, it might now be thought that if desert has a metaphysical ground in personal agency, this ground must also have to do with the causal dimension of such agency—that is, with *how* a person causally produces its actions. Of course, it is far from obvious that something like desert, which seems to be an essentially normative phenomenon, could have a strictly causal ground. But on the other hand, this book has not offered any argument to rule this out. And given that it has not ruled this out, it ought perhaps now to review its reasons for so resolutely ignoring the causal dimension of agency, and focusing on its normative dimension instead.

The focus was initially motivated by chapter 3's effort to clarify the notion of an agency-regarding relation, that is, the relation that arises when one agent (or person) attempts to influence another and yet aims not to hinder the other's agency. It was argued there that the question whether an effort to influence a person hinders its agency cannot be settled just by considering whether and how such influence might make a causal difference to what happens within the person's domain of intentional control, for the very same sort of causal intrusion into that domain (such as hypnosis) might be a hindrance to one person's agency while being a help to another's. Why? Because the question whether a person's agency has been hindered must be answered by appeal to whether what happens in the person's domain of intentional control *accords* with its rational point of view. It goes along with this conception of hindering agency that the exercise of agency itself must be nothing else than the attempt to achieve such accord. Indeed, that is one good way to understand what it is to act *for reasons*. And so it was concluded that that is the universal and defining goal of agency, namely, to bring the events within one's domain of intentional control into accord with the dictates of one's rational point of view so that what one does is what one takes oneself to have most reason to do. Once this universal goal of agency is placed at the center of an account of agency, the causal dimension of agency, which has specifically to do with *how* actions are *produced*, simply drops out—except insofar as it bears on the normative issue of whether the right sort of accord between the events within one's domain of intentional control and the dictates of one's rational point of view is in place.

On the largest and most complete project of explaining personal accountability, which seeks to give not merely a necessary condition, but a sufficient condition and a full justification for our notions of desert, punishment, and the like, the interrelated proposals in this book about agency, persons, and personal identity leave the ground open for different sorts of proposals. But it is compatible with any such further proposals, whether they are of the kind that justify punishment on evaluative grounds such as suggested by Strawson, or other proposals that more ambitiously seek the ground of justification of normative practices in sufficient conditions stressing purely causal and metaphysical conditions. Neither kind of such further proposal falsifies the relation between this book's proposal and desert. This is the relation of specifying a necessary condition, in terms of a particular conception of persons and the particular kind of agency they possess, for the *appropriateness* of the application of concepts like reward and punishment. The point is that first, the appropriateness in question does not amount to a sufficient condition for the practices of punishment and reward; second, granting it as a necessary condition is compatible with the standard directions that further proposals of such sufficient conditions can be expected to take; and third, no proposed sufficient condition will do its work unless the appropriateness in question is also respected.

A Rational Basis for Self-Concern

Chapter 3 observed that an account of the kind 'person' that wishes to proceed from an uncontroversial ethical assumption cannot begin with the assumption that persons have reason to be prudentially concerned for their own well-being. That assumption would raise far too many contentious issues, including the following: in what does personal well-being consist? what is the nature and extent of our reasons for prudential self-concern? how ought prudential considerations to be weighed against other ethical considerations? This brief discussion does not aim to settle any of these issues completely. Indeed, in keeping with this book's commitment to ethical uncontroversiality, it places absolutely no constraints on how the last issue might be sorted out. With respect to the first two issues, it will make some very limited and therefore appropriately uncontroversial claims.

First, in what does the well-being of a person consist? Some of the difficulty that this question presents is due to the dispute about personal identity. Animalists would naturally seek an answer in animal nature, or perhaps in specifically human nature as in the Aristotelian idea of human flourishing, while Lockeans might give a somewhat different answer, stressing more the quality of a person's experiences. But here is a partial answer to the question that seems beyond dispute: insofar as a person is an *agent*, then much of its well-being and suffering will consist, respectively, in the fulfillment and frustration of its desires, in the broad sense of "desire" that includes all of its motives and values and practical pursuits. And that is all that will here be taken for granted about the well-being of persons.

Now, it is impossible that a person, qua agent, can fail to be concerned for its present well-being, qua fulfillment of its present desires. Being an agent, it will naturally be concerned to act, and to act is nothing else than to strive to fulfill its desires, and thereby achieve the sort of well-being that comes with practical success. It is hard to see how we could define the very notion of desire without this point being true.

However, if the present aim theory of rationality is true, it would seem that a person, qua agent, does not necessarily have reason to be concerned for its future well-being as well, that is, reason to take measures in the present to ensure the fulfillment of its future desires. Yet it is something of a platitude that persons do have reason to be concerned for their future as well as their present well-being.

One virtue of the normative analysis of personal identity is that it preserves this platitude. It says that personal identity consists in the condition that gives rise to a commitment to overall rational unity. This condition consists in a set of rationally related intentional episodes that includes a commitment to a unifying project that brings in train a commitment to achieving overall rational unity within the set. It follows from the analysis that personal identity *over time* consists in a set of rationally related intentional episodes that includes a commitment to a *long-term activity* that brings in train a commitment to achieving overall rational unity over time. And a commitment to such a long-term activity gives a person reason in the present to take measures in the present to ensure the fulfillment of certain of its future desires. For in the context of such an activity, the success of my present actions will depend upon my completing the longer activity, and hence on the success of the future actions that will also figure in it. Since those future actions will spring from desires that I will have then, I have reason now to take measures to ensure the fulfillment of some of my future desires.

It might seem that such concern would really amount to present-directed, rather than future-directed, self-concern. What such concern aims to ensure, after all, is the success of a long-term activity to which I am *presently* committed. This is indeed true. And it *must* be true if future-directed concern is to be reconciled with the present aim theory. Within that theory, my future-directed self-concern must have a basis in my present aims. Why then is it a genuinely *future*-directed concern? Because it is a concern to fulfill desires that I will have in the future. And those desires may well be desires that I do not now have, for they may include other desires besides the desire which I now have to carry out the long-term activity, such as the following: desires to make certain specific contributions to my long-term activity that I do not now even envisage; desires that will be generated by future needs that I do not now have; desires that are not directly generated by my commitment to my long-term activity but whose frustration might compromise my general effectiveness in pursuing that activity. Since I do not now have these desires, my concern to ensure their fulfillment is a genuinely future-directed concern.

This explanation that the normative analysis provides, of why a person's attitude of self-concern may extend beyond the present so as to include concern for its future well-being, also sheds light on the self-concern of group and multiple persons. Like the scope of future-directed self-concern, the scope of their self-concern in general would be determined by the nature and needs of their unifying projects. And in their cases, this scope will not coincide with the boundaries of any particular human body or consciousness. Thus multiple persons within the same human being would not have any special concern to ensure the fulfillment of one another's desires—except insofar as such fulfillment bore on the success of their own projects. And group persons who were composed of many human beings would be concerned to fulfill a much larger range of desires.

The normative analysis entails that this rational basis of self-concern in a person's unifying project is, like the facts that ground personal identity itself, a matter of degree. Thus when individual human-size persons are engaged in a joint activity, their shared commitment to that activity gives them special reason to be concerned for one another's well-being. And this sort of partialist concern for one another differs only in degree from the sort of prudential concern that an individual group person who was composed of many human beings would have for its own well-being.

Is it an objection that the account does not make the basis of self-concern completely unlike partialist concern for others? No. For it still manages to preserve a crucial difference between the two cases. Persons need not have any special concern for one another, whereas they must be especially concerned for their own present and future well-being; such self-concern is *guaranteed* by the structure of their own personal agency. This is so despite the fact that partialist concern for others, when it is in place, differs only in degree from prudential self-concern. That this should be a difference of degree is the inevitable outcome of the book's larger account of personhood and personal identity. It entails that the boundaries between persons can be vague, in the sense that the facts that ground personal identity are a matter of degree. It is bound to follow that the first person relation itself is not so clear-cut. The last section showed that this is so on the strict normative understanding of it, as the relation that a person bears to the intentional episodes that constitute the basis of its deliberations. And it is also so in both of its ethical dimensions—rational accountability and self-concern.

The foregoing account of prudential self-concern might seem counterintuitive, not merely because it portrays self-concern in such a way as to reflect the vagueness of the boundaries between persons, but also because it fails to portray concern for one's *future* well-being as *basic*. Such concern is portrayed rather as being *derivative* from one's commitments to long-term activities.

Perhaps some agents are endowed with a basic commitment to their own well-being in the following sense: for them, the mere thought that a future desire will be *mine* directly supplies a reason to ensure its fulfillment—no matter when it might occur and no matter what other practical commitments the agent might have.[13] Nothing in this account precludes such a basic and ungrounded sort of future-directed self-concern. It simply aims to bring out that for agents who satisfy the ethical criterion of personhood, something else is basic, namely, their unifying projects, and these projects actually provide a *rational basis* for future-directed self-concern.

However, it ought not to go unobserved that the picture of self-concern as basic and ungrounded is somewhat problematic. Seeing why it is problematic will help to bring out some additional reasons for taking the normative analysis of personal identity seriously, over and above the reasons that have already been supplied in the course of the book's overall argument.

The problems emerge when we ask the following questions: Is the purportedly basic value of one's own future well-being something that persons are *bound* to recognize? And if so, *why*?

We cannot simply lay it down as a brute fact about persons that they do recognize this without also taking a stand on the dispute about personal identity, for doing so would narrow down the range of acceptable analyses of personal identity to those which are consistent with this brute fact. And note that the animalist analysis would appear not to be acceptable by this criterion. It is not a brute fact about human animals in general that they recognize a reason to take measures in the present to ensure the fulfillment of their future desires. Some are in fact unmoved to do so. And indeed, some might be moved *against* doing so. This is so in Parfit's example of the nineteenth-century Russian who anticipates that in the future he might lose his present com-

<hr>

[13] This is suggested by Thomas Nagel in *The Possibility of Altruism* (New York: Oxford University Press, 1970).

mitment to turning his estates over to the peasants, and who resolves to take measures to ensure that his present commitment to turning his estates over will override any future desire that he might later have to keeping them.[14]

Of course, much of the force of Parfit's example turns on the present aim theory of rationality, in the light of which it seems that the young Russian is within his rights to take measures against fulfilling his future conservative desires. And to insist on the basicness of future-directed concern is, in part, to make a criticism of that theory. But it is not the sort of criticism that can preclude the actual existence of persons who embrace and live by that theory. Such persons would not, at least not by their own lights, be bound to recognize the basic value of their own future well-being, irrespective of their other practical commitments. For them, this basic value might constitute a merely external reason. And they would regard themselves as within their rights to demand another reason, besides the mere fact that they will have certain desires in the future, to take measures in the present to ensure their future fulfillment.

It will do no good to respond to their demand simply by pointing out that those desires will be *theirs*. They have already granted this. And in any case, this response would serve only to raise the following uncomfortable question: since my past desires are just as much *mine* as my future desires, why do I not have just as much reason to take measures in the present to ensure their fulfillment as well?[15] This question cannot be dismissed on the ground that the past has already happened. Many past desires are such that they could still be fulfilled (I used to want to master Norwegian; unfortunately, I can take action now to fulfill that desire.)

The normative analysis provides a ready answer to this question. Long-term activities unfold in time. One's past contributions to it are already done and can be taken for granted in the present. It is one's future ability to complete the activity that is of special interest and concern. And this ability will rest in various ways on the fulfillment of one's future desires. Not every analysis of personal identity can afford such an explanation of the temporal bias of our extended self-concern. Again, consider the animalist analysis. It says that a desire is mine just in case it belongs to the animal life that constitutes my identity. This in itself does not show why I should be more concerned to fulfill my future desires than my past desires (insofar as I can). And indeed it also does not show why I should be concerned to fulfill *any* desires besides my present desires. We have already seen that the normative analysis supplies an

---

[14] Parfit, *Reasons and Persons*, pp. 327ff. Parfit's use of this example is somewhat different. He is concerned with questioning the animalist analysis of personal identity, partly through an examination of the following question: if the Russian's wife *promised* him to hold him to his present commitment, and if he did change in the way he feared he might, can we say that he would still be the same person to whom the wife had made the promise, and if not would she then be released from the promise?

[15] Parfit, ibid., has provided a very convincing discussion of why this question cannot be dismissed out of hand.

explanation of this too, and in doing so it ensures that persons have an *internal* reason to be concerned for their future well-being, at least insofar as such well-being rests on the fulfillment of their future desires. For according to it, anything that satisfies the condition for personal identity over time will have commitments to unifying projects that involve long-term activities, and these commitments will give the person reason in the present to ensure the fulfillment of many of its future desires.

It should now be clear that the account of self-concern that is entailed by the normative analysis really has three advantages: first, it explains why, even given the present aim theory, a person automatically has reason in the present to be concerned for its future well-being; second, it ensures that this reason is an *internal* reason that the person is bound to recognize; third, it explains the temporal bias of a person's extended self-concern, for the future and against the past. And *all* of these advantages rest squarely on the fact that it finds a *rational basis* for self-concern in a person's unifying projects. In other words, the normative analysis has all of these advantages precisely because it portrays future-directed self-concern as a *derivative* rather than a *basic* value. So it is a strength, rather than a weakness, of the normative analysis that it supplies this nonbasic, rational ground of a person's self-concern.

This rational basis of future-directed self-concern tracks the normative first person relation that a person generally bears to the future intentional episodes that constitute its temporally extended rational point of view.

In both cases, there is a question why a person ought to take certain future episodes—be they desires in particular, or all of its attitudes in general—into account in the present.

In both cases, the reason why the person ought to take these future episodes into account is the same: the person has present commitments to long-term activities that give it reason to do so.

In both cases, these practical commitments meet an *explanatory* demand: why is it that persons have reason to achieve overall rational unity within their rational points of view over time? and why is it that persons have reason to take measures in the present to secure the fulfillment of their future desires?

In both cases, it may initially appear that there can be no explanatory demand to meet: an individual person qua rational being is *by definition* committed to achieving overall rational unity within its rational point of view; it is a platitude that a person just *does* have reason to be especially concerned for its own well-being.

In both cases, problems of scope arise: what are the boundaries of a person's rational point of view, such that a person has reason to take all and only those intentional episodes into account in its deliberations that fall within those boundaries? what is the scope of a person's concern to fulfill its own desires such that a person has reason to take measures to fulfill its present and its future desires, but not its past desires?

And in both cases, these problems of scope are solved by appeal to a person's practical commitments to unifying projects. Insofar as it is built into the condition of personal identity that a person has such practical commitments, then it is guaranteed to be the case that a person has reason to take into account a particular set of intentional episodes when it deliberates and a particular set of desires when it is concerned for its own well-being—namely, its *own*.

The normative analysis, thus, even though because of its aspiration to ethical uncontroversiality it does not give a full story about all the ethical issues surrounding self-concern, nevertheless has a satisfying story to tell about the first personal relation that is involved in self-concern.

Postscript

THIS BOOK used an ethical premise about the nature of persons (the nature of the kind 'person') in order to argue for a metaphysical conclusion about the condition of personal identity. That metaphysical conclusion was unavoidably revisionist. But the ethical premise was not. Indeed, the unusual strategy of the book's argument depended on avoiding all ethical controversy, even while arguing for a metaphysical revision in our thinking about personal identity on an ethical basis. The strategy was to find a starting point for an account of the kind 'person' on which all parties to the philosophical dispute about personal identity can and should agree, no matter what position they might happen to take within ethical theory—including even an antitheoretical position, though not of course a completely nihilistic position that withholds ethical significance from everything. Yet it does seem reasonable to expect that a revisionist conclusion about personal identity, even if it issues from uncontroversial ethical premises, is bound to have *some* ethical *repercussions*. And it is only fitting to consider, even if regrettably briefly in the form of a Postscript, what they might be.

The most *obvious* repercussion is this. Insofar as the metaphysical possibilities argued for in this book were to be realized, of multiple persons composed of parts of human beings and group persons composed of many human beings, then prima facie, we ought to accord to them whatever treatment and consideration our ethical views dictate we ought to accord to persons generally—or rather to those persons who (unlike fetuses, infants, and the insane) are rationally competent. Of course many ethical views entail that all persons ought to be treated on a par, at least within legal and political contexts. And the introduction of multiple and group persons would inevitably raise difficulties and confusions for such views. (Ought multiple persons within a single human being to be given the right to own property and vote? Would it be wrong to restrict a group person's right to own property and vote?)

As far as this book is concerned, there is no reason why the recommended metaphysical revision should not, in the light of such difficulties and confusions, lead to ethical revision as well. In particular, the book allows that someone who is now committed to treating all persons on a par and to making no distinctions among them *might* reasonably begin drawing such distinctions and treating different sorts of persons differentially, in the event that multiple and group persons should come to exist alongside human-size persons.

This allowance might seem inconsistent with the book's defense of its ethical criterion of personhood, which rested on the claim that the criterion helps to define and expose a certain kind of prejudice against persons. For it might be thought that the whole point and importance of defining and exposing prejudice is precisely to *preclude* the differential treatment of persons. But this is not necessarily so. And to think so would be to misunderstand the point and importance of the particular kind of prejudice that figured in the book's argument for the ethical criterion. What sort of prejudice is that? A kind of prejudice that involves *hypocrisy*, in the sense that it explicitly denies personhood to something while at the very same time standing in a distinctively interpersonal relation with it (say, by rationally engaging it). Thus the form of prejudice does not *merely* consist in a differential treatment of persons; it also consists in a dishonest attempt to avoid having to *justify* such differential treatment. And at no point has this book argued or even suggested that differential treatment among persons could never be justified. To say that would be to commit oneself to a form of philosophical egalitarianism that would amount to a familiar sort of substantive ethical position. And that would be to embrace the kind of controversial stance in ethics that the book forswears. This point can be brought out concretely as follows. Suppose one discriminates against a person on account of race. And suppose one says, "That is not a person," by way of justification (not an unfamiliar move in the history of personal and social relations), while all the time engaging in distinctly interpersonal relations with it such as talking to it in rationally engaging ways. Then what one has precisely done is avoid the task of having to justify discriminatory treatment of the person. And this avoidance is an act of hypocrisy, given one's interpersonal relations with it. To expose this sort of prejudice is not to have simply taken the stance that all discrimination is prejudicial, for it leaves open that *some* differential treatment (*not* discrimination on racial grounds, but perhaps on some other grounds) may be justified. It is merely the distinctively hypocritical form of prejudice that the ethical criterion seeks to expose.

However, it might seem that the determination to leave the possibility open for such a justification of differential treatment is in its turn unjustifiable—even if this determination should derive from a commitment to ethical uncontroversiality and neutrality, for it might seem that leaving this possibility open is hardly distinct from inviting attempts to reaffirm the pernicious distinctions among persons that have been drawn in the past (on grounds of race and gender, for example) and against which significant political progress has been made in the last century or so. But the really crucial point that must not be lost sight of is that *those* distinctions were *not* justified *or* justifiable. Now, if we want to buttress this point with the further claim that *no* distinctions among *any* persons could *ever* be justified, then (given the book's metaphysical conclusions) we shall be stuck with treating multiple and group persons, should their possibility be actualized, on a par with human-size persons—even if that should wreak havoc on our legal and political systems. The general tendency of this book has been to provide reasons to think that nothing as strong as that can be gotten from the bare metaphysical conclusion that multiples and groups can be persons. Of course, *if* one is committed to the substantive egalitarian position, then one must treat multiple and group persons on a par with other persons. But the condition of personal identity formulated in this book undercuts one natural-seeming metaphysical defense of such egalitarianism. How does it do so?

Perhaps the most counterintuitive metaphysical claims of the book are these: (1) an individual person's commitment to being rational, in the sense of being committed to achieving overall rational unity within itself, is necessarily a conditional commitment which is grounded in the person's substantive practical commitments to unifying projects that require such overall rational unity; (2) it is therefore part of the very condition of a person's identity qua rational being with a commitment to achieving overall rational unity within itself that the person *have* such substantive commitments to unifying projects. Part of what makes these claims counterintuitive is that they render both a person's commitment to rational unity and its very existence as being *contingent* on substantive practical commitments to unifying projects; for we normally think of such substantive practical commitments as presupposing the prior existence of a person with a prior commitment to rational unity. The same contingency also intruded, with equally counterintuitive results, upon the book's account of the rational basis for self-concern that persons, in the sense defined by the ethical criterion of personhood, are automatically supplied with. Such self-concern, especially as it extends beyond the present so as to comprehend a person's future well-being, can be seen as grounded in a person's commitments to its unifying projects. More specifically, one reason why a person has reason in the present to take measures to ensure the fulfillment of its future desires is that this will help to promote the success of a project to which it is already committed in the present. Thus neither a person's normative commitment to achieving rational unity within itself nor its ethical commitment to securing its own future well-being has been portrayed in this book as undertaken *for its own sake*. These commitments have been portrayed rather as commitments that are undertaken for the sake of *something worth doing* (a unifying project). This means that the book's account of personhood and personal identity assigns no *intrinsic* value to the rational unity of persons, or to their well-being (in the sense of having their desires fulfilled)—or *even to their very existence*, since their existence itself is grounded in the same thing that grounds their own commitments to rational unity and self-concern, namely, their unifying projects.

How do these counterintuitive metaphysical claims affect the issue at hand, concerning whether the possibility ought to be left open that it might in principle be justifiable to treat different sorts of persons differentially, at least once the class of persons is extended to include multiple and group persons? Simply by bringing out that since the very existence of a person is inextricably linked with the pursuit of its projects, so too we can think of the *person itself* as having a *value* that is contingent on the value of its projects. And this is not just an external perspective that *others* might take on the person. Just as a person achieves rational unity and exercises prudential self-concern for the sake of something it finds worth doing, so also a person may think of its very existence as something that ought to be preserved for the sake of the very same thing. In consequence, a person may also *rethink* this matter by *comparing* the value of its unifying project (that is, the project for the sake of which it exists as well as acts) with other possible projects that might be pursued instead, but whose pursuit would require integrating with others into a larger person or fragmenting into smaller persons. Through such reflections, persons can literally reason their way out of existence by finding that there is something really worth doing that requires a different level of rational unity from their own. But if persons can take this perspective on themselves—that is, if they can reconsider the value of their own existence in the light of a larger question concerning what, among the things that could be done by various possible persons, would be most worth doing—who is to say that there could never be a perspective from which it was justifiable to draw distinctions among persons and to treat them in a differential manner? These need not be superficial distinctions based on insignificant differences among persons; they may be momentous distinctions based on the very values that ground persons' lives. (If this still sounds too dangerously accommodating of pernicious prejudice, consider how beneficial it might be to treat an extremely large and powerful person differentially from smaller and less powerful persons by putting constraints on the former's activities while allowing the others free rein.)

It should not be inferred from these remarks that it would be incoherent to adopt an ethical stance from which all the persons who in fact exist must be regarded and treated on a par. There is nothing at all incoherent in such a stance, and much to recommend it. But on the other hand, it must also be acknowledged that the metaphysical arguments of this book undercut one natural way to defend this stance, which assumes that the existence of a particular person, qua rational agent, is always something of intrinsic value. This assumption breaks down once we see the existence and identity of a particular person as contingent upon and inseparable from its unifying projects.

On a more positive note, it is a virtue of this metaphysical account of the person that it places self-regarding and other-regarding ethical attitudes on the same footing. It identifies a rational basis for future-directed self-concern in present commitments to unifying projects, and it identifies a similar basis for partialist concern for others in commitments to joint projects with them. In this matter, it follows, for a short way, the same path that Sidgwick and Nagel have taken.[1] Both of these philosophers have tried to show that the issues of prudence and altruism can be treated together in the following sense: insofar as persons can find prudential reasons for action, that is, reasons to ensure the fulfillment of future desires that they do not have at the time of action, they can also find altruistic reasons for action—reasons to ensure the fulfillment of desires that are not their own. But these rationalistic arguments

---

[1] See Henry Sidgwick, *The Methods of Ethics* (Indianapolis: Hackett, 1981); and Nagel, *Possibility of Altruism*.

are meant to lead us from our personal, temporally rooted practical perspectives to a more objective perspective, which is both timeless and impersonal, and ultimately impartial and universal in the sense of giving equal weight to all individual perspectives.

In contrast, the common basis that this book finds for self- and other-concern does not require us to adopt either an impartial or a universal perspective. It points to a quite other sort of objectivity, which is firmly rooted to the temporal and the personal. And that is the objective worth of particular projects, as entertained and pursued by particular persons at particular times. In the pursuit of such objective worth, persons can assess not only the worth of their actions and the meaning of their lives; they can assess heretofore unpursued practical possibilities, and in doing so, perhaps be led thereby to redraw the very boundaries that shape and define their identities as agents. That is, they may be led to realize the possibilities of multiple and group personhood. If one can reason one's way out of one's very existence on the basis of a commitment to the worth of a practical project, that gives the notion of a practical project a kind of objectivity that transcends one's individual perspective while at the same time still being tied to someone's perspective. This objectivity, thus, makes no appeal to an unsituated universal point of view for rationality. But it is a kind of objectivity nonetheless, an objectivity in the realm of ethics that is tied to a specifically revisionary metaphysics. It is a kind of objectivity in ethics that cannot, by its nature, bring with it any ethical controversy because its entire source lies in the idea that there are things worth doing, projects worth undertaking, an idea that no substantive ethical position could coherently disown.

Block, Ned. "Troubles with Functionalism." In *Perception and Cognition*, edited by W. Savage. Minnesota Studies in the Philosophy of Science, vol. 9. Minneapolis: University of Minnesota Press, 1978.

———. "Are Absent Qualia Impossible?" *Philosophical Review* 89 (1980): 257–74.

Bratman, Michael. *Intention, Plans and Practical Reason*. Cambridge: Harvard University Press, 1987.

Braude, Stephen E. *First Person Plural: Multiple Personality Disorder and the Philosophy of Mind*. Lanham, Md.: Rowman and Littlefield, 1995.

Butler, Joseph. *Analogies of Religion* (1736). Reprinted in *Personal Identity*, edited by John Perry. Berkeley: University of California Press, 1975.

Castaneda, Hector Neri. "He: A Study in the Logic of Self-Consciousness." *Ratio* 8 (1966): 130–57.

Chisholm, Roderick. *The First Person*. Minneapolis: University of Minnesota Press, 1981.

Chomsky, Noam. *Language and Problems of Knowledge*. Cambridge: MIT Press, 1988.

Dancy, Jonathan, ed. *Reading Parfit*. Oxford: Oxford University Press, forthcoming.

Davidson, Donald, *Essays on Actions and Events*. New York: Oxford University Press, 1980.

———. *Inquiries into Truth and Interpretation*. New York: Oxford University Press, 1984.

Della Rocca, Michael. "Essentialists and Essentialism." *Journal of Philosophy* 93 (1966): 186–202.

Dennett, Daniel. *Brainstorms*. Cambridge, Mass.: Bradford Books, 1978.

———. *Elbow Room: The Varieties of Free Will Worth Wanting*. Cambridge: MIT Press, 1984.

———. *Consciousness Explained*. Boston: Little, Brown and Co., 1991.

———. "Replies to Slote and Rovane," *Philosophical Topics* 22 (1994): 558–62.

Descartes, Rene. *The Philosophical Writings of Descartes*. Vol. 2. Translated by John Cottingham, Robert Stoothoff, Dugald Murdoch, and Anthony Kenny. Cambridge: Cambridge University Press, 1991.

Donellan, Keith. "Reference and Definite Descriptions." *Philosophical Review* 75 (1966): 281–304.

Elster, Jon. *Ulysses and the Sirens: Studies in Rationality and Irrationality*. New York: Cambridge University Press, 1979.

———. *Solomonic Judgments: Studies in the Limits of Rationality*. New York: Cambridge University Press, 1989.

———. *The Multiple Self*. New York: Cambridge University Press, 1985.

Evans, Gareth. *The Varieties of Reference*. New York: Oxford University Press, 1982.

Fodor, Jerry. *Psychological Explanation*. New York: Random House, 1968.

Frankfurt, Harry. "Freedom of the Will and the Concept of a Person." *Journal of Philosophy* 68 (1971): 5–20.

French, Peter. *Collective and Corporate Responsibility*. New York: Columbia University Press, 1984.

Gewirth, Alan. *Reason and Morality*. Chicago: University of Chicago Press, 1978.

Gibbard, Allan. "Contingent Identity." *Journal of Philosophical Logic* 4 (1975): 187–222.

Gilbert, Margaret. *On Social Facts*. London: Routledge, 1989.

Grice, Paul. *Studies in the Way of Words*. Cambridge: Harvard University Press, 1989.

Guttenplan, Samuel, ed. *Mind and Language*. New York: Oxford University Press, 1975.

Habermas, Jurgen. *The Theory of Communicative Action*. Boston: Beacon Press, 1989.

Hacking, Ian. *Rewriting the Soul: Multiple Personality and the Sciences of Memory*. Princeton: Princeton University Press, 1995.

Hume, David. *A Treatise of Human Nature*. Edited by L. A. Selby-Bigge. Oxford: Oxford University Press, 1888.

———. *Enquiries Concerning Human Understanding and Concerning the Principles of Morals*. Edited by P. H. Nidditch. New York: Oxford University Press, 1975.

Hurley, Susan. *Natural Reasons: Personality and Polity*. New York: Oxford University Press, 1989.

James, William. *The Principles of Psychology*. New York: Dover Press, 1950.

Kant, Immanuel. *Critique of Pure Reason*. Translated by Norman Kemp Smith. London: Macmillan Press, 1929.

———. *Foundations of the Metaphysics of Morals*. Translated by Robert Paul Wolff. Indianapolis: Bobbs-Merrill, 1969.

Kitcher, Patricia. *Kant's Transcendental Psychology*. New York: Oxford University Press, 1990.

Kolak, Daniel, and Ray Martin, eds. *Self and Identity*. New York: Macmillan Publishing Co., 1991.

Korsgaard, Christine. "Personal Identity and the Unity of Agency: A Kantian Response to Parfit." *Philosophy and Public Affairs* 28, no. 2 (1989).

Kripke, Saul. *Wittgenstein on Rules and Private Language*. Oxford: Basil Blackwell, 1982.

———. *Naming and Necessity*. Cambridge: Harvard University Press, 1990.

Lepore, Ernest, ed. *Truth and Interpretation: Perspectives on the Philosophy of Donald Davidson*. Oxford: Basil Blackwell, 1986.

Levi, Isaac. *Hard Choices*. New York: Cambridge University Press, 1985.

Lewis, David. *Philosophical Papers*. Vol. 1. New York: Oxford University Press, 1983.

Locke, John. *Essay Concerning Human Understanding*. Edited by P. Nidditch. Oxford: Oxford University Press, 1975.

MacIntyre, Alisdair. *After Virtue*. Notre Dame: Notre Dame University Press, 1981.

McDowell, John. "Functionalism and Anomalous Monism." In *Truth and Interpretation: Perspectives on the Philosophy of Donald Davidson*, edited by Ernest Lepore. Oxford: Basil Blackwell, 1986.

———. "Reductionism and the First Person." In *Reading Parfit*, edited by Jonathan Dancy. Oxford: Oxford University Press, forthcoming.

Merskey, Harold. "The Manufacture of Personalities: The Production of Multiple Personality Disorder." *British Journal of Psychiatry* 157 (1992): 327–40.

Nagel, Thomas. *The Possibility of Altruism*. New York: Oxford University Press, 1970.

———. "Brain Bisection and the Unity of Consciousness." *Synthese* 22 (1971): 396–413. Reprint in *Mortal Questions*, Cambridge: Cambridge University Press, 1979.

———. *Mortal Questions*. Cambridge: Cambridge University Press, 1979.

———. *The View from Nowhere*. New York: Oxford University Press, 1986.

Noonan, Harold. *Personal Identity*. New York: Routledge, 1989.

Nozick, Robert. *Philosophical Explanations.* Cambridge: Harvard University Press, 1981.

Parfit, Derek. *Reasons and Persons.* New York: Oxford University Press, 1984.

Perry, John. "Can the Self Divide?" *Journal of Philosophy* 73 (1972): 463–88.

———. *The Problem of the Essential Indexical and Other Essays.* New York: Oxford University Press, 1993.

———, ed. *Personal Identity.* Berkeley: University of California Press, 1975.

Prince, Morton. *The Dissociation of a Personality.* London: Longmans, Green, 1905. Reprint New York: Johnson Reprint Corp., 1968.

Quine, Willard van Orman. *Word and Object.* Cambridge: MIT Press, 1960.

Reid, Thomas. *Essay on the Intellectual Powers of Man.* Edinburgh, 1785. Reprint in *Personal Identity*, edited by John Perry. Berkeley: University of California Press, 1975.

Rorty, Amelie, ed. *The Identities of Persons.* Berkeley: University of California Press, 1979.

Rovane, Carol. "The Epistemology of First Person Reference." *Journal of Philosophy* 84 (1987): 147–67.

———. "Self-Reference: The Radicalization of Locke." *Journal of Philosophy* 90 (1993): 73–97.

———. "Critical Notice: Peter Unger's *Identity, Consciousness and Value*." *Canadian Journal of Philosophy* 24 (1994): 119–33.

Schiffer, Stephen. *Meaning.* New York: Oxford University Press, 1972.

Schreiber, Flora Rheta. *Sybil.* New York: Warner Books, 1973.

Scruton, Roger. "Corporate Persons." *Proceedings of the Aristotelian Society* 63 (1989): 239–66.

Shoemaker, Sydney. *Self-Knowledge and Self-Identity.* Ithaca: Cornell University Press, 1963.

———. "Self-Knowledge and Self-Awareness." *Journal of Philosophy* 65 (1968): 555–67.

———. "Persons and Their Pasts." *American Philosophical Quarterly* 7 (1970): 269–85.

———. "The Inverted Spectrum." *Journal of Philosophy* 79 (1982): 357–81.

Shoemaker, Sydney, and Richard Swinburne. *Personal Identity.* Oxford: Basil Blackwell, 1984.

Sidgwick, Henry. *The Methods of Ethics.* Indianapolis: Hackett, 1981.

Strawson, Sir Peter. *Individuals.* London: University Press, 1959.

———. *Freedom and Resentment and Other Essays.* London: Methuen, 1974.

Taylor, Charles. *Sources of the Self: The Making of Modern Identity.* Cambridge: Harvard University Press, 1989.

Thigpen, C. H., and H. M. Cleckly. *The Three Faces of Eve.* New York: Popular Library, 1957.

Unger, Peter. *Identity, Consciousness and Value.* New York: Oxford University Press, 1990.

White, Stephen. *The Unity of the Self.* Cambridge: MIT Press, 1994.

Wiggins, David. *Identity and Spatio-Temporal Continuity.* Oxford: Oxford University Press, 1967.

———. *Sameness and Substance.* New York: Oxford University Press, 1980.

Wilkes, Kathleen. *Real People: Personal Identity without Thought Experiments.* New York: Oxford University Press, 1988.

Williams, Bernard. *Problems of the Self.* Cambridge: Cambridge University Press, 1973.

———. *Moral Luck.* Cambridge: Cambridge University Press, 1981.

———. *Ethics and the Limits of Philosophy.* London: Fontana Press, 1985.

Wittgenstein, Ludwig. *Philosophical Investigations.* New York: Macmillan, 1953.

———. *The Blue and Brown Books.* Oxford: Basil Blackwell, 1958.

About the Author

CAROL ROVANE is Associate Professor of Philosophy at Yale University.